Bon Courage:
Essays on
Inheritance, Citizenship,
and a Creative Life

Bon Courage:
Essays on Inheritance, Citizenship, and a Creative Life

Ru Freeman

Etruscan Press

Etruscan Press
Wilkes University
84 West South Street
Wilkes-Barre, PA 18766
(570) 408-4546

 Wilkes University

www.etruscanpress.org

Published 2023 by Etruscan Press
Printed in the United States of America
Cover design by Lisa Reynolds
Cover image by Hasadri Freeman
Interior design and typesetting by Todd Espenshade
The text of this book is set in Minion Pro.

First Edition

17 18 19 20 5 4 3 2 1

Library of Congress Cataloguing-in-Publication Data

Names: Freeman, Ru, author.
Title: Bon courage : essays on inheritance, citizenship, and a creative
  life / Ru Freeman.
Description: First Edition. | Wilkes-Barre, PA : Etruscan Press, 2023. |
Identifiers: LCCN 2022024453 | ISBN 9781736494677 (paperback)
Subjects: LCGFT: Short stories.
Classification: LCC PS3606.R4455 B66 2023 | DDC 813/.6--dc23
LC record available at https://lccn.loc.gov/2022024453

Please turn to the back of this book for a list of the sustaining funders of Etruscan Press.

This book is printed on recycled, acid-free paper.

"Writing is *all* resistance."
—Zadie Smith

For my daughters
Duránya, Hasadrī, and Kisārā
&
For my nieces
Indi, Mithsi, and Dayadi

CONTENTS

Author's Note

There is a before and an after to every life. A before love, a before marriage, a before children, a before sickness, a before death. The year 2009 gave me an after that brought not merely deep sorrow, but terrifying perspective. It was the year that my first novel was published, a feat that became diminutive in the face of the reminder of finite time: my own diagnosis of cancer in the months preceding the splashy arrival of that novel, and the sudden death of my mother in the months immediately following. Forever after, I placed everything I said and did within the larger context of being unalterably human. I was, I am, a writer. But I was, and am, defined more truly by my relationship to those who raised me, and the country in which I came to be, Sri Lanka, as well as those whom I raise, and the country in which I do that, the United States—a place I work to transform—both of which are situated upon the global stage on which all of us unfold.

I am a writer the way actresses in South Asian cultures practice their art, unlimited by genre, required to register the emotive specifics of a character as flawlessly as they are able to also sing and dance. I am known as a novelist, but I am a maker of poems; I opine on politics and compose essays. In other words, my allegiance is to words—not form. They are my clay, the thing that I shape to suit the need at hand. Yet through it all there has also been this truth: the words I've chosen, and the forms into which I've poured them, have had a dual purpose. They have shaped the world, but, equally, they have shaped me.

What follows is a collage, an illustration of a writer's life. A life where the personal is understood as framed by the collective, where a gift must be used as assiduously for the good of a whole as it must also serve to assuage, comfort, or otherwise provide solid ground. It is a life where the gaze tries, though often it fails, to unite truth with compassion, sometimes separately, but more frequently in a single work, and where the evolution of the writer consistently weds the personal with civic, public life.

It is hard for any of us to separate what is imagined from what is real. We are all storytellers of our own lives, narrating what we observe, making sense of it all. What happens around us is equally complicated, for, as the writer Anaïs Nin put it, "We don't see the world as it is, we see it as we are." In that liminal space between what is and what we think it is, we write history: our own and that of others. That word, history, has its origins in the Greek term *historia*, which implies a dynamic process of finding out, of inquiry, rather than the passivity of recording. I consider this collection, then, a similar endeavor. It is a writer's attempt to train her eye on what is unfolding around her as well as herself, all of it viewed through a kaleidoscope constructed of the four mirrors: the larger ones of place, culture, and politics, and the smaller one of the self that shares its borders with all three. Words are the glass beads inside. Twist the instrument, and the world rearranges itself.

rf.
Marfa, Texas

Hero

You don't care that the music you hear has taken years to reach your country. You are a teenager, lying on the cold cement floor of a room in Colombo, Sri Lanka, listening through borrowed headphones to one of the few bootlegged cassette tapes you own: Top Ten Hits from David Bowie. You come from a culture comfortable with androgyny, so you stare up at a poster of the skinny blond boy that covers the cracks in your walls and feel your heart melt; you think he can do no wrong while wearing lipstick, bell-bottoms, and blue eyeshadow. You listen, and though you feel everything has already passed you by, and your head is all tangled up, the singer calls you "love," and you are not alone. When the one music show, *Pops in Germany*, that runs on the TVs the Japanese gifted your country, the one that plays the anti-war anthem "99 Luftballons" from the German band Nena every single week, adds Bowie and Jagger "Dancing in the Street" on repeat during and after Live Aid, you believe you've melded the family gift of understanding the link between capitalism and global poverty before you could walk, with your private satanic heart that loves pop music and all things American. You don't have enough fabric to stitch yourself a cheetah print jumpsuit, so you make do with a mini dress that hugs your boy-girl body as you dance. You listen to "Five Years," and you believe your poster boy made room in his head for "all the somebody people," which means he must have made room for you. You imagine that when he sings about how he "touched the very soul / of holding each and every life" at the kind of free festival you have no hope of ever attending, that he was holding you, even though you know that all the joy was imagined, was just a claim you wanted to make the same way he did. You can't afford the albums, but the tracks find you somehow, and when the Berlin Wall comes down, even though your family has made sure you know how to pronounce Gorbachev and *perestroika*, you believe much more in the idea of East Berliners gathering on the hard side of a wall to listen to Bowie serenade them. Time passes and different songs claim you, set your history to music. You grow up to become familiar with other walls from Arizona to Palestine, to face an American military arranged in battalions aiming their guns at your head, at the heads of your daughters. And yet. You still believe that walls can be torn down by the strength of sweet voices singing love songs and reciting poetry. You know now that singing to people he could not see moved him deeply and that he did not expect to be able to repeat the experience. You shrug and think that doing one brave and beautiful thing should be enough for any artist. You are sitting in a country far from the place where you were born, wrapped in a blanket and looking out on the waters of the Pacific, thinking about compassion and literature, when you hear the news. You close your eyes and turn on "Rock 'n' Roll Suicide," all quiet on the inside of your head. You imagine hands reaching all the way across the world. *Gimme your hands*, you say, *gimme your hands 'cause you're wonderful.*

Memory, Loss

I don't know which year it was, exactly.

It *couldn't* have been 1971, when my paternal uncle (my older-father, in the terminology of Sri Lankan culture) was bodyguard to the world's first female prime minister, Mrs. Sirimavo Bandaranaike, who rose to prominence and would forever be known as "The Mother" after her husband was assassinated—and this is true—by none other than a rabid Buddhist monk, and who presided over the mass murder of thousands of young men, and the rise in stature of the country in the World Bank reports, which hailed Sri Lanka as "the new Singapore."

It *couldn't* have been 1983, when the cities burned, and neighbors were butchered, and refugees filled our homes, and we children pretended to play in the gardens outside so nobody would think to come looking for the people with the wrong names in our houses where they sat, rendered speechless, clutching passports and identity cards and their bits and pieces of gold jewelry.

It *couldn't* have been 1986, when the death threats flew into our home from every available orifice like a determined summons to Hogwarts at Four Privet Drive, except that we lived at 601/2 Havelock Road, Colombo 6, and there was nothing magical about life in those times except that people disappeared, and eighteen-year-old boys were found arranged in rings like the circle of the Buddhist Dharma Chakra, decapitated, their limbs dismembered, or with tires around their necks, charred streaks of black on the pavements like chalk, the shaded avenues of the universities, on streets, by the riverbanks.

It *could* have been in 1987, when our house filled up with boys. My brothers, yes, but nine of their friends, all occupying my brothers' room, while I slept, alone—alas, I thought—in my bedroom. Among them, my boyfriend, in my preferred ilk—a girly boy, sweet faced, slender, sleepy eyes, a generous mouth, sensuous and seducible, who did, very late at night, sometimes knock softly on the door behind which I waited, having communicated with the subtle play of eyes that the goodnight murmured was not a farewell but an invitation to have one.

They were hiding in our home, and I know this will dismay and perhaps even horrify every real estate agent from coast to American coast, there were fourteen of us in the house and we had only one bathroom! Somehow, none of us ever needed to defecate elsewhere, urinate in our pants, or greet the day unwashed. There was never enough food in my parents' house, but fourteen of us had lunch—the most important meal for us—anyway. Mostly it was rice and okra, which we planted in the ground behind the house the day the boys moved in, and which sprang into life and fertility like Jack's beanstalk, providing the something-to-go-with that we needed for our rice. What should we make for lunch, we'd ask each other every afternoon, and each afternoon we'd give it some thought, the silence falling over us, until one of us blurted, with great excitement, "How about okra?" Yes, we'd say, Okra! and we'd high-five each other.

Were there people being murdered? Why, yes. But we were teenagers reveling in our version of the French resistance, playing our small parts in the great revolution that was not coming, it was already here! We wore red and called each other comrade and we quoted Marx, and so I now think it *must* have been 1989 because I remember, the younger less knowledgeable sister that I was, drawing one of my brothers and a few of the boys aside and asking, because oh how I loved that dizzyingly happy moral high ground, "But what about Tiananmen?" and there being a lot of head shaking and consideration and soothing murmurs of "someday," as in "someday you will understand," which lead as these things do to my hearing not the words but the beat of those words, "you will understand," which tripped not toward understanding but, with a light leap, into the "we shall overcome" that it recalled, and which I then proceeded to sing with religious fervor as though it were the new *Internationale* in the bathroom, which had a door that fell far short of the ceiling so that anybody passing, any of those boys, but particularly the boyfriend, could go up on his toes and watch me cavorting underneath a shower that had no shower head and merely fell like a forced waterfall, hard on my head and body, and I could turn my back, pretending I did not know this, and display my two finest assets.

Each night I unfurled a long pink carpet that my mother had purchased in the Black Market under the almost-Singapore policies of Mrs. Bandaranaike and laid down a sheet and fluffed the three available pillows and the cushions off my mother's rudimentary living room furniture—which remains, to this day, stiff and uncomfortable—and I made a bed for the boys, who lay down like sardines, each head to another's toes, and spoke only in whispers. Each morning I'd help them roll up the carpet, and put the bedding away, and we'd leave the curtains drawn over the shut windows because we lived within twelve feet of the house next door, a mirror image, except that it was filled up with army boys. Army boys, which meant government, which meant green, and the symbol of the elephant, and paramilitary forces called Black Tigers, and Yellow Cats, and all kinds of other two-legged felines who roamed the streets and picked up boys such as ours and did not ever bring them back. Ever.

And each morning my father went off to work for that government, civil servant that he was, called to duty and being dutiful, while his house filled up with boys from the villages. I remember now that it was the year when my father was appointed to head the Agrarian Research and Training Institute, which came with a house for its director. A house with two stories, in other words, the house of my dreams, because only rich people lived in two-story houses, and we had never been rich. My father, a Trotskyite to this day, refused the house but continued to direct, while we languished—and we did languish—in the bliss of being a part of Dangerous Times.

All, that is, except my oldest brother, the musician, the one who swore fidelity to the sage Sathya Sai Baba and all things spiritual, but also liked perfume, and did his hair just so, and was, therefore, the butt of many jokes within the family, but particularly among us, his younger brother, these nine friends, and his only sister. He did not care for politics, did not want to participate in the revolution, did not want to think about who was dead or dying, or might be killed or jailed, he never liked Marx, did not follow in his illustrious father's socialist footsteps, and was mostly deeply disappointed by his brother's equally determined desire to repeat what he called "the foolishness of that stupid man." He also acquired a British accent for words like that, "stupid."

Among us all, the one he loved best was my boyfriend, also a musician, whom he'd lure to some corner with his guitar while the boyfriend brought his Esraj (and that instrument had a special place in the bedroom, namely, on the one bed, because it was revered by everybody, this classical curved instrument belonging to a real musician), and the two of them played, very very quietly—remember those army boys?—in the farthest part of the house, which was, unfortunately, the kitchen, which was somewhat difficult for me, because the kitchen had cockroaches. The giant, flying kind. And though I loved nothing more than to sit with this particular brother—because it meant also sitting in the presence of, if not in intimate proximity to, the boyfriend, to have an opportunity (when my brother left the room to light a cigarette, or use the—one—bathroom) to stroke the boyfriend's inner arm in such a way that changed the tempo of his breathing, which made me feel very womanly—I did not like the cockroaches. And the cockroaches loved me.

It must have been on a day after one of those frustrating kitchen-music nights, as I called them, when the phone rang. Another friend, calling from a town where the disappearances had been the greatest, asking for refuge, asking to speak to one of the boys, Priyantha. Priyantha, whose features only seemed to improve when I hadn't seen him in a while—you know the way it happens, you don't see someone, and in your mind's eye, you intensify the good, the bad, and, in this case, the ugly, so it gets uglier and uglier until you finally see them again and are mightily surprised by how good looking they are. That's a theory he shared with me, by the way, when I commented on it once, how good he looked. Priyantha, who was only second to my other brother in terms of how passionately committed he was—despite the death of two of their closest friends—to the romance of the revolution, the defiance of it all, the bravado of breaking curfews and ducking into alleyways, and flaunting their red-hued slogans whenever they could, because they were convinced, and they convinced me, that we would win. Priyantha picked up the phone and began to speak in explicit terms about what was going on, the word on the streets, the hope in the air, the plans afoot, about who else was in residence in my parents' house. Until he heard the faint clicking on the line.

Did I forget to say that along with the death threats came the tapping of our phones?

Even Priyantha's voice faltered as Premasiri, on the other end of the line, asked, *Did you hear that?* And a silence fell between them. A silence from Priyantha, still holding the phone, that curled and twined around everybody in the house, even those not in sight of this one boy, until the whole house became unnaturally still and for the first time we became fearful, not brave.

When we talk about that moment now, we laugh. We don't speak of the way my mother took a bus to my father's office, to tell him in person, alone, of what had happened. We don't speak of how my father sent his official vehicle to help his family that had never had the use of this vehicle before, driven by a man, Mullegama, who had once revealed an allegiance that matched ours in response to my question: "So, how do you feel about the JVP?" The JVP being made up of those whose predecessors had been tipped into mass graves during that first year I told you about, 1971, the year of the advent of The Mother.

We do not talk about how Mullegama arrived, the Pajero painted the color of the ruling party, and how I bid the boys a sorrowful goodbye as they each slipped, quietly, their few belongings in tissue-paper–thin plastic plastic bags, into the Pajero, the pink and white carpet rolled and placed over their knees. There were tears, and we do not say, now, that the tears were for the time that we were losing, this time we'd had of hope and excitement and the charge of being a part of something massive, of having had the time of our lives play-acting change in the confines of our home, the danger all but invisible to us because the *feeling* of that time together was everything, *fuck* the revolution.

We do not talk about how it became, the way we abandoned our home, and how the boys hid in the new house my father had never wanted to accept, the rich people's house that came with furniture fit for such people, where our bottoms could find plush seats, where the floors gleamed, the kitchen had an oven—for baking what?—and mirrored almirahs in all our rooms even though everything we owned, all fourteen of us, could have fit into one. We do not talk about how we dug up a square of the ample backyard and planted okra anyway, even though the chef at the canteen now walked the quarter mile from the offices to the house carrying large plates of rice and bowls of curries, how the lemons dripped off the lemon tree at the back, piling up and rotting, and how we all got sick of lemon juice we could have for free without the sugar we couldn't afford.

We do not talk about how my paternal uncle, now the head of a security agency, hired the boys for pretend jobs, how they went to become security guards, because to be in the city without a reason to be there, when you were eighteen, and nineteen, and twenty, and twenty-one, was a death sentence.

We do not talk about the death threats that found a new address, or the army patrols that sometimes stopped in front of the high walls of that house and stayed there for hours, watching, listening, as we watched and listened on the other side. We do not talk about the security guards at the Agrarian Research and Training Institute who patrolled the premises late at night, causing the boys to quiet their voices, or how though the boyfriend now climbed the stairs at night, and though my room had a Juliet balcony complete with floor-to-ceiling drapes, though I still had my girl-only room, and though masses of printed and intoxicatingly fragrant airmail packages had arrived for me from colleges in the United States with offers of full scholarships, what I felt was a lack, not a gift.

What we talk about now of that day is this. How, *ha ha!* Thilak, who hailed from the most rural of the villages, grabbed the phone from Priyantha and slammed it down and called him a fucking donkey, how he rushed around the house and burned all the books, including the notebooks, and journals, that had any mention of themselves or their beliefs, how he stammered tearfully that it was over, it was all over, they were all going to die. But most of all, we talk about my oldest brother, how furious he became over what was to befall him, who had no damn interest in any of this nonsense, and how in that hour when we all gathered their belongings and erased the evidence of their stay, how he paced, and how he rushed over to Sathya Sai Baba's shrine, the shrine he had in his room, and stood there chanting inaudible prayers, and how he reached out to take some of the ash from the incense that gathered each night, and rubbed it on the forehead of each boy and, lastly, himself, and how in the final second, something overcame him, and he grabbed a fistful of that ash and shoved it into his mouth, a sob escaping his throat. Remember that, we say? Remember? Remember? And we laugh. We laugh far too long and far too loud, remembering everything.

I Am Not Now, Nor Have I Ever Been,
an Adolescent

Mine went MIA. I didn't look for it. I didn't know I was entitled to one. Perhaps it was merely lost in translation, there being no corresponding word in Sinhala for the term. It was not encouraged nor discussed, this uncomfortable period between being cared for and learning to care. The word was thrown around sometimes by my teacher-of-English-Literature-and-Western-Classics mother, but more often by my also-English-educated writer father, and when it was, they communicated it as something not to be tolerated. It was a sort of overly spelled four-letter-word for stupidity.

"The minister was at the cabinet meeting today. Bloody adolescent." Like that.

Neither my two older brothers nor I were inclined to be confused with that sort of behavior, whatever it was. Most particularly not I, the treasured one, the convent-educated only girl in the family: a special star reining over a galaxy of brothers and male cousins for the first decade of my life and, in effect, for much of my teenage years as well. We soldiered on, non-adolescently.

But there was an added dimension to the premise of our youth, something that we suddenly noticed as being other than what defined the three of us, this work we did to be child, then adult, nothing between: the bitter iteration of marriage that was our parents' primary contribution to the exterior emotional climate that we learned to navigate, relate to, and eventually recover from.

It had always been there, this constant tremor threatening earthquakes of discontent and vitriol flung every which way—even, in one singularly memorable moment, with a dish of curried pumpkin flung against a framed-without-glass oil painting of vegetables, where one small smudge, unnoticed in the frantic washing I did to restore appearances, still remains—but as we climbed over the peak of our first decade on earth, we saw with a particular clarity that our lives were not to be showcased or diminished by their relationship but rather that we had a responsibility to protect and disarm while we prepared to sever and excuse ourselves. And them, too.

So perhaps it was not so much that adolescence was missing but that it was missed. My brothers made a valiant attempt to do the things that their peers did. The oldest, a gifted pianist, contrived to fail his final London examinations and then hide the results from my mother. The other brother broke into his high school to ring the school bell after dark and managed to get himself incarcerated for a night. But I, The Girl, had too much minding to do. I had no margins in which to scribble the usual small and large escapades of those years. I tackled the Leviathan from the innocuous nib of a biro and the page-a-day diaries that my father's secretaries gave him, and which I hunched over in my pristine room. My pristine room with not a speck of dust in sight, with its shelves stacked with battered secondhand books whose spines stood exactly, exactly, exactly together, going toe-to-toe with each other, with photographs framing my dressing table and fresh newspaper changed regularly to cover my desk, and a bed whose sheets I snapped into hospital corners, a clean-swept room in which I went to sleep each eighty-degree tropical night, wrapped from head to toe in various lengths of cloth—an old sarong belonging to my father, old shirts too, and socks, and a verti draped over my head and tight across my mouth, only my eyes showing—and all the knives in the house, including the one butter knife, hidden under my bed.

What fears? What fears? Some, a few, all of them! The real, the surreal, the extraterrestrial, the inward, outward, flesh-mangling, dream-depriving things from which children are supposed to be saved. The things they are supposed to grow up and save their children from after they've passed over that brief covered bridge of madness, this adolescence of disposition when the ringing of school bells, the truancy of teens, the sneaking into adult-only movie theaters, the inhaling of someone else's cigarette, the time of air guitars and colored hair and perhaps, in the extreme, putting up posters of Che Guevara for the most left-wing group one could find, another effort of an older brother, should be the only hesitation.

No, no, to all of it. I lived by daylight, wrote in the evenings, and slept light. Awake at the intimations of discord: my father's drinks pouring into my mother's cut-glass; my mother's upper-caste rage pouring into my father's silent frame; the telephone ringing; the dishes clashing; some fight we children had got into; the discovery of that failed exam; a decision by a brother to switch from studying Physics and Math to English Literature and

Political Science; the lead-up to elections; the approach of an almsgiving to remember a dead grandfather; the arrival of a bill, or a death threat. Who could isolate a source? I was a child making sense without the inner quiet required to do so. With the burden of secrets withheld from parents who had unfolded into their own twisted, uncomplimentary, divergent lives without noticing the underfoot.

"Why don't you talk about Shanali?" my mother asked one evening. Once.

"They don't talk to me anymore," I said, my heart pounding. Could this be it? The longed-for moment of intervention? After round two in a second school? "Nobody does."

Silence.

"They call me Black Forest," I added, raising the stakes, "because of my hair."

My father glanced up from the chessboard that I had set up for him, that I set up for him it seemed a hundred times a day, for the endless replaying of games by Russians with beautiful faces and long fingers and names that rolled in my mouth. He glanced up and said, in his slow, exegetical way, "Marvelous! You should tell them that the Black Forest is a famous forest in southwestern Germany. It is bordered by the Atlantic watershed and the Black Sea." He paused to frown at the board, to move a white pawn in some direction towards the black queen. "The people there grew rich from the wood, and the silver, and the ore." His voice grew deep and mysterious for that word, dragging it out: *orrre*. He nodded, enhancing the gravitas. "Black forest gateau," he added at last, a non sequitur, as I waited, completely under the thrall of this explanation. And then he went back to Kasparov, leaving me to fade into the woven seat of smoothed-wood chairs that I carried in each night from the verandah before the front door was shut because those chairs seemed precious and thieves came both as human beings and monsoons.

They weren't bad people, they were flawed like the rest of them, haphazard in their attentions. My mother, however, had set me up for success: I had learned to elocute, to perform on stage, to sing, to dance, to run, to swim, and also to play the piano. That last was so that I could have "options" when—not if—I married *a despicable bastard* or, more often, *a lousy lout* who would keep me under lock and key and prevent me from gainful employment outside the home. I knew of nobody among my parents' entourage of friends, all superbly eccentric and colorful, and often homosexual, who labored in that kind of situation, but perhaps my mother felt this might be my lot. Perhaps it had to do with my flat chest, dark skin, and, for so much of my childhood, boy hair (I was a boy in my dream life, another of those unexamined penchants that could have helped the whys to come gushing forth), so unlike the curves and fair skin and curls that destined others for good marriages. She pictured me safe inside this potential tomb of deprival where I would give piano lessons to small children and earn a little something with which I would do—What? What? Buy my freedom? Send the houseboy out for lollipops? Which is perhaps why *The Maiden's Prayer* was my favorite piece. A learned-by-heart that I played with great reverence, *pianissimo* and *mezzo forte* coming from guts tied to fingertips, not pedals. Though what I prayed for was escape, and not with any man but solo. In a flat. An independent life during which I would fulfill my goals: be a lawyer, work for the UN, write books.

My father, when he was not upset with America and/or the government, which was such a rarity I remember the occasions, was funny. I confided in a brother once that I would run away. He had no patience.

"So what are you waiting for?"

"If I had money, I would!" I said, convinced, to his back, turned away from me, working on his own poetry, a squish even then of Neruda and Marquez, a literary cocktail that has dogged him into many books of poetry and translation and his professional writerly life as an adult.

My father, in transit between one refuge, the toilet seat, and another, the chessboard, peeked around the curtain. "What would you do if you had money?"

"I'd run away!" I said, longing for a concrete enemy, a faceable, nameable one.

His eyebrows went up quizzically. "Then you won't need money." He pumped his elbows in slow motion. "You'll be running."

Perhaps he only meant to lighten the gloom he knew waited just under the surfaces of his house, never quite his home. Under the polished tables, the day help who sometimes came but who most often went, the odd accomplished-yet-restless children, the ceaseless reminder of an unloved wife, the gone-wrong life. Or perhaps public integrity had its personal price.

Yes, they were not bad, not intentionally unkind, but when they drew near, they merely brushed the air around my head, the rest left well alone.

So I played normal at school. That was my challenge, the thing I needed to do to earn the right to grow up. A girl with not much parental presence at school events, parent-teacher conferences, or sports meets at private schools my mother had called on favors to enroll me in, where parents—how they looked, where they worked, what they contributed— was everything, I became brilliant, so I would be an asset, and unassailable, so no slight could faze me. Yes, I would run in multiple races, of course I'd audition for the lesser part of Rosencrantz for the school excerpt from *Romeo and Juliet*, and I would debate, and I would sing American ballads, and I would attend any extra classes held after school. Yes, yes, yes to everything. I would do everything so nothing about me could be questioned, except, of course, the frightening intensity of a forgotten child with verifiable parents who were wholly absent.

My classmates were busy doing their own growing up, and it usually took the form of swapping boyfriends and gossip, skipping classes, and sometimes turning their attention to my peculiarity, especially when it smacked of something better than whatever they had.

"Where did you get that Ocean Pacific t-shirt?" someone asked me once at ballad practice. I didn't know what an Ocean Pacific t-shirt was. I had been given it, a metal-grey shirt with a colorful strip of ocean creatures underlined by the letters for the brand separated fancifully by double spaces, by my host-brother, Cameron, an American exchange student who had washed up in our house against all odds. Two of them arrived on our doorstep that way. Perhaps something about the open-door, who-knows-whom-we-will-find-sleeping-in-the-house-by-morning, explosive, haphazard, incorrect conduct of a household in an otherwise properly maintained former British colony in South Asia appealed to these adolescents from America.

"Cameron," I said, and felt for a fleeting moment the sweetness of superiority. Cameron, an American name signifying all manner of possibilities. Everybody at school knew of Cameron, who wore the long white trousers and short-sleeved white shirt of all school boys and had to walk past the school to his previous host-family's home. And Cameron had become "mine."

Cameron and, before him, Daniel had found our house through serendipity, that concept that the Persians once used to name my country Serendip. They met my brothers, fell in to chatting with them, went with them for chess tournaments that lasted till midnight and beyond, and to camp on Horton Plains, which meant a single tent and no sleeping bags in the freezing cold of the mountains having traveled overnight on the night-mail and walking up seven miles. They did these things, and suddenly they wanted to be in the family that my brothers were fleeing and I was fighting to survive! They came and begged my mother to call the American Field Service offices and petition for reassignment. She did. They came. They became absorbed. They loved us, and we loved them. Cameron's mother had left his father and become a biker chic who rode around with her biker boyfriend in the usual cliché. What parallels he found in our life I do not know. But it was years later that I learned the rest of the lyrics to the words he scrawled in my autograph book, subsequently, poetically, lost at Grand Central Station: *freedom's just another word for nothing left to lose.* I thought he made those up. I thought he was so astute.

I also thought he made up the words he would sometimes sing tunelessly to me: *don't drink, don't smoke, what do you do? Subtle innuendos follow must be something inside, tu-tu-tu-tu…*I thought he knew there was something inside that wasn't quite aligned right. Something unhinged and tainted and wrong. And he became even more remarkable to me, this sixteen-year-old boy who had arrived from nowhere, unasked for, and settled in for a while, who brought me prestige at school and words to live by and functioned as a boyfriend at the parties we went to together, slow dancing in a madly platonic embrace as we giggled and referred to each other as sister and brother. And somewhere, buried under all the declamations against White America and White Americans and capitalism and Star Wars and Coca-Cola and conversations with my best friend that went like this—

Her: "I'm going to become an air hostess and find a blond American, Ru. That's what I want. I want a blond American to get me out of this shit hole!"

Me: "Gads. I'd never marry one of them. I need brown skin."

Her: "Well, I can ask him to get a tan!'

Me: "But you'd have to sleep with a *mostellaria* first!" (We were beginning to read Aristophanes' *The Ghost* for our Advanced Level examinations at the time; we called other people Kitchen Utensils and felt superior.)

—conversations that were followed by shrieks of laughter at how well we knew ourselves, beneath all that, what Cameron left behind along with the Ocean Pacific shirt he had once pressed into my hands and his tears of farewell at the Katunayake International Airport was a seed of belief, a small, porous, growing thing that must have whispered *American boy, American boy,* to me until I grew up and left for Maine with two suitcases carrying the bare essentials: dresses with puffed sleeves and bows on the back, high-heeled pumps to wear to dinner, gifts for my professors, Orex ballpoint pens, Signal toothpaste and toothbrush, and *Samahan* for coughs, colds, fevers, or anything else.

And in America I met real adolescents, not like Cameron. These ones swept, carefree, through the corridors of my dorm, getting drunk in the lounge, twitching pens and looking confused in my classes, gagging over the fantastic meals in the cafeteria of an expensive liberal arts college I now felt wildly, euphorically, thrilled to be at. These versions had no time for me, no time for songs.

It all seemed shameless to me, this discarding of their origins. As Parents Weekend drew near, my friends rolled their eyes and cursed, and I marveled. I would have given anything to have my long-misplaced parents visit the campus then. Anything to see them at dinner. Instead, I went out for Greek food with a beautiful girl named Phoebe and her gracious mother and articulate father. We had a mostly silent dinner where they asked me questions. I felt as though I had been the entertainment. Perhaps I had. At the time, I thought it was lovely of her to include me in a private reunion with her parents. Years later, she grew up and married a South African boy she had met while she had been a high school exchange student. The world did not turn so much as it returned to an older story.

But watching those friends, I rediscovered my parents' aversion to adolescence. It was not a period of time, I swore—still swear—it was an indulgence in stupidity. Who had the right to be so unconcerned with other people? With me? With Palestine? Who could be so uninformed as to believe that if people who couldn't place Kuwait on a map and had their own cars on campus marched around the college pond with candles, there would be no war on Iraq? I blamed all this on the condition of adolescence. I could spit that word out with the same contempt my father once had. He about his colleagues, and sometimes about America, I about my peers. I also learned to infuse every political piece I wrote with that same derision. Adolescence was, I felt, an absence of intellect, something to be ridiculed and disassociated from. In an effort to distinguish my unique perspective on adolescence from that of my parents, I changed their "bloody" to "fucking," or, for more panache, "bloody fucking."

Still, despite this new effort to lay a claim to an advantage, a dirge of sorts to that lost time in my own life, the things that Cameron, that once heroic, now near-mythical sage from the past had said came back to me repeatedly until I realized that I had, indeed, left my long-term, much beloved, wholly brown-skinned boyfriend and sung Joan Baez into the heart of another American boy. Another who, like me, had experienced adolescence in the absent-presence of parents, his father the son of a veteran, his mother a devotee of *The Feminine Mystique*, a member of MENSA, between Yale Business School and IBM.

And now, safe in an American home, where I do not intend to give piano lessons though I intend to, and do, pay for them, where I sleep unafraid, facing upward, naked if I feel like it, where all the sharp things spend the night in the kitchen and the underbelly of my bed collects dust balls, where the past has gone to where it should be left, a place for harvesting small diamonds, little treasures to be bartered for stories like this, for the longing poetry and truthful fictions that I write now, I have no fear of adolescence. I've experienced it in the form of all of my daughters, in their half (adolescent) American, half (lost/hidden/denied adolescent) Sri Lankan hearts. This lack of fear, it helps me write. The political notes that people love for their seeming courage, their unforgiving sight, the pieces that help me rid my head of problems: bombs in Beirut, the ruins of the national library in Baghdad, the hijacking of the presidential elections, the awarding of Oscars to misogynistic lyricists. But mostly it helps me write the stories that recreate unseen places, unknown times, a milieu in which The Girl could have been any girl.

Uncle Moe's Diner

In the late spring of my freshman year in college I, a non-beer-drinking but hard-dancing international student from Sri Lanka, was high on two things: enjoying the first freedom of being 10,000 miles away from home, and my very handsome American boyfriend. The former had manifested itself in a series of worthy accomplishments at Bates, ranging from being on the only team to represent America at a debate tournament in Montreal (an event I got to by hiding under blankets and pretending to be asleep in those easy-breezy, pre-9/11 days of border non-security), appearing in full-length theater and dance productions, and receiving straight As in all five classes I was taking. The latter, though, that was the real bliss.

Mark, a true-blue Connecticut Yankee, introduced me to all things American. He took me both to the top of the press box of the college football bleachers *and* the crown of the Statue of Liberty. He got me hooked on movies at the college library *and* eggs over-easy with sausage on the side at Denny's on Main Street, not to mention the cakes and pies which he always had to help me finish. He took me for walks around the campus *and* drives to the state parks of Maine, where we slept in the back of his Ford pickup truck and I tasted my first vaguely smoky hot dogs and s'mores. Like I said, American life—or, looking back now, the American life *he* knew, so vastly different from the one I came to know, a chasm that would prove one day to be too wide to be mitigated by history.

It stood to reason that I would want to share something that he didn't know about, something I could find in this country, since I was so far away from my own. I had been teaching dance for a month during what was called Short Term, a time for students to take just one class over an intense period of time, something many of us chose to do instead of leaving college for an early start on summer. Over the course of our travels to various public elementary and middle schools, I had taken in the areas surrounding the bubble of our highly competitive liberal arts college, the land rolling away into farms and mill towns. So it was that one night, after a drive to a local coffee shop, when Mark suggested that we keep on going to find an open area from where we could see the stars, I announced that I knew just the place.

I did know. Sort of. I had seen a path leading to a clearing off the main road that we'd taken earlier that afternoon on a school bus headed to a school where we would perform, and then teach modern dance pieces set to Middle Eastern music to little Mainers. Where, *exactly*, I didn't know. I have always just felt places. I don't know the names of roads, I travel by intuition and implicit trust that "something in my bones" will help me navigate everything, roads, people, places, life itself. In the late night, though, in semi-rural Maine, with no streetlights and the houses few, we were easily lost. Not simply lost, we were stuck in a mud bog. There I sat, ladylike in my very light cream sweater that I had purchased for five whole dollars at the Salvation Army and that I did not intend to ruin, while Mark attempted to get the front wheels of the pickup out of the swamp. I helped, eventually, but only when repeated suggestions that we *just ask the nice people who probably live in the house up the hill to help us* fell on deaf, obdurate ears. The farmer did help us, in the end. When he strolled out in the first pink-grey light of the morning with his son. It was a sweet victory to hear him inquire why we hadn't asked him for help in the first place, when all night long he had lain in his bed wondering about the sound of the revving engine across the street from his house, in the area where he kept his lumber. *There's an abandoned railway line at the far end of my farm,* he said, pointing as we said our goodbyes, after he had invited us in to wash up, *you can come and park there anytime.* He smiled as he said this, and Mark had the good sense to blush.

It was in that mood that we set off for home, which meant back to our dorms, a little contrite on his part, a little jazzed up on mine, never mind that it was I who had got us into the mess in the first place. By the time we stopped at Uncle Moe's Diner, a place we visited for decades after, whenever we were back in Lewiston, Maine, but that we had never heard of until that morning, Mark was a little tired of my crowing, and I was just getting started.

The diner was crowded that Sunday morning, old-timers filling up the tables, the waitresses busy. We got a table for two by a half-wall off to the side of the main room. For no good reason that I can recall, I started humming the melody to a song that my mother had taught me to sing when I was about seven years old: "The Star-Spangled Banner."

"Why don't you just sing the words?" Mark taunted.

I did.

"Why don't you sing it louder?" he said.

I did.

"I dare you to stand up by this table and sing it," he challenged me.

"I will," I said, and made to stand.

He said, "I bet you wouldn't go to the front of this diner and sing it there."

The waitress came by to take our order. I don't remember what I ordered. When she left, I followed her to the counter, which sat just to the left of the front door to the restaurant, open to the room and its diners. I spoke to the older woman standing there, told her I'd like to sing the national anthem. I love Maine, my first American home state, and I love Mainers, unfazed by just about anything. She asked me to wait a minute, she'd need to ask Moe.

"You want to sing the national anthem?" Uncle Moe asked me, a little furrow on his brow. "Why?"

I don't know how this fragment of information came back to me. It was either my international relations major or my debate prep, but it sprang to my lips with ease: "Because the troops are coming home."

Uncle Moe walked around that counter and stood beside me. "Excuse me, everybody," he said to his customers, "this young lady would like to sing the national anthem in honor of the troops coming home today." He turned to me and said, "Go ahead."

I began, glancing over with triumph at Mark, who sat with his fingers interlaced, utterly shocked. I began, but it was not the sweet song that my mother had taught me that rose to my lips, but a song-on-a-dare, the kind of song that could be any song. But when my eyes moved away from him and returned to the people in front of me, I saw that most of them had stood up and had their palms over their hearts. I earned my citizenship to this country more than a decade later, but I believe that I learned my love for this country in that moment. I could see so clearly what this anthem meant to each person there, the stooped veterans, the women and men on their way to church, the ones for whom the stop at this diner was a Sunday ritual. I could see not Americans but people for whom these words meant just as much as the words of my own country's anthem meant to me. I don't believe I have ever sung any song with more heart than that one, with more empathy than what I felt for that audience.

It isn't the applause that has stayed with me, or the *thank you for singing the anthem today* that I heard from a few of them who were leaving as we did, or the fact that Uncle Moe and his wife remembered me when Mark and I, by then married, went back years later, that they said, looking at me, *Aren't you the young lady who sang the anthem here?* What has stayed with me is the grace I learned in understanding that my song was a much smaller gift to those people than their gratitude was to me. For in that gratitude I saw a bridge, the one I walk on toward people I don't know, the one I lay down for them to walk toward me. It has no political stripe, no class, no gender, no agendas, it is itself: a bridge built of that grace, and recognition of each other's essential, deep, vulnerable humanity.

Black Skin White Skin

Many years ago, when I was working at an elite liberal arts college, I held a freelance job as a writer for the college magazine. Part of my duties included covering speakers who came to campus, one of whom was Cornel West. The piece I wrote, "Single Man March,"[1] was drawn from the six pages of notes that I took, notes that transcribed every word that was being uttered in the room, from the introduction of the speaker to the last response from Mr. West to a question from the audience. I don't always work that way. I've had the kind of education that trained me to pick out the important details from the mass of superfluous fluff that usually punctuates our speech. The things that give me a solid opening for an article, or those that highlight a point I wish to make, appear in the auditory version of highlighted text in a book, and I write it down.

Cornel West, however, is a different cup of tea. His eminence and his intellect combines with his fast-paced speech to make it impossible to simply wait for "the important pieces." Every word, every sentence carries something of note, something worth listening to, something worth capturing in an overview. I do not believe in disturbing everybody else at a gathering with the clacking of my keyboard, and Cornel West does not allow his speeches to be taped. The task before me then was to simply write down everything. Pen, paper, and my ears: these were my tools. In writing about Mr. West, I described him using the words of a faculty member who had called him, with a nod and a smile, during her introduction, "and, yes, the violent and eloquent public intellectual he is." She seemed, in her remarks, to be carrying over something they had talked about prior to their arrival on stage. At the private dinner. Maybe.

I used her words because, as I wrote this piece, I was asked to speak to her on account of the fact that she was, I suppose, the most prominent Black faculty member on campus. Since she had nothing to add to the story, and said so, I went back to my notes and used what she had said during her introduction of Mr. West. The day the magazine came out, this professor ripped into my editor, claiming that she had never said such a

---

[1] *Colby Magazine* vol. 93, no. 2, June 29th, 2004.

thing. I, initially willing to discuss this matter with the professor, sent her an email which she replied by calling me a racist, who needed to "examine the racism in my own head," and pointedly referencing her doctorate in her signature—I had made the additional mistake, apparently, of referring to her by her first name. She also emailed her message detailing her outrage to my editor and all the senior staff including the president of the college (via BCC, but of course).

It was the kind of attack that a member of the faculty would never make on someone of equal status—economic, professional, or minority hue. I, with no steady job on campus, an outlier without a department or any kind of official position within the college, was easy fodder. Mercifully, my editor, a fellow writer and the author of many novels, took my side. In the face of her behavior, I told him I would not apologize, I stood by my words and could share my six pages of notes with him and that if this person had some notes of her own that she could show, or could tell us what it was that she had said, we could talk. The correction from the editor was a "she says" that referred to her statement that she did not say such a thing, but issued no apology, although the online version has expunged the word "violent" from the text.

It amused me, over the years, that whenever I saw this professor in public she always seemed delighted to see me. On each occasion she addressed me warmly, though she never asked my name, quite as if we were old friends. On more than one occasion she paused to photograph me and a friend of mine, as we stood together at some event. I assume she photographed us because we were both of color, since neither my friend nor I were acquainted with her. It occurred to me that in her attack on me she never tried to learn who I might be, or what credentials I had to my name, or any history of integrity that might have given her pause. It was simply an easy attack to make, and she chose to make it on account, among other things, of my last name: Freeman, which, Morgan notwithstanding, is routinely assumed to be White, Jewish.

Time passed. I moved away.

On an everyday afternoon, when she was just a second grader, my youngest came home with a blotch on her name. While standing second in line behind a boy from her class, another boy came out of school, pushed past everyone and tried to take her place—do I have to note that he did not dare dislodge the boy, but felt fine dislodging the girl? She asked him how he got there and told him he needed to go to the back of the line since he had been last out of the school. The boy went home and told his parents, who informed the school principal that she had said, "I don't like Black people." It was a dirty way to wiggle out of the spot he was in because, of course, in a happily liberal, mostly White elementary school, that was a phrase that would have a certain response. Never mind that my daughter is, herself, of mixed race. Never mind that her mother is a brown-skinned immigrant and often referred to as being Black. All that mattered was, obviously, that she looks white (she is light skinned and has dark brown hair), and that made it okay to defame her character in a way that drew attention to the color of each of their bodies.

I won't go into the conversation I had with the principal, nor my opinion of parents who are raising that kid with that perspective. I will, however, go into the school board meeting that was held not long after, to elect a new member to the board due to the sudden retirement of one of the other members. There had been many difficulties for the school board in this district, much of them related to race, and the meeting was full of people, both in the audience and as administrators, who had come there carrying a lot of baggage from that past. I went with the express intention of speaking on behalf of one of the candidates who happened to be White. The candidate of the hour, however, was the wife of a pastor, who happened to be Black. As I listened to the proceedings, and to the interview of this particular candidate, I began to feel that she had something unique to bring to the table, a historical perspective and experience that could, perhaps, add something that was not already covered by one or more of the people currently serving on the board. And so though I got up and spoke, eloquently, I'm told, on behalf of my friend, I also acknowledged the merits of the other person's candidacy, something I had come to understand in light of the information I had gathered during the proceedings. I agreed publicly, in fact, during the course of that speech, that her election would possibly be of more benefit to the district than that of my friend.

What struck me, however, was the tone of many of those who stood up to speak on her behalf, and the room was almost entirely filled with her supporters. Far too many of them, *both Black and White*, made derogatory remarks about the complexion of the current board, their very "Whiteness" somehow a problem that made them "lesser" and "incapable of understanding." Doing the right thing, as one after the other got up to say, was to "take a look in the mirror." In other words, there was something inherently wrong about all the White people, something about their "Whiteness" that prevented them from, I suppose, caring about their kids (who also attend these same schools), the schools themselves, and neighborhood communities, the achievement gap, the budget, etc. etc. It made me wonder what would have happened if any one person, let alone dozens of them, had got up and said there was something wrong about the candidate who was Black who, because of her "Blackness," could not "understand" the issues pertinent to a district that is predominantly White? (The breakdown of the district at the time is as follows: White 83.1 percent; Black 7.9 percent; Asian/Pacific Islander 6.8 percent; and American Indian/Alaska Native 0.3 percent). What was *not* addressed, in all of these speeches, would turn out to be the very things that my second grader and her friends would grow up to address: the fact that the district was inaccessible to many Black families because of class, and the historical disenfranchisement of Black people, conditions that Cornel West would be tasked for referencing when arguing against the liberal embrace of Ta-Nehisi Coates and his certainly excellent tome, *We Had Eight Years in Power*;[2] and that Nikole Hannah-Jones would one day cover in the 1619 Project, in which the essay by Matthew Desmond, on the brutality of American capitalism, stands out.[3] Conditions that were, in fact, beyond the administrative duties of the school board but were certainly well within the purview of their personal lives, voting patterns, purchasing power, and advocacy in the world beyond it.

The liberal minded are quick to agree that it is never okay for someone who is White to say something derogatory about someone who is Black. The standard is, of course, justified, for we consider power differentials when we look at these demographics objectively. But not, as we all also agree, when we consider each other individually, i.e., subjectively. Why is it then that we are all so comfortable with saying anything we like about people who are White? I count myself in that group, by the way. My rants, albeit private, often carry the term "White People" as a group that is engaging in some stupidity, incompetence, lack, in the same way that I feel

---

[2] West, Cornel. "Ta-Nehisi Coates is the Neoliberal Face of the Black Freedom Struggle." *The Guardian*, December 17th, 2017.

[3] Desmond, Matthew. "In order to Understand the Brutality of American Capitalism, You Have to Start on the Plantation." *New York Times*, "The 1619 Project." August 14th, 2019.

perfectly justified ranting about "Americans," all within these unalterable facts: three decades of life with a partner who is both White and American, three daughters who are also half White and all American, not to mention my own joint-citizenship of this country.

I can claim that my prejudices are justifiable. My entire career as a journalist began when I had it up to my eyeballs with White women assuming that I was the hired help whenever I was with my light-skinned firstborn daughter. (Their children never made that mistake, it was always the adults; children notice interactions, they notice the mothering that is so distinct from the work of a nanny.) I once sat in the office of a health care specialist at the nation's top pediatric hospital, CHOP, and had the bizarre experience of having her turn to me—after I'd filled out all the paperwork, along with my oldest daughter, after we'd been there for about half an hour— and ask me with more than a little doubt if I was her mother. I will not write here what I could have said there. What I did say was, simply, "yes," and then I mentally took a step back to evaluate the conversation. Perhaps, I thought charitably, she feels I looked too young to be the mother of this tall young girl, something I hear often. But that was because I was taking the time to be generous. In other words, I was taking the time to reflect on relationships.

My life in America and my political work have certainly given me enough cause to feel that it is entirely within the realm of reason and good behavior for me to trash both Americans and White people whenever the American government commits some fresh crime or vast swaths of Americans (of every race and ethnicity), under the Tea Party or "Proud Boys" or some other banner, utter some blasphemy (against immigrants, the gay community, artists, women, etc.), or whenever another private slight comes in my direction from an inattentive/insensitive person. My White friends laugh along with me, poking fun at themselves for their "Whiteness"—their inability to eat flaming hot curries, for instance, or some other trait that is associated with their race. Perhaps in the correct context, where affection (for friends), or love (for one's partner), is not in question, such speeches are allowable. Perhaps within the privacy of one's home it is innocuous to let fly at all the petty and large things we cannot control. And perhaps the depth of my obvious civic and other commitments to America, my nurturing and writing in support of its good, and my equally obvious happy co-existence with innumerable White people suffice to absolve me. But perhaps not. Because in the end, what we talk about around a dining table has a way of filtering out into the world in the minds and hearts of the children we raise.

Mine will never be heard saying anything derogatory about Black people (or any BIPOC). That is an out-of-bounds that holds within these four walls as steadfastly as it holds outside them. And they will not be heard saying they don't like White people because that would indicate a level of self-loathing that they are too joyous to carry within them. But somewhere in the midst of the goodwill that they embody sits their mother who feels just as comfortable expressing strong and public support for White people as she does expressing equally strong dislike for them. So what, exactly, am I teaching them? Quite possibly the same thing that was taught to all those people—Black and White—who got up and felt comfortable looking directly into the faces of fellow hard-working, all-volunteer, much beleaguered elected officials and trashing them for the whiteness of their skin.

It is far too late for the professor, but not for us. I hope that as I sit here mulling over these issues, somewhere else in this neighborhood, there's another mother reevaluating her prejudices tonight. Perhaps it will be possible for both her son and my daughter to grow up in a world where nobody, of any color, uses race as an easy out or an easy in, and where the humanity of a person—even a person whose politics they dislike—is never obscured in their eyes by the color of their skin.

Then again, I believe that was asked of us more than half a century ago by a man of cloth, and we, divergent-minded flock that we are, keep failing to rise to that dream.

Many Rights, Few Responsibilities

I became a citizen of the United States on the eve of the invasion of Iraq. Sitting in a room at the University of Maine, holding my infant daughter, I listened to a speech made by an administrator who spoke not of the benefits of citizenship but of its responsibilities: to participate in civic engagement, to vote, to speak out against injustice. There was a note of despair to the address, in that way things sound when we speak of what we hope will happen while being fully conscious of the horror of what is actually going to come to pass.

"Why do you want to become a citizen?" I was asked this by a local TV reporter as I strode up, decked in my sari, to cut a large chocolate cake decorated to resemble the American flag—not because I had been appointed to do so, but because everybody else seemed too nervous to disrupt the red, white, and blue. "I want to demonstrate what it means to be a citizen," I replied. "I want to give my American daughters a model of citizenship where pride in one's country does not absolve one of working to mend its ills."

All these years later, I find that my answer to the reporter still stands. I have a deep allegiance to Sri Lanka, the country in which I was born, and the call-and-response of America, where I now live, comes to me as a responsibility. To teach my daughters the same loyalty to the land of their birth that I feel for my own, I have to let the country where I have raised them get under my skin. In the face of overwhelming evidence of my love for Sri Lanka, I must demonstrate my love for America in ever-more meaningful ways.

Love for a country must surely carry with it love for its many parts. To claim love for this country and yet care not a whit for the public education of other people's children, or the fate of young people too poor to have any other choice but to risk their lives at war, or the abandonment of people whose skin color marks them for a lifetime of injustice, is to exist in a vacuum where you possess but a superficial understanding of those two words: love, and country.

I have discovered that love is a responsibility that has little to do with rights. I have listened, time and again, to Americans who can quote the First, the Second, the Fourth, and the Fifth Constitutional Amendments. Rarely have I heard my fellow citizens speak up on behalf of the other amendments—the Thirteenth, the Fourteenth, and the Fifteenth, for instance, crafted to ensure dignity, due process, and equality, respectively, whose language speaks to the creation of the perfect union that we all seek, and requires us to make a more nuanced reading of those other, more popular amendments.

An interpretation of rights unrelated to responsibility does not speak to me of love of country or of patriotism. We live among others in a social agreement where the laws governing our rights provide a guide to the responsibility each of us has toward others. Those laws should be the last resort in our interactions, to be summoned when all conversation is spent, when all negotiation is done—in other words, when we are broken.

As a Sri Lankan, I grew up understanding that what is given freely must still be earned. A free education must be earned by upholding respect for education and rigorous intellectual pursuits. Free health care must still be earned by the purchase and consumption and, if possible, the cultivation of native vegetables, fruits, and herbs. The freely given affections of parents and grandparents and extended family must be earned by a willingness to tend to the elderly, a consideration for the dying, and the transmission of those values to a younger generation.

The freedoms that Americans are so quick to mention are no different. They, too, ought to be earned. We ought to deserve them, somehow. That somehow, to me, does not come on the wings of a recitation of the Pledge of Allegiance but on the heels of attentiveness to the work that must be done in any neighborhood, in any community, in any state, in any given moment.

As I teach my daughters the American anthems that my own mother taught me to sing long before this American life came to pass, I favor less the bombast of "The Star-Spangled Banner;" rather, it is that other anthem of a beautiful country that I sing most often. And, perhaps because words are the foundation of my life, my daughters can hear in my voice the note of care that accompanies the celebration of a bountiful nation: to mend our flaws, to confirm our souls in self-control, to refine our goals, to ennoble our successes, to ensure that selfish gain no longer stains the banner of the free. Perhaps most of all, I hope that they hear in those words the reminder that we are asking for, not demanding, the grace that might bring us the brotherhood we still lack, that I commit to making beauty possible, and expect them to do the same.

This past June, I found myself walking down a highway with that child I had held while being sworn in long ago. She was there, now seventeen, along with one of her older sisters, several of their friends, and thousands of Philadelphians demanding an end to police violence. In a single afternoon, she witnessed the dream articulated by a constitution that gave her the right to speak on behalf of brotherhood, itself evidenced by the fierce solidarity of those around her. She also experienced a state-sanctioned assault, in direct opposition to that constitutionally guaranteed right, with weapons banned by the Geneva Convention even in times of war, an atrocity that generated an international outcry. On the one hand, beauty, on the other, what must change. A right directly related to responsibility.

Among the regular speakers at Black Lives Matter rallies in Philadelphia is Mike Africa Junior, a father of four who was born in prison to wrongfully convicted parents who were jailed for forty years. He is also a spokesperson for the Black-liberation organization MOVE, which was bombed by Philadelphia police in 1985, who killed six adults and five children, incinerated sixty-one homes, and left more than 250 Philadelphians destitute, a precursor to the attack that took place against us on June 1, 2020, on that highway. "There is so much injustice in this country," he said, standing in Malcolm X Park on June 13th at the end of a march that wound through West Philadelphia thirty-five years after the MOVE bombing, "that we the people are forced to step into the streets to fight for justice in the middle of a fucking global pandemic."

Streets in small towns and big cities have been filled with dutifully masked people who've shared hand sanitizer, home-cooked food, extra masks, and water, as they've called for the dismantling of racist institutions. My daughters in Philadelphia and in Denver are among them, all acting in flagrant defiance of a curfew designed to stifle dissent. On July 4th, they were at another rally calling for the freeing of the wrongfully detained, and for resources earmarked for a brutal police force to be instead reallocated to community-building initiatives, to schools, and to the arts. It does not escape my notice that my daughters live in wealthy townships where they are afforded all those things in spades, in and outside their schools and places of work. Their presence on the streets on behalf of their fellow Americans is the real testament to the strength of their citizenship. It also does not escape my notice that they have no difficulty drawing parallels between the segregated streets of American cities and the apartheid walls running through the West Bank in Palestine.

I come full circle now, remembering the oath I made at that long-ago ceremony, and the words I spoke to the reporter after. I look at my daughters and I see that I have done what so many immigrants did before me: passed on a necessary fire in service of the real American dream of equality. I watch it burn in their fearless hands.

A Fight in Good Hands

I say what I think. Perhaps that's a bit of an understatement. I say what I think about a multitude of things, and often when I'm saying what I think I am in direct conflict with what a majority of people may be thinking about the same thing, or I am at odds with a more comfortable point of view. For people who don't know me personally it may seem as though I am constantly in the thick of one sort of battle or another, usually against forces far greater than any I could muster, often against those who are going to cream me in the long run.

I learned from the best: my father is now in retirement and lives as he does because he stuck to his guns through decades of service to multiple governments; my late mother was, and in memory remains, beloved precisely for her willingness to tell it like it is. My brothers and I carry the torch. (Only one of us, the oldest, is able to let some things go unsaid, and I attribute that to his deeper involvement in Buddhist scripture and his renunciation of much of the noise produced by politics.)

What sustains me is what sustained and sustains them: a belief that, if I do not shy away from doing my small part, in the end, good will prevail for us all. To paraphrase the Pink Floyd song, I guess the "walk-on part in the war" has always seemed more preferable to the people in my family than the "lead role in a cage." And though my mother, in particular, often worried about our fate, and sometimes tried to tell us how hard the fall would be from the edge of that limb up high in the sky, or how bare our necks looked, exposed as they were, what could we do but as she did, as our father did: keep climbing, keep sticking our necks out.

People who do know me know that, whatever it looks like from the outside, I try to live a peaceable, compassionate life, attending just as much to moments of grace as I do to the injustices that plague us. And, as a rule, I tend to take people at their word, to accept that they are who they say they are, to believe that they are well-intentioned until proven otherwise. When I do find something that gets under my skin, more often than not what I can bring to a cause is my voice. If I have been given the gift of words, then it stands to reason that I should use it to honor the gift giver by using it to the best of my abilities. But passion and words are both double-edged swords.

One weekend, I fell into conversation with a neighbor. We had both been concerned about the misuse of authority on the part of an individual employed by the school district in which we live, and we had talked about bringing our concerns to the relevant people. He, however, had decided, in consultation with his wife, that it would be better *not to become involved*. What he said gave me pause. Touching my shoulder in genuine reassurance, he said, *We know the fight is in good hands*, i.e., mine.

Like I said, I learned from the best. I learned to speak up. I also learned that nobody gets anything done by themselves. Audre Lorde pointed out that our issues are not unrelated. The Occupy Wall Street movement is a perfect example of what she was talking about, despite the fact that so many seemed not to understand the reason for its seeming "chaos." But we also do not fight our battles alone. The perhaps-mythical boy with his finger in the dyke may have prevented the town from being inundated and countless human beings from drowning, but he suffered greatly while doing it. I do not imagine that I am that important, or that anything I do is comparable to that story, but I do know that standing alone is, well, lonely, often futile, and usually fatal to one's well-being. One only needs to look at the most recent spate of depression and fatalities among young activists of color—like Ashley Yates and Erica Garner—to understand the toll.

In another lifetime, it seems, in the months after I had returned to the US after an extended stay back home, when I was still looking for work and spent my time watching the Senate hearings on TV, hour by endless hour, I went to Newark, New Jersey, to stand on a street corner to protest the attacks against Bill Clinton in the throes of the Lewinsky scandal. It was an event organized by a relatively small group called Censure and Move On, a group that has since become MoveOn.org, a behemoth power in politics whose refusal to stand with communities I care about has made it far less impressive in my eyes. As we drove up, we saw that, on a grey and rainy afternoon, there were two people standing on the corner with umbrellas. My companion, whose constant charge has been to save me from myself, surveying the embarrassing scene from a fair distance, said, "Ru, don't be nuts. Let's not make fools of ourselves standing in the rain with two people." The words that sprang to my lips came not from me but from generations of people who had felt the same way I did right then: "That's when it is important to stand out there," I said. "What is the use of joining something when there are a thousand people there? *This*, when it is difficult and uncomfortable, *this* is when it counts." With that I stormed off, and, as he often does, he soon followed, even though this type of shenanigan is not his thing, has never been; it will always be difficult for him, but, to his everlasting credit (much more than I deserve, because, hard though it may be, I grew up learning to be comfortable with being uncomfortable), he has always done it when it counts, even when it meant, as it did that day, dragging along a two-year-old who held up her own borrowed poster with two declarations, both of which were patently false: "My Memory Is Long and I Vote!"

I may have the words to write persuasively about my case, and those words probably give the impression that the "fight," whatever it is, can be successfully won by me. I may speak with passion for my candidate, my cause, my peeve, and that passion probably makes people believe that I'm "passionate enough for the both of us." Neither is true. Nothing, absolutely nothing, except for love for another and enlightenment of the soul, can be accomplished alone. No matter how strong the words, no matter how great the passion. Everything takes a village. And then many villages. And entire regions. And a country. And many countries. But mostly, it takes more than one. The fight is not in good hands if it remains in the hands of a single person because that is usually a fight that is going to be lost. These are the words I should have said to that neighbor: if you ever wonder if it is really necessary to raise your hand and be counted when somebody else seems to have it covered, or if it seems a little out of your comfort zone, even though you are invested in the outcome, or if you are worried about what this one or that one might think of you, even though you really hope the fight will be won, rest assured, it is. It is always necessary. Unless you are equally invested, equally hopeful that the fight is going to be lost. If that is the case, by all means, leave it all to one person.

When in Doubt, Climb the Roof

I was a tomboy who would rather be caught scaling the roof than reading, a child who couldn't tell the difference between the letter "b" and the letter "d" long after it ceased to be adorable, in a family that could ill afford, but loved, books. And yet I grew up to be someone for whom the instruments of writing and the printed word are essential for both livelihood and life.

It might seem that the shift from one set of predispositions (the wild, devil-may-care play and restlessness of my childhood) to the other (the focused, inward-seeking determination of the adult) would have been tortuous for me, but it wasn't. In a family like mine, filled with parents and older brothers who reveled in the glory of words, written, read aloud, recited, performed, the matter of writing was a given. What else would anybody do but read and write? For me to resist words would have been like Anoushka Shankar resisting music. It is easy to run away from family, and I certainly did, carrying myself from Sri Lanka and establishing a homestead in the often-unforgiving landscape of America, but the family and traditions that run in our veins—these would require a bloodletting that could be fatal. Far better to give in. Far better to figure out how to write on top of the roof with a stolen guava for company.

And so, I did.

I am seven years old. My father has suffered the first of many events that could be described as strokes, or "cardiac events." He has been rushed away in an army ambulance summoned by his best friend, then retired, now late Brigadier Eustace Fonseka, to the ICU. It is an event that is significant enough for me to begin a journal. This journal is a very small notebook with about ten ruled pieces of paper bound together, four inches by seven inches, the kind of notebooks used by my grandfather to keep track of the number of coconuts plucked in his fields each season.

I write: *Today Appatchi was taken in an ambulance to the accident service. Uncle Eustace took him. He had a heart attack.*

I cover the exterior of this book with brown paper very, very neatly, exactly as I had learned how to do from my mother, a teacher of English literature. I write my name on the front. I am only seven, but I have no reason not to believe that whatever I write down is both important and worth a great deal of attention, not to mention being preserved for posterity. I continue to write in books small and large through all the changes in my life, my words growing from simple to complex sentences, to paragraphs that detail many things. My concerns include:

—The coming of television to Sri Lanka;
—Domestic abuse;
—My oldest brother winning a trophy half his size for the Light of Asia contest in which he recites the words of Edwin Arnold's *Prince Siddhartha*;
—The receipt of a signed Christmas card from Ranjan Madugalle, then captain of the Royal College cricket team, eventually to play for and captain Sri Lanka's team, and afterward to serve as chief referee of the International Cricket Council;
—Much later, the receipt of an email from that same Ranjan Madugalle, upon having been given my first novel during a transatlantic flight between world test matches, and the way my heart skipped beats in precisely the same way it did when I was twelve years old;
—The way he came and stood by my mother's coffin, silent, his head bowed, during the wake and on the day of her funeral. That same Ranjan given a starring role in anecdote and conjecture in my second novel, the way that life comes full circle;
—Death threats that came routinely, all addressed to my father;
—Our flight from our own home to an official house, and the boys— Priyantha, Thilak, Ananda, Premasiri, Saman, and sometimes Nishadh and Malta, other friends of my brothers—whom we took with us for fear that they would be disappeared;
—Multiple boyfriends;
—The necessary heartbreak of first true love;
—An older brother leaving for Harvard University, the only institution to which he agreed to apply, and which preempted his determination never to come to America by calling his bluff with the award of a full scholarship; the way Cornell University followed suit for graduate studies;
—His incarceration as a political prisoner upon his return between the two;
—An entire class of students deciding not to speak to me for most of my eighth-grade year;

—An entire class of students in a different school deciding not to speak to me for most of my two last years of high school;
—Not merely surviving but thriving in the face of these things;
—My brothers' love affairs, their marriages, separations, and second marriages;
—Sexual abuse;
—The Tiananmen Square massacre;
—Leaving for university in Sri Lanka;
—Leaving to join my father to study for almost a year in Australia;
—Leaving for college in America;
—The diagnosis of cancer;
—Leaving for the Bread Loaf Writers' Conference, the bliss found there;
—Marriage, its rewards and challenges;
—Daughters, their rewards and challenges;
—Estrangement, divorce;
—The loss of my mother;
—The loss of my mother;
—The loss of my mother;
—Hope that I will survive, that my heart will be healed, and that I will be loved;
—Etc.

What I never write in my journals: ideas for stories, essays, or my novels.

*

I am eighteen, between having taken the G.C.E. A/L Examination and receiving results. I work as a temp for J. Walter Thompson Advertising Ltd. at an office where fabulously cosmopolitan women talk about sleeping around and insufferably fatuous men order their secretaries about. I notice the peon, an old man, who comes around to serve tea at ten a.m. and three p.m. each day. I'm low on the totem pole; mine is often more lukewarm than hot by the time it gets to me, and yet I am very grateful. I find out that the man has a son who has taken his A/Ls too and is also awaiting results. I write a short story about this boy, making him the peon, turning him into a fellow student who will one day attend the same campus I will, a story about a picture he might draw for me. It wins the national prize for creative writing in English and I am awarded a certificate by the President of Sri Lanka at the annual ceremony. My mother ensures that I have a blouse made to go with the new sari I am to wear for this occasion, but both my parents despise the president, Ranasinghe Premadasa, and so I go to the gala alone, not realizing then that this will be the story of my life at gala after gala after gala. In a show of solidarity with my parents, I refuse to bring my hands together in the traditional greeting for the president and simply gather my certificate with a certain haughty air. I doubt he noticed.

This, too, is my birthright, this idea that whatever I do in life, it must be conscious of politics, of social justice, of basic rights, that the privilege of being capacitated with language and opportunity can only be gilded by speaking for and of.

And so, I do.

In the wake of that award, I gather with other young writers and set down poetry and prose that speaks to the *bheeshanaya* that we were trying to survive. Those friends of my brothers, the ones who call me *nangi*, and indulge me and nurture me and tease me like they would their own younger sisters, I write of them. About the way they hide in our city home, how they sleep in my brothers' room, lined like fish drying in the sun, how silent they are with army boys living next door to us, how we buy extra rice, but secretly so as not to arouse suspicions, how we say nothing of note on the tapped telephone, how we can't afford to buy so much extra food and so plant fast-growing okra and cook it in different ways to pretend that it is some new vegetable. I write about how they have been given work as security guards by my father's older brother, and how my own brother refuses to break the pact he has made with his friend, Thilak, who is afraid to go to work without the closed shoes he's been borrowing from my brother, who has only that pair of good shoes.

He says: *If I wear my security uniform and go on the buses without real shoes, they will know I am not one. They will take me away.*

My brother says: *Don't worry, you take them.*

My mother, unaware of this bargain, says: *Malinda, you made me feel so ashamed in front of Lakshmi, showing up in rubber slippers at Pradeep's wedding.*

I write of my brother's silence. And I rewrite a poem written by my father, adding the completely unoriginal *cri de coeur* of youth against the older generation, realigning his words with my own decade of protest, graciously offering him, too, a role as I set these two poems next to each other and send them off as supplementary material with my applications to American colleges, all of which award me full scholarships.

In college, I dedicate my thesis on the exploitation of five South Asian countries—Sri Lanka, Bangladesh, Pakistan, Nepal, and India—by USAID, a thesis that closes with a quote from Audre Lorde, to the lady who cleans our dorms, Patricia Draper. She shows the page to the college president when she retires. I visit her for as long as I can whenever I go back to Maine, until, decades after, she dies of lung cancer from a lifetime of smoking.

Also in college I write, against the persuasion of my entire class, in defense of cultures like mine where the sharing of food and money is a given, where what we might consider crass has to do with making a fuss about those things. I get an A in that class from a teacher who smiles with delight as I argue my case. Years later, I get to mention her name in the acknowledgements at the back of my first novel, *A Disobedient Girl*, a book I could not have foreseen writing then, but is an *of course* now. I don't know if she knows this.

I confront widespread misuse of company funds and perks at my first job out of college as an administrative assistant. I do this in writing, never once doubting the power of a persuasively composed argument. As a result, I find myself six months pregnant with my first baby and appointed to direct the program for five states and the capitol solo. I soldier on.

Writing never fails to soothe me. And just as I had done as a very young child, writing to the newspapers when the president showed up on TV during what should have been Sesame Street, I know that setting down the details of whatever is tormenting me energizes me. In doing so, too, I learn to unite my passion for social justice with my personal life, in exactly the same way that my older brothers do as journalists and activists. Every moment, every interaction, is a point of takeoff for certain kinds of writing, and the unwavering faith I had in my words as a seven-year-old has not left me.

The slang term for the English language in Sinhala is *kaduwa*, which means sword. It is used to describe the way the acquisition of that language is used like a sword to fell those who do not possess a command of it. This language, English, is one that I have learned to use as a weapon, albeit not against the hapless, but against those who wield a power greater than my own—or that of those with whom I identify—in some capacity, be it through privilege, wealth, or politics.

∗

I wield it this way:

I am in the showers of the YMCA in Madison, New Jersey, where my four-year-old daughter is rinsing off after swim class, and I am standing by holding her shampoo and towel. A woman addresses me as my daughter's nanny, from Jamaica, no less. I have been taken for a nanny to my light-skinned daughter many times, but this is the veritable last straw. I write my anger to the newspapers, eviscerating the provincialism of upper-class suburban Americans in Morris County (the tenth richest county in the nation), and highlighting the racism that has, as of yet, escaped their off-spring. The newspaper contacts me to ask if I would write regularly to the paper. It begins my career as a journalist who pens opinion pieces on a range of subjects, from Hillary Clinton's lack of cultural savvy to the religious underpinnings of Iranian President Ahmadinejad's letter to George Bush, my support of Palestine on every front, about politics in Sri Lanka, and politics in the United States but also about popular American culture, literature, poets, writers, and books. And also anthologies that cajole other writers to put their pens to paper on behalf of Palestine, on behalf of an idea that our security, our places of sanctuary must be all-encompassing, not mirages or fortresses built always against an "other."

And for all the things that a newspaper cannot do, for getting to the very heart of things that matter to me in life, there is fiction. When the personal essay I was working on regarding the end of the war in Sri Lanka did not conform to the sterile untruths required by the renowned newspaper to which it had been promised, I took the truth I knew in my bones and turned it into the fiction of my second novel, *On Sal Mal Lane*, which is set in the five years leading up to the riots of 1983 in Sri Lanka that preceded another quarter century of war. This particular war was personal to me, a story of my country, but the larger issue of the inner psychic dislocations wrought by wars was central to the work of that book. In other words, it was, as all of my writing has been, a marriage between the personal (outrage at the story preferred by the Western media about Sri Lanka) and the universal (the unsung and unmourned details of war, any war).

It seems then, in retrospect, that my approach to writing is grounded deeply in the way I came to it in the first place, from within the parameters set by family and culture. The child who ran amok in the neighborhood, collecting dirt, bruises, injuries even, broken violins *and* broken roof tiles, and who wrote of those experiences in single-ruled notebooks is the same one who goes fearlessly into life as an adult, as willing to join a protest with only a handful of people against a pernicious invasion of an innocent nation as she is content to knock on doors with thousands in support of an American presidential candidate whose very name reminds this country of the existence of a world beyond its borders, as moved to write about the importance of respecting our teachers in public schools as she is to write novels about foreign wars.

I write to transmit the life that I have lived, that others have lived. When I write as a journalist, I do so to put my rage at ease, to bring myself to a place where I no longer feel impotent in the face of injustice. When I write nonfiction essays, I do so to look closely at the culture that raised me and the culture that holds me now. When I write fiction, I do so to dwell in compassion, to love the unlovable, to understand the humanity of those with whom I would disagree to the bitter end. When I write poetry, I do so to share myself, unfiltered, an asking rather than a telling.

Writing = joy + gratitude. I am blessed, and I cannot and never will see writing as work. It is, every step of the way, a gift to dwell within words. And my gratitude for that gift must be laid at the feet of my family, particularly my mother, who stood by and let me climb that roof and also read every word I put down on paper, whether essays or articles or stories. I encourage my daughters to climb that same roof when we visit home, and I shoo away the neighbors—who express their concern, their faces etched in horror at this "jungly behavior." I don't know if my daughters know why I join them on that roof sometimes, or why I bring them food for imaginary journeys taken up there as well as pieces of paper and pens, if asked.

A Brief for the Defense of a White Man

On December 10th, 2016, Patti Smith sang Bob Dylan's "A Hard Rain's A-Gonna Fall," backed by the Royal Stockholm Philharmonic Orchestra conducted by Hans Ek. She was there as part of the celebration that would present the Nobel Prize for Literature to Bob Dylan, and she chose, at the last minute, to substitute one of his songs for one of hers. As a *New Yorker* (Petrusich, December 10th, 2016) wrap on the event put it, the choice of Dylan by the Nobel Prize Committee "incited plenty of pearl clutching across the globe" on the part of people who felt that his lyrics—transcendent to one of America's most famous decades, which brought citizens out in force to protest a range of atrocities, including Stonewall, the incarceration of Rubin "Hurricane" Carter, and, of course, the war on Vietnam—were too lowbrow.

The disruption in my own corner of our communal puzzle was relatively mild, albeit forcefully communicated, my apparent error being having the gall to commend those who had maintained neutrality in the face of the announcement from the Nobel committee. The exchanges that took place between my friends, mostly poets, and myself, were rife with all the necessary bluster and flourish, and the usual incendiary language around citizenship, class, and race, not to mention genre: Would I feel the same sanguinity were it a novelist of, allegedly, no great acclaim who had been recognized? What poets would I choose, were I doing the choosing? Apart from the fact that I do not possess the vital distinction of having 31 million Swedish kronor to establish and endow a prize in my name (and yes, we could talk about how wealth becomes concentrated in the hands of those who don't generally tend to favor my hue, nation of birth, or gender, not to mention the fact that the accrual of such wealth usually depends upon the oppression of those like me), my feelings about which of my poet idols might better deserve the accolade is worth about a whole red cent. More useful is the consideration of the intent of the award as stated by Alfred Nobel: *en som inom litteraturen had producerat det mest framstående verket i en idealisk riktning.* Or, in plain English, an award for a body of work in *an ideal direction*, a concept that carries with it an implicit awareness of the fact that the author of the work should be working not toward a simple cre-ation of interesting, even brilliant work, but rather demonstrating a track record of speaking toward an ideal version of the world. The sort of work that depends first upon having the moral fortitude to name what ails us.

I've had occasion to think of this latest bout of *non alors!* that gripped the nation, particularly the literary set, in light of the election that followed. It is vital, of course, in the aftermath of that disaster to continue with, to borrow from James Wood, the "thisness" of a life in letters: the sincere observance of our rituals of praise and blame, our ordinary—yet deeply felt—notions of what makes for good, notable, necessary, mind-expand-ing, world-transforming high art. And yet, this other matter of the elec-tion of a dangerous, ignorant sociopath at the helm of an army of proven bigots and racists. And yet, the unalterable fact that they are bolstered by a vanguard of sixty-three million, many of them armed, marching behind, lock-step with policies that would dismantle whatever marginal progress has been achieved thus far, and affirmed in their hatreds. How quickly the incendiary pro/con rhetoric about Dylan's win faded into the navel-gazing abstraction whence it had sprung. The two seemed so utterly unrelated in importance and repercussion. One of these things was not like the other. Except that they both involved white men and all the hallelujahs and um-brage that, too often justifiably, bedevil those of their ilk.

In seeking to defend my position—about not taking a position—about the Nobel, I said many things, but there was one thing I did not say. I did not say it because it would have meant taking a side, and not just any side but the side of a white man, something that isn't easy to do on the best of days, and certainly not for an immigrant woman of color. However, after this election, when it seems that it would be even less advisable to take the side of a white man, it seems important to do so.

Here's why. Because white men, as a category, are a part of this country and their relevance is neither lesser nor greater than any other citizen or undocumented human being. Because specific white men do terrible things and incite terrible violence, and others, like Dylan, do the opposite. Because it is as important to point out the good done by the latter as it is to call out the bad perpetrated by the former. Because "of course it's a White/man" offers as little clarity—and absolutely no humanism or compassion—as "of course it's a Black/man." Because our progress depends not upon excoriating or marginalizing or ostracizing others as we ourselves have been excoriated, marginalized, or ostracized, but rather upon setting forth and observing a policy of equality that takes honest measure of what each of us can, has, or will contribute toward an ideal world. Because even as we are willing to point out the evils perpetrated by this country and its legions of miscreants, a shame that stains us too as citizens, we must have equal ability to rejoice in the good work done by others, and have the grace to bask in the glow that reflects off of their excellence. And because, when it comes down to it, Dylan gifted his voice to the movements that mattered the most to us: for equality, for justice, for peace, and for global citizenship.

Dylan was not ambitious, or, if he was, he was ambitious to a fault in the business of speaking truth to power. In doing so, he wept for many with whom he had no observable common ground based on genetics, color, or race, but only that of sharing human sorrow. "Oxford Town" (1963) mourned the riots in Oxford, Mississippi, whose issues of segregation are starkly apparent in our present-day battles over low- and high-performing institutions of public education; "The Lonesome Death of Hattie Carroll" (1964) gave voice to the death of the fifty-one-year-old black barmaid Hattie Carroll, murdered by a rich Maryland tobacco farmer who got off with six months, a verdict that carries resonance still; "Hurricane" (1976) turned a spotlight on racial profiling, another national shame that has stood the test of time and is newly girded through the recent election; "The Times They Are A-Changin'" (1964) captured the zeitgeist of a restless young populace, a restlessness that a new generation of protesters spilling onto the streets of American cities feel today; "Chimes of Freedom" (1964) addressed the downtrodden, including the abandoned, the forsaken, the outcast, the luckless, who number into the millions today; and "A Hard Rain's A-Gonna Fall" (1962) spoke, in Dylan's own words, "of the lies that people get told on their radios and in their newspapers," words that hold chilling resonance fifty-four years on in 2016 as I write this. To mention a few.

In the speech he sent to be read on his behalf at the ceremony, Dylan pointed out the difference between playing for fifty thousand people and fifty people, where the smaller number is the harder gig. As poets and writers, we understand the point he makes: with a smaller audience, we are forced to address each person as "an individual, separate identity, a world unto themselves," that their perception of our work is more clear, and more obvious to us, that we are forced into a state of becoming as intimate and vulnerable as we were when we first sat down to write whatever brought us and those individuals together in the same room. Similarly, as he pointed out, when we sit down to create a work of art, if we wish to create anything of lasting value, anything that addresses our common human condition, we do not ask if our own work is worthy of accolades or fame, big advances or literary junkets. Like Shakespeare, said Dylan—surely with a nod to those who recognized that few considered the bard (the bard!) a serious literary contender in his time—"Some things never change, even in 400 years. Not once have I ever had the time to ask myself, 'Are my songs literature?'"

Oddly enough, in the way that these things go, I first read, rather than heard, Dylan's work as poetry, in Sri Lanka. Having been colonized by the British, this small tropical island in the Indian subcontinent followed, and still follows, the British system of education. The standards of our curriculum are high, a fact borne out by the thousands of Sri Lankans who arrive in the United States and other so-called "first world countries," miraculously armed with the ability to absorb complex material not imparted in their mother tongue and do not simply manage but excel. When we studied poetry or prose we did not simply read it, we learned to recite it from memory. We learned the milieu in which it was produced. We learned who else was writing at the time. We learned the political context of the work. In other words, we learned to place that work against a broad canvas against which its relevance was judged. Dylan's poetry was included in the poetry syllabus not because, as one critic suggested, its simple rhythms were being used to instruct me in rudimentary ESL (and yes, we could talk about the myopia of the above/average American who imagines that if an immigrant dares to have an opinion about English literature, it must have been something acquired in an ESL classroom), but because it was part of our university entrance examinations, in preparation for which we analyzed the texts not over a scant month or two but over two and a half years. The same texts. Dylan's "poems" could stand such scrutiny alongside the work of countless others, from John Donne to Wole Soyinka.

Dylan penned the hurt of this nation, and it was heard across the world. In America, a country whose literati seem, for the most part, unnaturally shy in sticking their necks out for the poor and the disenfranchised, he put pen to paper and set it to music. I read it in a poetry syllabus in Sri Lanka, others took to the streets rallying to his songs-become-anthems in many countries, most particularly in the United States.

The election of Donald Trump, the latest in a long line of despicable white men who have been given power over vast numbers of human beings within and beyond America's shores, did not happen overnight. It happened for a number of reasons, only some of which relate to racism and sexism. It happened also because we people of letters forgot the power of our own pens to provide a call to action, to sound a warning, to offer solace and comfort, but also to encourage our fellow citizens to write the truth. It might be time to consider that the prize was perhaps a nudge to the rest of us, of all colors and genders, to do as Dylan, no ordinary White man, did, to say what needs to be said: to hell with our notions of personal safety and, more importantly, personal advancement.

Was his work literature?

How many roads must a man walk down
Before you call him a man?
The answer, my friend, is blowin' in the wind
The answer is blowin' in the wind

Circumstances

The matter of breath, breath turning into only air, no human life sustained by it, no force expelled into heart and voices lifted against injustice, has been on our minds. There's a recent essay by one of my favorites, Jesmyn Ward, that I teach across genres. The essay, "On Witness and Respire,"[4] reminds me of how we are defined by our attention to the way our private lives brush up against public realities, the way what happens to us and ours must surely come with an awareness of what happens to them and theirs. It is a parallel that for me is invariably connected to how what happens in a "there" is tied to what happens "here." I'll tell you a story within a story.

One evening almost two decades ago, something happened in my house that held up a mirror to my face—in it, I could see that I was not an everyday angel, not a demigoddess who could make everything right with the world for my children. That evening, during dinner, my baby choked on a banana and lost consciousness. The nightmare lasted perhaps four minutes. In that time, my husband, trained in CPR, fished out the banana and tried to revive her. In that time, I called 911, ran for neighbors, had others pouring out of their homes. In that time, cell phones rang with more calls to 911. The police arrived in less than two minutes, the ambulance right behind. In that time, while struggling with her outside our house, on the grass, she came to and started to cry. The emergency team checked her out, the police reassured us, I rode with her in the ambulance to Morristown Memorial Hospital, which serves one of the bedroom communities that nourish the brokers on Wall Street. The volunteer nurse on board gave her a koala bear to cheer her up. Afterwards, at the hospital, other volunteers came by to blow bubbles for her, give her a musical toy. The doctors checked her, made sure she was all right. We stayed on in the small but private and comfortable cubicle of the emergency room's pediatric unit until it was time for her X-ray. The radiologist gave us a warmed blanket for her.

---

[4] Ward, Jesmyn. "On Witness and Respire." *Vanity Fair*, September 1st, 2020.

As I sat outside waiting for the staff to bring her back after her X-ray, the helplessness I had felt when I saw her limp in my husband's arms, blue and unconscious, came back to me. It's a feeling that is inexplicable—like the inside of your body becoming liquid even as you do things like hold the baby, pump her chest, yell for help—a feeling of such despair that "my baby" is beyond my help. I remembered the fierce and childlike words that I kept repeating to myself during those seemingly interminable moments—"she will be fine when the ambulance gets here because they know what to do, they've got machines and they'll revive her!" These things I relived as I sat in the spotless corridor watching for her return. As I comforted myself that it was really going to be okay, a feature I had read in an issue of *Mother Jones* the previous year came jolting, unbidden, into my mind.

*

Basra, Iraq

The story was about an American doctor from Milwaukee who specialized in pulmonary and critical-care medicine who visited the Iraqi town of Basra during the summer of 2000. He traveled there with a reporter and a photographer in a visit arranged by a Chicago-based organization called Voices in the Wilderness. While there he visited the Basra Pediatric Hospital in the company of its director, Ali Faisal. The story described the director as a man who wore the worn-out look of someone punished too long by impossible circumstances. He had witnessed the end result of malnutrition, contaminated water, and the collapse of Iraq's health care system. He could not speak safely against Saddam Hussein, although nobody would argue that he, Hussein, had been responsible for indescribable horrors within Iraq. Ali Faisal noted, however, that the economic sanctions were also responsible, saying, "even microscopes are not allowed. And one of the major difficulties is a shortage of oxygen." Waleed Najeeb, the American doctor, saw the oxygen problem on his trip:

> Najeeb and the reporters arrived at the pediatric hospital on a hot August afternoon. While they were talking, a woman down the hall shouted for a physician. Najeeb and the others hurried to the room. Inside, they saw eight children in metal beds pushed up against dirty, cream-colored walls. The moth-

er of a six-month-old boy named Hassan had screamed for help. Her baby was gasping for breath. He was no more than 12 pounds, half the normal body weight for his age.

"Get him oxygen," Najeeb told an Iraqi physician. A length of plastic tubing was fit into Hassan's right nostril and taped clumsily to his face; it was then attached to a worn green cylinder of industrial oxygen, the stuff mechanics use for acetylene torches. Hassan began convulsing. His arms and legs quivered. His skin turned pallid. His eyes rolled backward in their sockets. Najeeb told the doctor that the boy needed to be placed on a ventilator. "Do you think I don't know this?" the Iraqi doctor responded. "None of our ventilators are working. We couldn't obtain the parts."

Hassan drifted into unconsciousness. The doctors looked on. The mother sobbed. She explained that her family lived in a town near Basra. Hassan had come down with a high fever and an earache a week earlier. She had taken him to a doctor who prescribed an antibiotic, but she hadn't been able to find the medicine anywhere nearby. She told Najeeb that she had located it, finally, in a pharmacy near the Jordanian border, hundreds of miles away, but hadn't been able to buy it because she was the equivalent of 12 cents short. She had brought Hassan to the hospital after he began having seizures.

The Iraqi doctor whispered in Najeeb's ear, "Look at the gauge on the tank." The needle hadn't moved since the tank had been hooked up. It stood on empty. "We're looking for a new tank on the market now."

"Why do you have this one connected?" Najeeb asked.

"We're calming the parents down."

Hassan's hands turned cold. Najeeb observed that the boy was barely inhaling. He was slowly suffocating. The doctor knew it. And he knew that there was nothing he could do. About 10 hours later, the doctors told Hasan's mother to take her child in her arms. In a few more minutes he was dead.[5]

*

I've thought often about my four minutes of hell. The desperation my husband and I had felt. I thought about my older daughter crying and asking on repeat "Is she going to die?" and the neighbor who held

---

[5] Sudetik, Chuck. "The Betrayal of Basra." *Mother Jones*, November/December, 2001.

her and comforted her, and told her that her sister was going to be fine. Who took her in and gave her a bath and put her to sleep and carried her home afterwards and put her into her bunk bed when we got back from the hospital. I thought about the paramedics who came, and the police, the volunteers, the hospital staff, the doctor who had time to come out and show us how to get back to our car. Who had smiled and joked with my sleepy baby. And then I thought again about Hassan's mother—waiting, like me, holding her baby, like me.

It was an experience that made me write, repeatedly, about the wars we unleashed in Iraq and elsewhere in the years since. I wrote in the name of the mothers like me whose lives were nothing like mine. I wrote to keep sight of what was true in a country whose rulers were intent on selling false news to my fellow citizens, a fact easily overlooked then, when it related to those unseen others felled in our faraway wars, but suddenly placed front and center when #altfacts became all the rage for freshly woke Americans. And because it is vital to recollect those occasions on which we remained silent and deliberately ignorant, I offer a sample of those reflections on a series of events that set America on the irreversible path that led to five absurdly titled "operations" (Iraqi Freedom, New Dawn, Enduring Freedom, Inherent Resolve, Freedom's Sentinel) over two decades. Decades during which there was neither freedom nor resolution, only the suffering endured by human beings impacted both directly and indirectly by our violence.

Lest We Forget

1.
With God (and Weapons of Mass Destruction) On Our Side
September 2003

I have filled, with no great fear or impatience, several old milk bottles with water. I choose not to think about the origin of this liquid and its chemical contents. Born in a country where "boiled" equals "purified," I trust in the scorching heat of the water gushing out of taps. Every now and again, while preparing grocery lists, I catch myself taking inventory of canned goods. Sometimes my dreams involve bunkers and a gasping need to find oxygen for my three daughters. I wake from these thoughts to freshly squeezed orange juice and French toast, to mild scoldings directed at the usual laggards in the house to get ready for the day. Get ready for the day. What a concept. What hope in that simple belief that today will be as the day was before. School to go to, newspapers to read, articles to write, a baby burped, a toddler cajoled, an oldest dropped at her Montessori school, jobs done, careers advanced, dinners made, post opened. This is my current reality.

Today's newspaper carries a small note about people such as myself in Baghdad who are stocking up on gasoline, canned goods, bottled water, antiseptics, and antibiotics. Their reality includes a few sundry items that I don't—yet—have to cross off my list. Sanctions that deprive them of all but the most basic necessities. Three hundred thousand trigger-happy American troops lining their borders. The UN monitored fence between Iraq and Kuwait forcibly breached by American soldiers under orders for war even as their president postures in front of the world claiming to be the guardian of peace, security, democracy. Troops based in Kuwait and in every other country on the Arabian Peninsula except Yemen. Five aircraft carrier battle groups, each with 50-strike aircraft, which include thirty to forty vessels armed with Tomahawk land-attack cruise missiles. Three dozen ships carrying weaponry and equipment to spearhead the attack from Turkey biding time in the Mediterranean. Upgraded Patriot missiles awaiting testing in Iraq. Dirty Bombs pretested by the Americans possibly lying in wait for use on real live subjects, and, perhaps, planted as evidence against the Iraqi people. More damage was wrought on Iraq in 1990 and the years since than twenty attacks on the World Trade Centers could manage. So claimed a veteran of that war. The forces being organized today against Iraq have ten times the capability. Much more than Hiroshima and Nagasaki. Imagine that.

New York City, the city whose name is being used as a fig leaf by an administration that can only be termed barbaric, passed its own resolution against this war five days ago. "We of all cities must uphold the precious-ness and sanctity of human life," said Councilman Alan Gerson, a Dem-ocrat who voted for the resolution and whose district includes the World Trade Center site, where 2,792 people were killed in the attacks. What else might persuade our home-grown fanatic that the nation he stole power from is against this war? It seems as though this is a matter of a religious zealot attacking a secular lunatic. The religious madman being the one with the weapons of mass destruction inexorably aimed at ordinary people going about their lives. That would be Mr. Bush. Small man, big weapons.

Apparently, this man reads the bible every morning, particularly the Book of Psalms. Another favorite goodnight book is Oswald Chambers's book, *My Utmost for His Highest*, which asserts, among other things, that God writes all history. All vices to which he laid claim—like drinking—were apparently stopped with the aid of God. Racketeering, arms deals, election-rigging, destroying the environment, mass-murder, weaponizing diplomacy, plotting coups, lying, cheating, stealing, these types of things must have been done outside the purview of God. Perhaps God was turning his other cheek at the time and forgot to look back. The White House is also full not of relevance but of reverence. Bible study meetings are held in various corners. With war clouds being whipped up by this oh-so-merciful God, the little man, this mere mortal, has little to do but wait. So, apparently, he is in bed by ten after reading two—short—briefs. Brevity has been his hallmark, after all. Brief in all things. In words, in manner, in intellect, in action. Condemning millions with the stroke of a pen. Perhaps that is the power of small men: small hearts.

The odd thing is that those whom he has ordered to wreak fury and death upon other mothers—such as myself—and other children—such as mine—in Baghdad are confused. Chaplain Darren Stennett, out with the

3rd Battalion, 4th Marines, has tried to assuage their fears with a bit of twisted logic. "'Thou shalt not kill' really should be translated as 'Thou shalt not murder.' Killing for a just cause, on behalf of your nation, is a totally different situation."[6] Well, your reverence, we are thankful that suicide bombers and guerrilla fighters all over the world have thus been embraced into the bosom of the Lord. Reverend Bill Devine, a Catholic priest, requests that God protect "us" from "men of violence and keep us safe from weapons of hate."[7] He also prays for peace and no war. That covers Bush, then. God will, we hope, protect us from him. Dunbar, a Navy Corpsman, places his faith in good old-fashioned classroom debate. He doesn't see killing, in this context, as wrong. "God can't see it that way," he says, "it's just what they have to do."[8] Amass the weapons of mass destruction as we head off to mass—sorry, war. Meanwhile, we heard nothing of the Papal emissary to the White House sent to preach some sense into this truly prodigal son. Pope John Paul II, clearly not in God's Good Books, if we are to believe Bush, has been calling on Catholics to fast in the name of peace. Apparently he has called this an unjust war in every single sermon since—in the now infamous words of the Bushites—the "new product" (war on Iraq) was introduced into the "market" (the American public).

Colin Powell is quoted as saying with regard to North Korea, "We are not going to simply fall into what I believe is bad practice of saying the only way you can talk to us is directly." Washington says the Security Council should handle the North Korean nuclear problem. Would that be the same council you have defied and lied to at every twist and turn? The same council that Powell addressed with false claims and fake documents, that "testimony" by this so-called paragon of virtue that is now being investigated by the UN? Nobel Peace Laureate Eli Wiesel says he thinks the war is okay. Because Colin Powell says it's so, and Powell would never sacrifice his integrity, career, and honor on an empty claim.[9] Sorry, Eli, Powell has no honor or integrity, and he kissed his career goodbye when he decided to silence his brain and pucker up to his boss's posterior. Is God keeping track?

---

[6] Koopman, John. "Faith in the shadow of war / U.S. troops in Kuwait find themselves turning to their God." *San Francisco Chronicle*, February 24th, 2003.

[7] Ibid.

[8] Ibid.

[9] Wiesel, Eli. "Peace Isn't Possible in Evil's Face." *Los Angeles Times*, March 11th, 2003.

In Maine, vague allegations have been made against a schoolteacher who has apparently uttered the terrible untruth that "soldiers die because that's what happens in wars" to a child of a soldier. The national Patriot Act has now seeped into local use, whereby no names need be mentioned. It is simply enough to suggest some "outrage," and they have effectively silenced all teachers. We are all looking over our shoulders now. We are not afraid of terrorists. We are afraid of this government. So last night, during an unseasonably warm night for Maine, I collected my family and went and stood on a street corner along with other hopefuls, carrying five wavering candles. We are very much afraid. But perhaps God is on the side of us ordinary human beings after all. Because, quite clearly, God seems only to reside camouflaged in paper, bound by a leather cover, on a dim bedside table in Washington, DC.

Tonight, I will watch a special report on Iraq on public television. I will put my children to bed and bemoan my petty problems of colicky babies and empty refrigerators. But in the dead of night I will wake up to check on my three daughters. I will touch their heads and whisper blessings in another language. I will know that the mothers in Iraq are doing the same.

2.
The Fear Factor
October 2004

One of the most popular "reality shows" in America these days is something called *Fear Factor*. The underlying premise is that Americans will eat excrement (dead rats, glasses of worms, pounds of slugs, you get the picture) for money. Three finalists from the Miss USA pageant dove into 500 pounds of fish scales and ate rotting squid on national TV in a special telecast of *Fear Factor*. It's the modern version of an oft-misattributed discussion between Canadian-British media magnate and politician Max Aitken and a lady who, having agreed to sleep with him for a million dollars, exclaimed, when he proposed a lesser amount, that she wasn't a prostitute. He reportedly said, "We've agreed on what you are, we're just negotiating the price." Well, the price for Americans to take off their clothes *(Are You Hot?)*, French kiss with live hissing cockroaches in their mouths *(Fear Factor)*, engage in sexual activity with someone other than their betrothed *(Temptation Island)*, and demonstrate traits that we would attribute to slimeballs, bottom-feeders, backstabbers, etc. *(Survivor)*, ranges from a few minutes of infamy to a million dollars.

Oddly enough, last night's television also spoke of another nation whose people are apparently protecting their sovereignty due to, in the words of General Tommy Franks, "the fear factor." Ordinary Iraqis, armed with a pistol or two, sometimes not even that, are walking about in broad daylight, unafraid of the more than 1000 missiles that have been fired at them during the last few days, of the amphibious tanks, of the "Mother of All Bombs," which weighs 21,000 pounds, or the soldiers clad head to foot in the most state-of-the-art equipment. (Everything is state-of-the-art in America, so much so that people forget to question the art of the State that is slowly eroding their rights, bleeding them dry, and impoverishing the pop-ulace.) Now that is what I would call being truly without fear. ABC News finally showed us a few images of anti-American protests in the Middle East. The News Hour translated the words of one of the protesters in Iraq, who said, "Bush might be dreaming of Iraqis welcoming Americans here, but we are going to fight for our country." How perfectly ludicrous this must seem to ordinary Americans. What? No movie deal? No talk show circuit? No recording contract? No model tryouts? *No money?!!!!* What could they possibly be thinking?

Like the news that comes out of Israel regarding Palestinian suicide bombers who, if we are to believe the Israelis, spring fully armed from their mother's wombs, the picture we get of the average Iraqi, if we are to believe Bush's media moguls, is one of a dehumanized backward cave dweller. Colonel W. Patrick Lang, the pundit often contracted by Jim Lehrer for PBS, characterized them as an essentially brutal people. No mother's sons, these. Of the twenty-two Americans who have been killed so far, two were from Maine. There have been eloquent editorials about them, their parents, and other kin in the newspapers. We have grown to know these young men and the tragedy of their deaths. We have come to mourn alongside their mothers, one of whom had the courage to note in the midst of her own loss that it did not matter what technology was being used, murders were being perpetrated. The Bushites expected that daily prayers towards Mecca would be transformed into salaams towards the West. They expected no resistance. No dead Americans. Twenty-two Americans have died so far, fourteen are missing. We make much of these people, and we should. They, too, are human beings. I look at my husband, who is of an age that makes him recruitable, and I imagine the horror of a military man carrying a folded flag and knocking on my door at midnight. I also think about the fact that there are no such ceremonies for the Iraqi dead. One sentence in the newspaper, one quick running headline at the bottom of my TV screen, notes that 500 Iraqi "soldiers" have been killed. In the past two days. We all know the bias of "official figures." What of their families? Their mothers? Their burial rights?

Mr. Bush has returned from a quick retreat to chastise the Iraqis who were interviewing captured American soldiers and asking them why they were in Iraq. He is invoking the Geneva Convention on the treatment of Prisoners of War. Those prisoners should not be identifiable on TV, he says. He is right. No prisoners should be shown on TV. So why are we being shown endless pictures of perfectly identifiable Iraqi prisoners in extremely demoralizing situations on our TVs? Or does Mr. Bush think that they all look the same so it does not matter? Or does he think that UN conventions are only applicable to other nations? Are only American soldiers human beings? These are questions to which we already know the bitter answers.

Meanwhile, a challenge posed during a press briefing to White House Press Secretary Ari Fleisher regarding the treatment of POWs held by the US in Guantánamo and in Iraq brought this odd response: "The war on terrorism is different from this more traditional war." When you think about it, this "war" *is* a departure for the US. "Tradition" has favored covert terrorism and assassinations to get rid of democratically elected governments in places like Chile, Nicaragua, and Mexico. But the more relevant question is, can this be called a war at all? Commanding the elected leader of another nation to step down while a foreign army lays siege at his door is reminiscent of our ancient histories. And, like then, we call it what it is: an invasion. This is no preemptive strike, no war, this is an invasion. The TV channels should rename this The Invasion of Iraq and not attempt to legitimize Mr. Bush's despicable activities by calling this a war. Wars are fought among equals. When a schoolyard bully picks on the bespectacled, skinny nerd, kids yell "no fair!" When 300,000 soldiers take aim with tomahawk land missiles at men and women going about their lives with confused looks on their faces, we want to say, *go pick on somebody your own size*. Or, if that's too hard to do, *stay at home and consume less, for god's sake!* Unfortunately, that is not likely. We like our freedom to do what we want when we want (barring the Patriot Act and, more frighteningly, Patriot Act II). We like to drive when we can walk. We like our couches large, our portions big, and our guns biggest of all. We buy gas-guzzling, four-wheel drive, all-terrain vehicles, and we drive them around our cozy suburbs. We like our shit supersized, thank you.

Dianne Feinstein, a relatively strong opponent of this invasion, appeared on TV to say that now that we have soldiers out there in harm's way, we should rally behind the president. In other words, all the man's got to do is put Americans in harm's way (that's already been done, thank the lord), and we all have to shut up. Michael Moore may have been booed during his speech at the Oscars last Sunday, but that is par for the course for an ignorant nation. He had it right when he said, "We live in fictitious times, after a fictitious election, with a fictitious president who sends us out to war for fictitious reasons."[10] The reason was supposed to be to punish the Iraqi regime for disregarding the UN. So off we must go, disregarding the UN in

---

[10] "Michael Moore booed as he slams Iraq war at Oscars." *Sydney Morning Herald*, March 24th, 2003.

order to punish somebody who is disregarding the UN (though we don't do this when it comes to Israel, of course, which has, as of today, ignored close to 121 UN resolutions pertaining to its massacres and treatment of Palestinians). Mr. Bush tried to convince people there were legitimate reasons. There were those WMDs. But, as of now, within thirty miles of Baghdad, American soldiers have overrun one suspected site after another and found nothing.

I am beginning to gain a new respect for Mr. Hussein. The man seems to be better than Houdini at hiding not only himself but thousands of scud missiles, nuclear weapons, enriched uranium, and hundreds of pounds of chemical and biological weapons. Where is he putting all these things? If he was the size of your average American I'd say he'd stuffed them up where the sun don't shine, but he's a relatively small man. Where oh where could they be? That's not to say there aren't any such weapons in the immediate vicinity of Baghdad. After all, what can we call Apache Attack Helicopters, Unmanned Drones, Tomahawk and Patriot Cruise Missiles, Tomcats, Hornets, Super Hornets, Longbows, Paladin Howitzers, Massive Ordnance Air Blast Bombs, Multiple Launch Rocket Systems, Amphibious Assault Ships, Bunker Busters (the names go on, and there's a handy-dandy comparative list produced by CNN[11]), but weapons of mass destruction? It's almost like a trade show run entirely by the Americans. A multimedia presentation on what's up for sale these days in the weapons industry. And is it any wonder when the United States accounts for 43 percent of the world's military expenditure?[12] Chances are that if America is responsible for that alarming percentage of the global total on defense spending, we are the ones with anger-management issues and we're the ones who are a threat to global peace. But I digress.[13]

I'm recollecting here something General Tommy Franks said during a press briefing in Qatar: that this assault is based on "Sensitive Site Exploitation."[14] He nailed it on the head. What, after all, is more all-American,

---

[11] https://edition.cnn.com/SPECIALS/2003/iraq/forces/weapons/index.html.

[12] Stokholm International Peace Research Institute (SIPRI). Military Expenditure, SIPRI Yearbook, 2003.

[13] Although I direct attention toward the helpful website globalfirepower.com, which allows the average citizen to choose to compare the military might of any two countries in the world.

[14] Central Command Briefing in Qatar, March 24th, 2003. Broadcast via C-Span.

more True-Blue than Exploitation? We exploit resources, people, each other, entire nations, the moment, whatever we can lay our covetous hands on.

Yes, this isn't a match among equals. Well-paid, well-fed American soldiers (one of the meals before the onslaught for the 101st Airborne was lobster and steak)[15] murdering people on behalf of an illegitimate president desiring to control his own oil wells are not the equals of Iraqi people who are fighting with their bare hands to protect their dignity. Bush has sent other people's sons and daughters to get a hold of local oil pipelines from Basra to Saudi Arabia, from Baiji to Baghdad, from Baghdad to Khanagin, and from Kirkuk to Turkey's port of Ceyhan. Iraq's people live upon the second-largest proven oil reserves. According to oil industry experts, new exploration will probably raise Iraq's reserves to 200–300 billion barrels of cheaply produced high-grade crude, leading to a goldrush of profits for international oil firms in a post-Saddam setting. The four giant firms located in the US and the UK have been keen to get back into Iraq, from which they were excluded with the 1972 nationalization of oil. In a postwar climate, the US-UK companies expect to gain lucrative oil deals that will be worth trillions of dollars in profits in the coming decades. Those barrels of oil will no doubt be transported along a swollen river of blood.

What are the Iraqis fighting for? One general dismissed the entire country, saying, "There's just one city, that's what it's like in these third world countries...they only have one city." Really? Modern Iraq is (was) replete with tuition-free public schools, six major universities, forty-four teacher-training schools and institutes, and three colleges and technical institutes, all owned and operated by the government. It has (had) also displayed a 45 percent increase in the numbers of female primary students and a literacy rate of 70 percent. It has (had) functioning electricity grids, well-maintained roads, sewerage systems, and all the accoutrements of industrial development. But that is not what is at stake.

Iraq is the old Mesopotamia, at the core of the history of Babylon, Assyria, of the Abbasid empire of Harun al Rashid, of Persian invasions and four hundred years of Turkish rule. Baghdad, the center of the Muslim world starting in the 760s, is the still-beating heart of a long-ago cradle of civilization, a country whose history is as dramatic as that of ancient

---

[15] "Lobster, Steak, and a War Dance: US Troops Get Ready for Attack." *Quad-City Times*, March 20th, 2003.

Greece. Baghdad took four years to build, and Mansur employed a hundred thousand architects, craftsmen, and workers from all over the Islamic world to create the Round City, with double brick walls, a moat, a third innermost wall ninety feet high, four highways radiating out of four gates, and the Caliph's palace topped with a green dome. Its name means "founded by God," and Arabs call it the City of Peace. But one couldn't expect a man presiding over a country with a little over 200 years of Caucasian history to understand what those things might mean to the people to whom it belongs. America is the land of standardization, patriotism expressed in meaningless clichés, a flag desecrated on a daily basis as it is sold to people on everything from condoms to toilet paper. In his 1854 poem "The Charge of the Light Brigade," Tennyson immortalized the sad men who died on misguided orders when he wrote of the six hundred soldiers who rode into the valley of death. Fighting for a barrel of oil versus fighting for culture, tradition, history. You decide who makes the better soldier. Our poets are silent.

3.
Counting the Dead
October 2005

This past week, I have, along with thousands of others around America, been engaged in a curiously ghoulish phenomenon: we have all been waiting for the two thousandth American soldier to die in Iraq. We were planning vigils, wakes, memorials, and various other such events to commemorate this eventuality. While in the midst of this, I received a copy of a feature written by my journalist brother in Sri Lanka of a boy named Abhilash, an infant born to Jenita and Murugupillai Jeyarajah, whom the world will remember only, eventually, as Baby No. 81, an infant claimed by nine sets of parents afterward.[16] The article spoke of the importance of recognizing individual human beings, of resisting the attempts that are and will always be made to assign numbers—and therefore anonymity—to our histories.

Staff Sgt. George T. Alexander Jr., according to one report, was a father who could not keep the promise he made to his children—an eight-year-old son and a six-year-old daughter—that he would be home in Killeen, TX, soon after Christmas.[17] He could not because he succumbed to the injuries he suffered when his Bradley exploded in Samara. On October 25th, Alexander became the two thousandth soldier whose death set the stage for the protests and memorials that will happen throughout the country this week.

The Senate held a moment of silence, and the names of the two thousand soldiers who have died were read in the Capitol that day. On Sunday, there will be white flags erected to remember each one of them in downtown Waterville where I live.

I support and will participate in these activities. But I cannot shake off the fact that while we made our preparations on every side of the political aisle, we were all waiting for "someone" to die. A two thousandth soldier— whoever he or she was going to be—had to die. John Cory once said that "Politics is the luxury of the safe-at-home. War is a lottery of survival."

---

[16] "Baby 81 Reunited with Parents." *The Guardian*, February 14th, 2005.
[17] "Family Mourns Soldier Killed in Iraq." ABC News, October 26th, 2005.

Alexander lost that lottery, but perhaps we can help him and his family win it back. We can stop counting the dead and begin remembering them. We can stop waiting for them to die and begin helping them to live.

At thirty-four years of age, Alexander's platoon called him "Grandpa" because he was their oldest member. His sister Sasha Spence says that "he was a wonderful brother and I would give anything to have him back." There are others who feel that way.

For those to whom numbers matter, here are some from CNN. There have been, as of today, 2,201 coalition troop deaths in the war in Iraq: 2,004 Americans, 98 Britons, 13 Bulgarians, 2 Danes, 2 Dutch, 2 Estonians, 1 Hungarian, 26 Italians, 1 Kazakh, 1 Latvian, 17 Poles, 1 Salvadoran, 3 Slovaks, 11 Spaniards, 2 Thai, and 18 Ukrainians. From ABC News I found out that in March 2003, in the days after the start of the bombing of Iraq, 59 American soldiers died in Iraq. So far, in the most recent month, October 2005, 60 soldiers have died.

For those who want to remember that these were human beings, here are a few, very few, details. Sgt. Sean C. Reynolds, twenty-five years old, of East Lansing, Michigan, was killed on May 3rd, in Iraq. Uday Singh was twenty-one years old and had not yet become an American citizen when he died in an ambush near Habbaniyah Air Force base on December 1, 2004. I don't know what number either of them were.

In Brook Park, Ohio, a town that lost fourteen marines in a single car bombing this past summer, there's a man named Ronald Griffin. He lost his son two and a half years ago. This is what he said on the occasion of the announcement from the Pentagon: "I only look at the individuals. I don't think it's a significant number at all unless you think about the individuals who make it up. Who was ninety-eight? Who was ninety-nine? Who is going to be two thousand and one?"

This morning I woke up, as usual, to National Public Radio. It was a story from Iraq. The story of a man named Manadel al-Jamadi who died in Abu Ghraib, hours after his capture by the Navy SEALs and the CIA. His bruised, bloodied corpse was seen around the world, stuffed in a box of ice, with Sgt. Charles Graner giving a thumbs up sign and grinning over it. I went online to see what else I could find out about this story. There I found a picture of Manadel al-Jamadi's widow and his son, who looks about eight years old. They have no names. Nor do the children of George T. Alexander Jr.

4.
Ahmadinejad v. Bush: The Village Druid v. The Zygote
May 2006

On January 20th, 1977, for the first time in history, a newly inaugurated American president, Jimmy Carter, got out of his limousine and walked to the White House. In 2001, a president appointed by the Supreme Court sped up his limousine as it sought the refuge of the gates. That is not the only dissimilarity between former President Jimmy Carter and Mr. Bush. Carter spoke the bottom line of Christianity before it became fashionable to pose for pictures on your knees in a pew. Carter publicly rejected America's "inordinate fear of communism" in favor of supporting the more important matter of human rights, condemned the oil industry for executing "the biggest rip-off in history," and faced and successfully negotiated the release of American hostages in Iran.

Religion, oil, and Iran are once more front and center in America. Then, ostensibly because Carter allowed the Shah to enter the United States for medical treatment, sixty-six Americans were held hostage for 444 days before he was able to secure their release. Today, Americans and all American interests are perceived to be under threat from Iran in response to the Bush administration's aggression towards that country. I'm speaking of the amassing of forces along the borders of Iran and of the conduct of covert operations against that country, both of which have been going on since long before this latest justification for war was put into public motion. Sadly, Mr. Bush does not have the capability to release a single American from the vice of that threat.

Iranian President Mahmoud Ahmadinejad's eighteen-page letter to Mr. Bush is now old news, though it would serve every American well, even at this late stage, to read it.[18] For a brief while, there had been a sense of euphoria in the streets of Tehran as Iranians contemplated the possibility of civil discourse. Unfortunately for them, they didn't know that Mr. Bush is illiterate. There was no Carter to take note of this gesture, not even a Clintonesque Rhodes Scholar to be able to respond in kind. All America had was "Condi" to summarily dismiss the letter, its intent, its

---

[18] "Iran: Text Of Ahmadinejad's Letter To Bush." Radio Free Europe, May 11th, 2006.

writer, its nation of origin, the very culture that created it, and, perhaps most disturbingly, the eloquent philosophical debate laid bare within it.

The history of Iran began around 4000 BC. The Caucasian history of the United States began about 250 years ago. Conversation between Iran and America is like a discussion between a wizened village druid and a zygote. Still, since both have to inhabit the same universe, conversation is what the Iranians were hoping for.

The cultural impasse between America and the Arab, and indeed much of the non-European, world has always been wide, and sadly, in the absence of a credible translator, it is growing. A leader from any other part of the world, in the event of receiving an epistle of erudition such as this one, would, far from dismissing it, rise to the challenge of bringing their own intellect to the negotiating table. Leaders, after all, are supposed to engage in the type of esoteric discussions that the nations they represent have elected them to manage.

Non-Western cultures are noted for their reliance on symbolic gestures. There is a story I recall from my undergraduate days in Washington, DC. A young Middle Eastern student, freshly in the United States, got involved in an argument at a club. Before the situation deteriorated, this student removed his watch and asked his American friends to hold it for him, because he was not going to have it broken in a fistfight. His friends did just that: they held on to his watch as the argument escalated, and he ended up on the street with serious bruises. He could not understand what had happened. "I gave them my watch," he said, later, "they were supposed to stop me from having to go and fight with those people!"

It's a familiar tale. In most non-Western villages and street corners around the world, people get to a point in an argument where they utter some variation of the following: "You better hold on to me because otherwise I'm going to beat X, Y, or Z to a pulp." At this point, each person's friends step up, literally hold on to the person, and "prevent" the fight by negotiating an amicable settlement. No war.

Defending one's honor, saving face, avoiding bloodshed. All entirely doable. Yes, simultaneously doable. But there has to be a consensual agreement that these are the rules of engagement. That there must be dignity left intact for both parties. That both parties meet as equals, leave as equals. They both get to rattle their sabers and display their might but may withdraw without seeming to. Braggadocio is for the stage. Diplomacy is conducted at the quiet ethnic restaurant down the street from the theater over a nice dinner, good wine, and great conversation.

When the Iraqi people said "we will fight unto death," they were hoping to be spared that grim burden. Unfortunately, they were dealing with Americans, who said "bring it on," and meant it. When Americans said "bring it on," they thought they were at the half-time show of the Super Bowl. Unfortunately, when the Iraqis said "we will fight unto death," they were prepared, if forced, to keep their word.

Carter was condemned at home as being tolerant of dictators. How could he spend New Year's Eve with the Shah, and toast him as leading "an island of stability" in a troubled region? How could a Christian man kiss the atheist Russian Brezhnev? What kind of madman sends his wife, and later his mother, to the funeral of a pope? The kind who understood that gestures speak louder than words, that sending one's wife or mother is a statement of respect far greater than quibbling over which ex-presidents get to attend and showing up with an entourage of uninvited politicians in tow, such as happened at the funeral of the last pontiff.

Yes, Carter was a president who understood the culture of other nations. A president who once said, "The same rocket technology that delivers nuclear warheads has also taken us peacefully into space. From that perspective, we see our Earth as it really is—a small and fragile and beautiful blue globe, the only home we have. We see no barriers of race or religion or country. We see the essential unity of our species and our planet; and with faith and common sense, that bright vision will ultimately prevail."[19] If only common sense were not so uncommon.

Now we have Iran. Now we have this missive from the Iranian president. I am praying that the zygote has learned something.

---

[19] Carter, Jimmy. "Farewell Address to the Nation." The American Presidency Project, January 14th, 1981.

5.
American Shame
July 2006

Americans, it seems, have no shame. Today, online in *The New York Times*,[20] is a picture of a neighborhood in Beirut. It looks like the pictures Americans wept over in the days following 9/11. The difference is that the rest of New York City was still standing after the towers fell. The rest of America went on. It went on to commit such atrocities against the rest of humankind, including its own citizens, that I regret that resilience. Perhaps if it had been brought to its knees it would have remembered God.

Right next to that photograph is this headline: "U.S. Appears to Be Waiting to Act on Israeli Airstrikes." Waiting for whom? Godot? Apparently, Americans—and I hold every single silent American responsible—are waiting for Israel to "bombard" Lebanon for another week, ostensibly to "weaken Hezbollah."

Are these people for real? How much weakening has gone on in Afghanistan and Iraq? Lord knows the Americans have been searching for signs of weakening there and have had as much success as they did in locating President Saddam Hussein's stockpile of Weapons of Mass Destruction. So, really, it is not about weakening Hezbollah. Not at all. It is about something else, and I will get to it in due course. But first, a little trip down memory lane.

When the Americans invaded Iraq, they were set to protect a few sites related to national heritage. They were called oil wells. A few others were left to burn: Baghdad's National Library and State Archives and its National Museum,[21] an event with echoes of the incineration of the library of Alexandria, a detail so aptly used to punctuate the poem "Closing Time; Iskandariya" by the poet Brigit Pegeen Kelly.[22] On April 13th,

---

[20] Cooper, Helene and Steven Erlanger, Steven. "U.S. Appears to Be Waiting to Act on Israeli Airstrikes." *New York Times*, July 18th, 2006.

[21] Burkeman, Oliver. "Ancient Archive Lost in Baghdad Library Blaze." *The Guardian*, April 15th, 2003. For the ongoing impact, read Bahrani, Zainab and Lemoyne, Roger (Photography)."In 2003, Bagdad's National Library was Reduced to Rubble—Changing my Life and Iraqi Society Forever." *Document*, May 26th, 2013.

[22] *New York Times*, December 21st, 2005.

2003, Americans watched as the library and archives burned, destroying manuscripts that were centuries old. They had practice doing it. They had already watched one of the world's greatest museums be razed to the ground, and they had watched as artifacts from the Sumerian, Babylonian, and Assyrian civilizations were plundered. They watched while sixteen bronze Assyrian door panels from the nineteenth century were stolen. Even more heinous, though sadly not surprising, were the allegations that the Americans had been persuaded by private art collectors—namely the American Council for Cultural Policy, which had reportedly met with the Bush team to insist that all antiquities laws should be relaxed in the aftermath of the invasion—to turn a blind eye.[23] Not even Mounir Bouchenaki, the Deputy Director-General of UNESCO, could intervene.

Fast forward three years. Despite its protestations that there was no deliberate attempt to destroy the cultural heritage of Iraq and, indeed, much of the civilized world (among which, for reasons it makes more obvious with each passing day, I do not count America), the Army of One decided to literally grind that history into the dust by constructing a helipad in the heart of Babylon.[24] They bulldozed the ancient sites and filled their sandbags with shattered artifacts and earth. They brought in soil from other sites, thereby creating a muddle of archeological material that would take innumerable decades to sift. Daily takeoffs and landings caused such tremors in the ground that the wall of the Temple of Nabu and the roof of the sixth century BC Temple of Ninmah collapsed.[25]

I could go on—about the military camp in the ancient city of Ur, about the craters in the Sumerian cities of Lagash, Uruk, and Larsa, about the destruction of the pre-Akkadian region of Umma. But why bother? I simply ask you to remember this: the two Bamiyan Buddha statues. The Taliban's destruction of these two statues of great beauty and historical significance to Buddhists and non-Buddhists alike came in the wake of a visit by foreign dignitaries who wished to conduct repairs to the statues, but not discuss humanitarian assistance to the Afghan people. The American destruction of Iraq's treasures, complete and ongoing, has not even that faint—if bizarre and utterly backward—claim to rationality.

---

[23] Bailey, Martin. "International Outrage as Iraq's National Museum is Sacked by Civilians." *The Art Newspaper*, April 30th, 2003.

[24] "U.S. Admits Military Damaged Babylon Ruins." NBC News, April 14th, 2006.

[25] "Babylon's history damaged by modern day war." Al Arabiya News, December 9th, 2008.

Or does it? The Iraqi people have argued that the Americans were determined to erase the history of a culture more than nineteen times as ancient as theirs. They were determined to create a world defined by American values, begun on the date of the American invasion. I am inclined to agree. And I am inclined to add this: the Americans desire the destruction not only of your history, this administration desires the annihilation of your people.

In 1999, the Americans went to war in Kosovo to prevent the deaths of Albanians. A few years before then, in April 1994, the Americans, after actively aiding in the genocide that was to come, turned their backs on Rwanda.[26] A Canadian general, Romeo Dallaire, who was in charge of the UN Peacekeeping Force, was responsible for the order that the Belgians from that force protect the Rwandan officials. Their subsequent deaths led to the withdrawal of all UN peacekeepers. The rest is history. In his reflections, both printed and spoken, Dallaire asks this important question: Why did ten Belgians matter so much and why did 100,000 Rwandans matter so little? The answer is implicit in the question.

Americans like to think that racism is "so 1960s." They have actually convinced themselves that Affirmative Action has closed the book on that history. Perhaps in some ways it has. That was volumes one through ten. Volumes eleven onwards cover the present day. They cover the murder of Allende, the strangling of Cuba, the abandonment of Rwanda, the destruction of Babylon, and the massacre of the Lebanese. They cover the genocide in Palestine and the succor given to Israeli terrorism.

If the Lebanese were white there would be no waiting for Israel to finish ejaculating over Beirut.

It has taken the deaths of thousands of American soldiers for some Americans to wake up and smell the gasoline. It takes just one near black-and-white photograph for the rest of the world to realize that black and white is what Americans are about. By then, it will be too late for Americans to feel shame.

---

[26] For a long read on the influence that America wielded in Rwanda: Epstein, Helen C. "America's secret role in the Rwandan Genocide." *The Guardian*, September 12th, 2017.

6.
I Cannot Weep for Mariane Pearl
July 2007

On January 27th, 2002, the alleged captors of Daniel Pearl sent out their first emails, demanding the better treatment of detainees in Guantánamo Bay, Cuba. On January 27th, 2002, Dick Cheney called the detainees "the worst of a very bad lot. They are very dangerous. They are devoted to killing millions of Americans." Four years later, only ten of those people have been charged with anything.[27]

Meanwhile, Mariane Pearl has, as of this month, filed a lawsuit on behalf of her husband, the murdered journalist Daniel Pearl, and their son Adam, against eighteen defendants, including two dead men and the estates and families of others, two trusts, the whole of Al Qaeda, and the largest bank in Pakistan, Habeeb Bank Ltd., with headquarters in Karachi and branches all over the world including the Middle East, Europe, Asia, and an outpost in New York City.[28] This odd collection was chosen by her because they were either those who were directly responsible for the kidnapping, torture, and execution of her husband or organizations that aided and abetted those who were. Two of those are Islamic charities: the Al Rashid Trust and Al Akhtar Trust International, also known as Al Akhtar Trust.[29] The bank, according to Mariane Pearl's attorneys, supported those charities through its financial services.[30]

Now, there are a couple of things we can't forget here. For instance, the little fact that the government of Pakistan owns 49 percent of the bank's stocks. Or that the Aga Khan Fund for Economic Development (AKFED) owns the remaining 51 percent, which it acquired two years after the death of Daniel Pearl.[31] AKFED is active in sixteen countries in the so-called

---

[27] Hina Shamsi, Director of the ACLU National Security Project notes that, twenty years on, few have ever been charged. "20 Years Later, Guantánamo Remains a Disgraceful Stain on Our Nation. It Needs to End." ACLU.org, January 11th, 2022.

[28] Simpson, R. Glenn. "Mariane Pearl Sues Bank, Claims It Knew of Terror Tie." *Wall Street Journal*, July 19th, 2007.

[29] "Pearl's wife sues Pakistani bank, Al-Qaeda." *The Hindustan Times*, July 19th, 2007.

[30] Goldstein, Bonnie. "Mariane Pearl v. the Aga Khan." *Slate*, July 20th, 2007.

[31] "PC hands over Habib Bank to Aga Khan Fund." *Dawn*, February 27th, 2004.

developing world, including Afghanistan, India, and Pakistan. It's not a nonprofit organization; it is more along the lines of those other harbingers of doom, the IMF and the World Bank, (i.e., rah-rah capitalism). Oh, and by the way, a branch of the World Bank, the International Finance Corporation, is, allegedly, about to invest $125 million in Habeeb Bank Limited.[32] And, just to get all our ducks lined up here, Pakistan is, according to some people in Washington and thereabouts, America's closest ally *as well as* the front line in "The War on Terror."

I'm with Mariane Pearl in that there is a stinky trail that leads to a particularly filthy swamp here, although to claim that the trail begins with the death of Daniel Pearl is perhaps somewhat self-aggrandizing and frankly myopic. Still, for a woman who chose a white American (Angelina Jolie) to play a black woman in the movie about her life, myopia probably lurks quite close to the surface. Does adopting African infants make white actresses black? If there was no way to find any unknown women of color to play the sadly familiar role of loss and marginalization, surely there was the very well-known, extremely accomplished Halle Berry, for crying out loud!

No, the trail most certainly does not begin with the death of an American journalist from *The Wall Street Journal*. His death, while tragic, was no more significant than, say, the number of Iraqi civilians who have died by the conservative estimates provided by Iraqi Body Count: 67,945–74,336 (by its own admission, the site only provides the tally of media-reported civilian deaths, and you and I both know that the mainstream media has long since abandoned its raison d'être by neglecting to be independent, investigative, thorough, or unbiased).[33] As Chris Rock quipped in a recent segment on the "War on Terror" that took us to Iraq, "If it was so dangerous how come we took over the whole fucking country in two weeks? You can't take over Baltimore in two weeks!"[34] But only the Chris Rocks of the world had the gumption to say that. Not our friends with the newspapers. Not our pals on TV.

---

[32] International Finance Corporation report, The World Bank, "The First Six Decades: Leading the Way in Private Sector Development."

[33] https://www.iraqbodycount.org.

[34] "Everybody Loves Chris." *The Guardian*, January 7th, 2008.

Mariane Pearl is right to go after the friend of the relative of the colleague who killed her husband. On July 17th, in an interview with National Public Radio, one of her attorneys, Jodi Flowers from the firm of Motley Rice, LLC, said, "...a terrorist sponsor does not have to buy the very bullets or the very bombs that do the harm...it is enough that they provide the material support knowing the intention of the group. And that support can include financial services."[35] She's right, too. (Motley Rice, LLC, has, incidentally, brought other cases against Middle Eastern banks and companies on behalf of victims, presumably American victims, of 9/11).

They are so right that what I'm waiting for is that other lawsuit with the other list of names: the names of the 299.89 million Americans who constitute the entire population of the United States as of January 1st, 2007.[36] The people, for instance, who served the burgers at McDonald's to Navy pilot J.J. Cummings before he left for Afghanistan and wrote the names of those Americans who died on 9/11 in the United States on the 500-pound laser-guided bomb he dropped "in support of operations that resulted in the Taliban collapses at Kabul and Mazar-e-Sharif." Someone call Mariane Pearl and ask her to take Al Qaeda off her list there. Apparently the Taliban has collapsed. Al Qaeda should be close behind.

After all, while we're trying to figure out who did what to whom, we should unfurl the whole nine yards. Justice is not the special prerogative of the Mariane Pearls of this world, is it? And if we are all to agree that we don't have to do the actual buying and selling of bullets and bombs to have colluded in the deaths of thousands of people around the world, then we are all equally culpable. Hell, we probably brought down those towers in New York! Wait, I think somebody already laid out that theory. I think they were French. Goddamn French, they beat us to the truth every time. Throw out the French fries, French wine, and French kissing. Out with the French lettuce!

Somewhere in Guantánamo are the ghosts of three unnamed men who hanged themselves in full view of their guards. Apparently, according to Navy Rear Admiral Harry Harris, they did this because "they have no

---

[35] The record of this interview, and all records of representation by Motley Rice LLC have since been scrubbed. The firm dropped the lawsuit in October. "Daniel Pearl Widow Drops Lawsuit." CBS News, October 25th, 2007.

[36] https://www.multpl.com/united-states-population/table/by-month.

regard for human life."[37] As opposed, of course, to us Americans, who have the utmost regard for it. So much so that we never interfere in democratic elections in places like Chile or Palestine, for instance, and we ensure that when other countries like Cuba establish social welfare programs or conduct health care in a manner that gives equal weight to all human life we give them our full support. We don't go starting wars in other countries because we want their oil, or their diamonds. Oh no, not us.

Somewhere in Yemen and in Saudi Arabia are three women, mothers, perhaps, like Mariane Pearl, or, like her, widows. Or both. They don't know about paper so sharp it can kill you, or shined-up glass doors that whoosh air conditioning in and out when you approach from either side, and telephones with fancy rings and business lunches consumed with chopsticks, or deals made over sangria. They don't know about the Motley Rice, LLCs of the world, and they probably don't know about Mariane Pearl either. But unlike them, Mariane Pearl gets to talk about her dead husband. She gets to mourn him, bury him, honor him, write a book about him, make a movie about him, and now sue the world over his death.

Somewhere around the Potomac, they are expanding the American military with robot warriors. According to John Pike of the nonprofit think tank globalsecurity.org, this is a good thing because "if they are damaged you can recycle their parts or take them to a repair shop…there is no condolence letter or funeral." In addition, it can kill without qualms. The thing is, there are no condolence letters and funerals now. We write names on bombs. And qualms? We don't have those either.

So I leave you with this poem by Jumah al Dossari, a prisoner at Guantánamo Bay, who has been in solitary confinement since 2003.[38] He's a Bahraini who has tried to kill himself twelve times. His lawyer once found him in a bedsheet noose with a deep gash in one wrist.

Take my blood.
Take my death shroud and
The remnants of my body.
Take photographs of my corpse at the grave, lonely.

---

[37] For the full story of the suicides, read Horton, Scott. "The Guantánamo 'Suicides.'" *Harpers,* March, 2010.

[38] *Poems from Guantánamo: Detainees Speak,* University of Iowa Press, 2007.

Send them to the world,
To the judges and
To the people of conscience,
Send them to the principled men and the fair-minded.

And let them bear the guilty burden, before the world,
Of this innocent soul.
Let them bear the burden, before their children and before
*   history,*
Of this wasted, sinless soul,
Of this soul which has suffered at the hands of the
*   "protectors of peace."*

I wish Mariane Pearl good luck with her lawsuit. I wish her son a sense of security even as he grows up without his biological father. But if they really want peace I suggest that they terminate the services of Motley Rice and return to the place she was in when she wrote these words for her post on the Forgiveness Project: "Revenge is a basic human instinct, the animal part of man, and it gets us nowhere…Dialogue is the ultimate act of courage, far more courageous than killing someone."

And I suggest that those who can and do weep for Mariane Pearl try to find out the names of those three men who hanged themselves in Guantánamo Bay.

7.
The First Mistake: Barack Obama's Silence on Gaza
January 2009

In seven days, Barack Obama will be sworn in as the forty-fourth president of the United States. The UK *Telegraph* reports today that people have been willing to pay 25,000 British Pounds for one of the 240,000 tickets, most of them standing, to the inauguration.[39] The streets of Washington, DC, are flush with cash, the Kuwaiti ambassador's wife, Reema Al-Sabah, is throwing one of the flashiest parties in the Diplomatic Circle, every hotel room is booked, every couch taken, and every ball gown picked.

Meanwhile, the skies over Gaza, already lacking in any silver-lined clouds, are now thick with leaflets stating that Israel plans to escalate its war, and will begin a new phase in the aggression it launched, with cruel irony, on Christmas Day. As Glenn Greenwald exposes in a piece for Salon.com, there has to be a particularly horrific level of self-delusion for Americans to support this level of inhumanity.[40] The kind of inhumanity that purports, as the Israeli government does, and the American media dutifully reports, to "warn" people already imprisoned in camps—for there are no homes we in the so-called civilized world would recognize as such inside the occupied territories of Palestine—that death is imminent, for instance, for to which point of safety could they run? The refugee camps in Palestine and the deprivation within them are not different from the camps and deprivation that people pretended did not exist in Hamburg, Nordhausen, and Munich, and the forefathers of today's Israeli citizens were once given those same intimations of death with the same macabre regularity. We remember the names of those camps, Dora-Mittenbau, Sanchsenhausen, Dachau, even as we do not know how to pronounce the names of today's iterations of those same camps: Nuseirat, Deir el-Balah, Khan Younis.

Over the weekend I was offered tickets to the inauguration, including space in a hotel room close to the parade route. The offer came with the

---

[39] Spillius Alex. "Barack Obama Supporters Offer £25000 for Inauguration Tickets." *The Telegraph*, November 11th, 2008.
[40] Greenwald, Glenn. "Orwell, blinding tribalism, selective Terrorism, and Israel/Gaza." Salon.com, January 4th, 2009.

promise of chauffeured transport from my Philadelphia home to the hotel and back and the company of good friends. I have one day to make what ought to be an easy decision for someone who worked daily for twenty solid months by spoken and written word, by physical and ether-based deed, by personal and financial sacrifice, for the election of Barack Obama.

The inauguration of America's first Black president is a notable event. The millions who worked on this campaign and the millions who never thought they would see the day should celebrate an achievement that was as unexpected by our natural tendency toward pessimism as it was preordained by the march of history. No doubt the eyes of the world will be watching on the 20th of January with the same attention with which they watched his victory on November 4th.

But what does an activist like me say to that same world of a man who has refused to comment on the massacre of the Palestinian people, including children who are the age of his own daughters, because there can be "only one president at a time," but who has been front and center stage in flagrant disregard of the current Commander-in-Chief with regard to the American economy? Is this our first intimation that the change we can believe in is really an unbelievable continuation of the policy of America first, the rest be damned?

The German newspaper *Süddeutsche Zeitung*, no less, scorned Obama for his stance, stating that "Gaza is burning, and Israel's bombs are causing daily casualties, but the world can only expect change at twelve noon sharp on January 20."[41] And, all the way in the Philippines, columnist for the *Philippine Daily Inquirer*, Randy David, writes thus on his personal blog: "By any measure, this is not a war but a slaughter, not a retaliatory response but an outrageous massacre. The Jewish nation's transformation from colossal victim to callous aggressor is complete…As Israelis and Palestinians stared menacingly at each other on Christmas Day, the rest of us stared indifferently, forgetting that, in the last analysis, we are all Gazans."[42]

Is it, then, only our future president who has not understood the situation? Is it, then, only us Americans who have the power to intervene in

[41] "World Waits for Signal, Obama Keeps Own Counsel on Gaza." Deutsche Welle online, January 7th, 2009.
[42] David, Randy. "Israel's War: An Eye For a Tooth." http://www.randydavid.com/2009/01/israels-war-an-eye-for-a-tooth/ January 10th, 2009.

this monstrous daylight butchery of an entire tribe of people, who feel that good work must wait until the partying is over? Seven years ago, another American president took the sympathy of the world and transformed it into hatred. Just two months ago, Barack Obama won it back on the backs of ordinary Americans. Today he stands on the brink of repeating the biggest mistake of his predecessor. As a man with Barack Obama's upbringing, his global reach, his demonstrated intelligence and humanity, and his oft-repeated commitment to justice for all, that will be unforgivable. We do not expect great vision from fools, but we demand it of our heroes.

8.
Osama bin Laden and America's Celebration of Death
May 2011

One of America's foremost writers, Joan Didion, in a memoir reflecting on the death of her husband (*The Year of Magical Thinking*), quotes the English anthropologist Geoffrey Gorer's words from his own book *Death, Grief and Mourning*. In that book he writes that Americans (and the British) were pressured by "an ethical duty to enjoy oneself…to treat mourning as morbid self-indulgence, and to give social admiration to the bereaved who hide their grief so fully that no one would guess anything had happened."

It is a trend that has been taken to its extreme in the white swaths of this country where not only are the bereaved expected to not mourn publicly, but their public burials are sometimes beset by rabid groups who disrupt the restrained funereal proceedings by shouting slogans that denounce the dead, a strange custom that was recently approved as a "fundamental right" by none other than the Supreme Court of the United States.

For an immigrant American such as myself, whose cultural attitude toward death is clothed not only in deep respect and centuries old traditions but also a communal approach to grief—that this death is not mine alone to bear—it has often been disturbing to be present at the White American tradition of memorial services, held long after the funeral is over, where the focus is on a joyful remembrance of the life lived and then a moving on to other business as if that life had never been, all sorrow hidden deep inside the individual. It is as though death is unique and uniquely mourned, that the only expression of emotion that would make the mourner acceptable to society is equanimity, if not outright happiness.

How is it, then, that the youth in a country so uncomfortable with death could gather itself together to cheer the death of Osama bin Laden? Is there something about the American conscience, or lack thereof, that makes it impossible for an American to mourn their dead but makes it not only possible but, by some accounts lighting up the blogosphere, positively commendable to cheer the death of someone whose crimes they barely remember? And if, as the American media has repeatedly emphasized, particularly during these last few days, Osama bin Laden was American's

Public Enemy #1, could it be that these kids know nothing of how their obscene celebrations might be perceived abroad or of the people who might support bin Laden, and even less as to the reasons why? Here's a quick list that I include from the first part of a blog by Asim Rafiqui, an American photographer. The entirety of it is worth reading in full:

> We have invaded two nations because we were told that we must. Both illegally and in violation of all known international law.
>
> We have murdered possibly over a million Afghanis and Iraqis and Pakistanis and others in the process. And continue to kill them at will in Afghanistan and Iraq.
>
> We have displaced and dislocated from Iraq, Afghanistan, and Pakistan other millions, forever ruining their lives and humanity. And forever consigning them to the void of suspicion, fear, and prejudice.
>
> We constructed hundreds of millions of dollars' worth of military bases and detention centers in Afghanistan and Iraq. And now use them for "forward projection" in the so-called war against a noun.
>
> We continue to occupy Iraq and Afghanistan and use massive military force to retain our jackboots over their necks while funding and supporting illegal and completely illegitimate governments that we described as "democratic" and "parliamentary."
>
> We have invited private militia and corporate mercenaries to the party and given out contracts worth billions to make it appealing for them.
>
> We have detained innocents, including American citizens, indefinitely and still refuse to give them appropriate justice. President Obama willingly continuing the illegal and unjust policies of his predecessors.
>
> We have tortured them relentlessly (oh, sorry, we have enhanced interrogated them!) and strong-armed our civilized courts and bureaucratic apparatchiks to justify our actions.
>
> We have renditioned them and sent them off to our "allies" in other parts of the world to be tortured, maimed, and killed.
>
> And there is no end to this program.[43]

---

[43] Rafiqui, Asim. "The Dead Can't Dance and I Refuse to Either, or, Why I Insist on Remembering While Others Insist on Drinking to Forget." *The Spinning Head*, May 3rd, 2011. https://tinyurl.com/bdhjavff.

Chances are, yes, they do not know and, worse, do not care. Chances are that when the kids took to the streets in Washington, DC, in Camden, DE, and in Chicago, IL, those kids weren't thinking. Or if they were, their thoughts were on being swept up in the euphoria of groups. How telling that America's teenagers spill out into the streets to celebrate death while the teenagers of Egypt and Tunisia spill out to claim freedom and justice.

And what of the parents who look on with a smile? What of my friend and fellow writer, a mother of four, who wrote: *Don't shame the young for releasing their pent-up fear...Let them remember that they raised their voices, loudly, together. It's a good skill to learn because maybe before the next war starts, they'll be the ones who learned to take to the streets, chanting; maybe next time it will be in protest against war. They were claiming their voices. Let them remember it proudly.*

In what order of the universe does a child that learns to whoop with joy over death, destruction, and war learn to lift their voice for peace? It seems to me to be a chilling reminder of the social reality within this country, a reality where while this nation is waging two wars of invasion and occupation, most of America's elite don't know anybody fighting in it. Perhaps it is because these unjust wars are being fought by the poor—those people who are routinely excluded from the so-called "American dream" even as they are asked to fight and die to preserve other people's right to pursue that dream. It is a war that the educated elite of Georgetown chanting *Yes, we did!* outside the White House have never met. And it is a war that, thanks to their blindness, may very well come here to meet them.

I do not expect the appropriate response from a nation that has never been predisposed to learn the cultural sensibilities of other nations or other faiths, or to express circumspection in its group activities. It is a sad fact of American life that the sobriety exhibited by President Obama (of whom it can at least be said that he asked for the burial at sea that followed the customs of Islam after funereal rites, unlike a previous president who paraded his old friend-suddenly-turned-enemy, Saddam Hussein, for the TV cameras) does not seem to have permeated the minds of the people in the country he leads. Americans are so fond of describing other people's customs, the hijab, for example, as barbaric, and yet I can find nothing more barbaric than dancing over the death of another human being, nothing more macabre than teaching children that this is a good thing. Then again, what more should we expect of a country whose national sport was, at one time, the public lynching of people based on the color of their skin?

In this historic moment I feel that the only hope that still remains for America rests in her immigrant and minority populations. The ones who know what it is to mourn, loud and clear and without protest, what it is to absorb someone else's grief as their own. The ones who raise their children to live by a different set of rules, ones that can acknowledge tragedy with humanity.

My middle daughter was six months old when the Twin Towers fell. I did not go to work at my office in the federal building on Varick and Houston in New York City that day. She is now ten. This is what she had to say on Monday: "Kids at school were saying how happy they were about bin Laden being killed. Seth and I disagreed. I said it doesn't seem right to be happy about death. Whatever he did, he was somebody's son." Those are the hearts, my daughter's, her friend's, that will learn the ways of other cultures, that will be able to associate crime with cause, who will be able to see that there cannot be two sets of rules, one for "us" and another for "them." The ones who can understand the madness of claiming the right to nuclear arms for "us" but no nuclear power for "them." The ones who know that the leaders they cherish and revere, like President Obama, and on whose behest they march off to die, are not that far removed from the leaders cherished by other people in other lands. And in realizing these parallels, theirs are the voices that will be raised for peace.

And though this country has done so little to deserve it, we can only hope that the rest of the world will wait patiently for those children to grow up. God knows that billions around the world have seen enough of the other kind.

9.
Whose Wars Are These?
November 2011

The wars that permeated my childhood were those that were internal to my country, Sri Lanka. Therefore, everybody was involved. There was no refuge from it, no matter your social status, particularly if you were male. You could be killed going to market, you could be abducted from your dorm room, you could be left to burn with a tire around your head, you could be shot, you could die with dozens of others in a suicide attack. Everybody knew where everybody else stood, where their sympathies lay, what hue colored their politics. More than that, everybody knew someone who had died, and most of us knew more than a few. We did not have a particular love for living in a state of war, far from it. But they were the circumstances of our history for nearly three decades, and we lived or died along with the fortunes of our country.

I would like to believe that the fact that America's wars have been waged overseas is the reason why this kind of intimacy with mayhem and loss does not pervade every home here. I would like to imagine that it is universally mystifying to Americans that America could be fighting several major wars and the vast majority of people could go on with their lives knowing not one soul who has been dispatched to kill and die, nor any who returned injured or in a casket. I know only three, none of them untouched by their years of service, one of them lost entirely: the husband of my college roommate; the son of a veterinarian in the town I used to live in; and a fellow writer and photographer whose concerns mirror mine:[44] How strange it must have been for these three young men to return home to people fretting about organic apple cider and homemade iced tea, about peanut-free classrooms and special activities for those who do not celebrate any one of the national holidays. "Americans and their damn bottles of water," one of them quipped to me. "What a joke. Like they really imagine they might suddenly die of thirst without an easily accessible source of water."

---

[44] That last is Elliott Woods, whose most recent work is captured in the brilliant podcast *Third Squad*, a moving and wide-ranging exploration of the American psyche of individual soldiers, and the culture that has shaped them.

How strange that when I posted a link to an essay by one of those veterans ("One Afghan Refugee's Quest to Recover the Past"[45]) on Facebook, nobody clicked it. This is what I said in my note:

> Just read this piece of reporting by Elliott Woods. Between poppy palaces and architecture and 100 minefields still waiting to explode in greater Kabul, between 15,000 troops and up to 1.5 million Afghans killed during the reign of the Soviets and the advent and departure of the Americans is a story that too few of us know. Even those of us who in one way or another contribute to the "donor money" that accounts for four-fifths of the $14 billion GDP in Afghanistan.

I decided to see if it was the case that nobody was paying attention or if nobody cared. I followed up with a joke about Facebook, cut and pasted from some online source for a thousand and one jokes. There were the comments I had been missing. Yes, nobody cared. We care about the here, the now, and the here/now does not involve Afghanistan, Iraq, Iran, Pakistan, Palestine, vast swaths of Africa, or most of the rest of the planet, and certainly not those who were forced to go there to commit the acts no mother raises her child to perpetrate and who must then return to our midst, shattered and frayed, this generation's particular brand of invisible men and women.

How strange that Marine Lance Cpl. Scott Olsen went down in a hail of enemy fire aimed at him by American police during the course of a peaceful protest in the streets of Oakland, California. After two tours of duty in Iraq with the 3rd Battalion, 4th Marine Regiment in Iraq's Anbar province, site of some of the war's fiercest battles, this young man who had been just fourteen years old when we experienced the events of 9/11 lay on the streets on Tuesday the 25th. Why? Because he had divined that much of the economic inequity in America was fueled by the military industrial complex and chose to say that out aloud.[46] That, and the fact that nobody gave a damn where he had been and what he had done or seen, just pass the cocktail shrimp and Moscato.

---

[45] Woods, Elliott D. "One Afghan Refugee's Quest to Recover the Past." *Virginia Quarterly Review* vol. 87, no. 4, Fall 2011: 167–VIII.
[46] "Injured Marine Scott Olson Is A Network Engineer Who Can't Stand American Inequality." *Business Insider*, October 27th, 2011.

According to a report released by the Center for a New American Security, from 2005 to 2010, service members took their own lives at a rate of approximately one every thirty-six hours.[47] Scroll down on the report and we find the statement that the "VA estimates that 18 veterans take their lives every day." The report then goes on to state that they have no way of knowing the accurate number because of insufficient data.

Long ago, I used to watch The News Hour on the Public Broadcasting Service for my one hour of not doing, by which I mean not being a mother, a wife. The segment used to end with a silent screen on which appeared the names of the new dead Americans. I don't know that they still do it, I no longer watch, but I do know there is a searchable database on the PBS website that lists the dead, from 1 all the way through 4,885. That list stopped on August 2010. We cannot know how many people have died. I remember writing about the two thousandth soldier, Staff Sgt. George T. Alexander Jr., back in 2005 for the local paper in Waterville, Maine.

Michael Meade, in an interview done by John Malkin in The Sun Magazine, speaks, among other things, about the distinction between warriors and soldiers:

> Mass culture distorts our instincts and inclinations. Some people are natural fighters so they become soldiers. But soldiers are the opposite of warriors: soldiers do what they're told; warriors do what they feel is best for everybody...A warrior isn't looking for war. A warrior looks to be of service to something beyond him or herself...What's happened is that the culture uses that willingness to serve its own narrow ends. When you take the willingness to sacrifice and aim it in the wrong direction for the wrong reasons, you get damage, and not just to the individual. That damage is inherited by future generations. For healing to occur, the truth has to come out, and by "truth" I don't mean which side was right. That's the small argument. The truth is that souls were hurt, and healing is required for the individuals as well as the collective.[48]

---

[47] Berglass, Nancy and Harrell, Margaret C. "Losing the Battle: The Challenge of Military Suicide." Center for New American Security, October 31st, 2011.

[48] Malkin, John. "Your Own Damn Life: Michael Meade On The Story We're Born With." The Sun Magazine, November, 2011.

That burden of tragedy—of wars waged, of warriors forced into the servitude of soldiering—that burden belongs, surely, to all of us in whose name these things were perpetrated, not just the servicemen coming home to places that are irreconcilable with the places they've been in, with people who don't recognize them and in some ways never saw them to begin with. What is a human being to do, ever, about war? What is an artist to do? What can a writer say? If my words cannot move anybody to see more clearly, listen more closely, of what use are they?

It is the fifth of November. I know why I felt compelled to write about war and veterans today. I write about them because I'm thinking about a witty, talented writer who is my friend. I have never met anybody in her family. I know nothing about her brother. She never spoke of him until I emailed her to tell her that I had lost my mother and did not know how I would go on. She told me about him then, about his time in Iraq and the fact that upon his return, he had found it impossible to reconcile himself to all that he had witnessed and participated in, and had killed himself.

On each anniversary of his passing I have nothing to offer her or to any other family that has gone through this particular kind of loss, except my attention to the whole of their experience, the whole of their grief.

Pineapple & Roasted Nuts

When I was a child, there was nothing much to do in my house but write. Reading was desired, of course, but books were hard to come by, and that meant several things: my two older brothers and I read with great appetite. We fought over books, we memorized what we saw in black and white, and we dreamed of caravans, midnight feasts, puddings, and snow, things we had never experienced in our own lives. We begged for books from our friends at school, from neighbors our own age and much older. Books were passed around and packed away quickly into schoolbags as though they might be confiscated. They were brought out and read with deep pleasure. They were traded for favors of all kinds. The brother closest in age to me and I often exacted payment in pages of a book. *The book you borrowed has only 253 pages*, one of us might say, *so you can only read 253 pages of the book I borrowed.* And so we had to also turn into book thieves, risking fisticuffs in order to get at the final pages of the other's book.

But writing. That was different. That could be done without servility, or becoming emotionally indentured to one's siblings. What I couldn't memorize in its entirety, I wrote down in notebooks.

Hooloovoo, a hyper-intelligent shade of the color blue, I took from Douglas Adams as a child.

> *But why take all this quite so badly?*
> *I would not, had I world and time*
> *To wait for reason, rhythm, rhyme,*
> *To reassert themselves, but sadly,*
> *The time is not remote when I*
> *Will not be here to wait. That's why.*

I wrote down in more elaborate script as a teenager in the back page of a notebook that I kept for gems like that one from Vikram Seth (*The Golden Gate*, Vintage 1991). This habit of being able to recognize the unique voice of writers I had no idea I would ever meet in person was one I could not shake. I recall noting—even as I speed-read the passages and questions on my ACT in Literature, en route to an American college—the particular sentence that described our human fear of insects. I don't remember the precise words, but the line noted that insects were the embodiment of our deepest human fears: the insides on the out, all spikes and gesturing, and the power of a determined collective. I left enough time at the end of the examination to jot down the two sentences on the back of a bus ticket in writing that mimicked, due to the constraints of space, the footprints of ants.

Much later, applying to colleges, when asked to write about a book that transformed my life, I reached back in time to another set of quotes that had made it into my notebook. They did not come from the great Russians I had by now read, nor from the English poetry and literature I had studied in my Advanced Level classes, nor from the Greeks whom I'd also read, but from William Peter Blatty's *The Exorcist*. The two quotes, about good and evil, and about hope, defined a worldview for me, one that continues to resonate in the way I live my life now. I wrote then, as a nineteen-year-old, about the place of things in a universe that had its own wisdom and reason. More than that, I wrote, quoting Blatty, that sobriety was vital in times of despair as well as in times of hope. I used his words without ever having seen the revenge exacted by a fall on a spring, or the spring on fall. It was the poetry and musicality of the words that gripped me. Those words made sense.

There's a particularity to the way language is acquired by a non-native speaker such as myself, and how it is manipulated. My English texts in Sri Lanka were full of the rudiments of basic English that were required for the entire school population, but at home I was immersed in a version so elevated from that kind of ordinary usage that there was little to do but learn how to become conversant in it. My parents spoke that way, as did my brothers, and therefore so did I. There was no value placed on knowing the latest information on pop stars, though a working knowledge of politics was expected within the family. We did not own a functional pair of scissors, sticking plasters (Band-Aids) were bought one at a time and only when required, and shopping in general was undertaken for only the most necessary items, but there was a dictionary in the house to which my brothers and I were frequently directed. We cursed and swore (in our elegant tongues), but we reached for it anyway.

This was our underlying message: what we needed to know could be found in books, and if we failed to find our answers there, we would at least have acquired the language with which to ask for help from smart adults. And since this acquisition was so varied, our sense of its usage was correspondingly without limits; there was an internal rhythm to our understanding of the English language that did not seek to obey any single aesthetic, but instead let our intuitive sense of the world unfold on the page however we wished.

During those years, Sri Lanka had no tradition of public readings of work in English, though those who wrote in Sinhala and Tamil had their own multitudinous audiences. As such, we, along with our peers, performed for private audiences in full-length theater productions or during examinations where we declaimed the words of others rather than our own. Pulsing beneath what was taking place among those like me who wrote in English was an entirely different scene: one where Sri Lankan writers saw their own work performed on stage. For those who wrote in English, publication meant collections of poetry rather than prose, though there were always exceptions, and that work was assigned for study in university. It was, in other words, a more cerebral activity, rather than one that included the out-loud utterance.

It has been fascinating to discover, then, the more recent establishment of festivals of literature in Sri Lanka and, more importantly, readings of new work, as well as the local publication of fiction in English. The Galle Literary Festival is known beyond Sri Lanka's shores and has had its share of critics for its lack of inclusion of literature in translation, but it is a festival that has brought international writers to Sri Lanka. More than that, though, are the smaller local festivals that have taken on the matter of engaging with literature in a way that continues a cultural tradition of respect for language and books. Of these, *Annasi & Kadala Gotu* (which translates into pineapple and handheld cones of roasted nuts) is perhaps the most interesting. It spanned just one day, but included panels of people discussing literature and the creative process in all three languages: Sinhala, Tamil, and English. Its very name is an acknowledgement of a particularly local love for nutritious, delicious, and completely addictive street food, and an attempt to demystify literature and literary culture.

It stood to reason that the organizers of that festival were intrigued to hear of an endeavor that I have been pursuing along with my brother, Malinda Seneviratne (also a writer, journalist, poet, and winner of both the Gratiaen Prize for Literature in Translation in 2013 and 2022, and the Gratiaen Prize for Poetry in 2015, established by Michael Ondaatje): the establishment of an international festival of literature in translation, which we called IF/LIT. A few years ago, in the wee hours of a morning, I Skyped in from the US to join an afternoon gathering in Colombo. Assembled there were my brother, two young men who were active in the local literary scene, Rick Simonson from Elliott Bay Book Company, who was visiting my father in Sri Lanka after speaking at the Jaipur Literary Festival (JLF), and a group of Sri Lankans, all women, who had been brought together by a former school friend of mine. The most interesting thing about this group was that none of the Sri Lankans (other than my brother) were writers, but they were all extremely well-read, continuing into this present day our tendency to place great value on the worth of books. Further, all of the women were in positions of power, most of them heads of private corporations, from hotels and tourism to exports and finance, and all of them active patrons of the arts. Even more importantly, they were committed to sharing their love of learning of the world through its literature with as wide an audience as was possible, and willing to volunteer their time to make that happen.

I don't know if that drive to invest so personally in literature is unique to Sri Lanka, but I can say unequivocally that it is rare here in the US where I live now. I was somewhat transfixed by that conversation, by the energy in that beautifully appointed room, by the intense practicality regarding the logistics of putting such a festival together that at no point diminished the bright enthusiasm for and embrace of the festival itself, an ambiance that harkened back to those Blatty quotes I'd jotted down.

When I was in Sri Lanka, I met with the young organizer of *Annasi & Kadala Gotu*. He made an appointment with me, sat bolt upright in a chair, asked questions, and took notes. He made suggestions informed by considerations that I had not stopped to think about and explained which people could take on which tasks in putting a festival of this magnitude, our IF/LIT, together. The person who began the festival he had just run was an airline pilot, a non-writer. He himself was a computer programmer. His friends who would handle publicity and tickets and every other conceivable detail that goes into producing a festival were mostly engineers and accountants. What were they doing immersed in books? Simply this: they loved literature. They loved literature because they had been taught, as we had been taught, about the significance of the imagination, and of the way our minds expanded through the simple act of inhabiting other people's reality. Our children are not relegated to certain aisles at a bookstore or library. There is no concept of Young Adult literature, they read as their parents do; they are as likely to pick up Enid Blyton as they are to memorize Donne and Soyinka, quote Achebe and Shakespeare.

During a visit that took place in the wake of JFL, at which I'd spoken with him, I attended a book launch for Romesh Gunasekara (author of *Noon Tide Toll* and others). The event took place at Barefoot, a favorite haunt of expatriates and well-shod Sri Lankans, and the whole evening had an elegance that was unusual in my experience; readings in America, with the notable exception of Seattle, seem largely unpredictable. This launch took place in the open-air courtyard, with tables decorated with lamps and flowers; a porch provided the stage-setting for the reading, and books were bought and signed before a word was read. The evening concluded with hors d'oeuvres and red and white wine served by waitstaff. An airy reverence hung over the assembled. Most significantly, I noted the way in which the London-based author of the hour spent time with the guests, who were almost all known in some fashion to him or to his family. He chatted a little to Shyam Selvadurai and me, both of whom he knew well, but I also noticed the care he took to pull up a chair and sit with my father, himself a poet and reviewer. I listened as they reminisced about various Sri Lankan writers, their own families, and conversed about books read and those yet to be written. They were of a different time, there was mutual respect, but my father was the older man and Romesh had lost none of the affection reserved for those who served not only as friends but as teachers, whether or not they stood in front of a chalkboard in classrooms. He had lost none of that particularly subtle language of regard, a lexicon that is a blend of a quintessentially Sri Lankan character sweetening this foreign tongue.

Many months later, I heard Romesh's voice again. He was back in London, and I was back in the United States, and we were connected on air on a BBC program, being interviewed by Rana Mitter. It was a program devoted to a conversation with writer Tony Harrison, the 2015 winner of the David Cohen Prize for a body of work. On a program devoted to an artist who welcomed political debate on topics ranging from the Persian Gulf to Bosnia, Mitter felt it would be interesting to have two writers from Sri Lanka, a country of much turbulence, and recent peace, to speak about our experience writing of it. Over the course of the program, I listened to Romesh's soothing inflections, and my own much less mellow delivery. We were of different generations, a world apart, speaking about our nation of origin. We left it off air, discussing IF/LIT and the importance of literature. We were not that different. We had read different books growing up, and our phrasing was correspondingly divergent, but we were in agreement: our country, despite all that had ravaged it, still pulsed with that same yearning for the benediction of books that we had once experienced, and we, having been blessed by that culture, saw with intimate clarity the importance of continuing to participate in the vitality of a well-read citizenry. I took off my headphones and headed to Miami, where I was due to speak the next day. I took my country and my countrymen with me, that unique communality that we bring to our embrace of the written word, the way in which poetry and stories are so universally regarded as being essential to human life.

Five Books That Shaped My Life

1.
Staying Hungry on Enid Blyton

Enid Blyton, the British author who penned 753 books before she died in 1968, came to me all the way in Sri Lanka in the form of her many series of books about children—The Famous Five, the Secret Seven, the girls at Malory Towers and St. Clare's and fairy characters such as Noddy, Big Ears, Dame Washalot, Moon-face, Silky the fairy, the Saucepan Man, and the Angry Pixie. Her books, which my brothers and I borrowed one at a time from the boys next door, sat among the many that were brought lovingly into our home by our English literature and Greek and Roman Classics teaching mother and by our poet and writer father. We did not have money, though we weren't poor, an important distinction, and the books that came to us were often stamped "Gift of the Asia Foundation" (a peace-directed initiative headquartered in San Francisco that donates books to countries in Asia), or purchased for next to nothing at the People's Publishing House, an equally laudable initiative of the Soviet Union that thrived in socialist-leaning countries such as mine.

In 2008, the Costa Book Awards voted Enid Blyton the best-loved author, ahead of Roald Dahl, J.K. Rowling, and Shakespeare. A new breed of academic, however, has tagged Blyton as a snob and racist whose books were populated by "golliwogs" who in appearance resembled the actors who appeared in blackface on stages across the United States. Her books have been purged of these characters and her language updated in consideration to present, more global, sensitivities. Another group of academics, including Dr. Rudd (*Mysteries of Children's Literature*, Macmillan), contends that "of the children who were not previously aware of the equation 'golliwog equals ethnically black person,' none made it."[49] I was one of those children. Alongside the millions of other children in places where we were not being described as being "of color," the golliwog remained a golliwog. And, waltzing between books from America and books from the Soviet Union and the borrowed books from England, the stories that caught my

---

[49] Ward, David. "Golly! Blyton is not Guilty of Race Slurs." *The Guardian*, July 3rd, 2000.

attention were those that dealt with gumption, resilience, the magic of fairy tales, and escape.

My life as an only girl growing up with nothing but boys in every direction within the family, not to mention those my mother taught at an all-boys school, was devoid of the usual fluff of girlhood. I was tough, my life was full of adult complexities, and I could out-fight, out-talk, out-climb, and out-run the boys, skills necessary in my world, but skills nonetheless that made me less of a girl in a culture where how to be one was quite easy to understand for those so inclined. How sweet it was, then, to read *The Wonderful Wishing Chair* by Enid Blyton, in which two children named Mollie and Peter (dully named, for a kid growing up around Medhavis and Arjunas!) come upon a chair that takes them out of their ordinary lives and into magical places. Places like the Magic Faraway Tree whose uppermost branches graze different lands and where it is equally possible to step one day into the Land of Dame Slap—a particularly terrible schoolteacher—as it is to find oneself in the Lands of Birthday, Goodies, or Take-What-You-Want!

Most books take readers away from their familiar settings, but children's books are required to do so. Good children's books transport in ways that go beyond the usual nonsense of moralistic tales that preach and preach and leave nothing to the imagination. The best ones reach into a child's world and identify yearning: for the forbidden thing, the unknown place, balm for a secret hurt, calm for an unuttered desperation, syrup for the unspeakable thirst. Enid Blyton knew those longings and found their antidote in an ordinary-looking antique chair that could fly away from their house (in my mind, from mine) to far more exciting places. Among their adventures was the escape of the brownie, Winks, rescued from Mr. Grim's School for Bad Brownies, who is subsequently returned there with a gift from Peter. This gift, a Tidbit Dish (won from the Island of Surprises), is a tiffin-carrier that, whenever it is opened, contains a tasty morsel of food. How it warmed my heart to imagine that box, filled as it was with foods I'd never seen but could picture, trifles and puddings and watercress sandwiches, all of which sounded insanely complex and divinely delectable to a child raised on fiery spices.

At the tuck shop run by the nuns at the convent I attended, where I rarely had money to buy anything, I would barter my services as a girl at ease with boyish mannerisms—to sweat and toil and be aggressive if I had to—to purchase treats for my friends so I could share a bite. In that world, where getting to school was hard enough for our mother and her sons and daughter, I did not expect a packed lunch after the first grade. I made do with food when I got it, I made do without it when I needed to. And I dreamed in terms of Tidbit Dishes.

Years later, on a full scholarship at Bates College in Maine, I continued to marvel at food as it is presented in American schools: smorgasbords offering multiple choices in every single food group, dozens of cereals, varieties of breads, arrays of juices, and less-and-more-fat milk in flavors, desserts at every meal. Deep within the gratitude I felt for being so well fed was a hunger I desired. A full belly addled my brain; it was no longer possible to yearn when every craving was fulfilled in this manner. A grotesqueness colored the matter of dining. In my heart I had always been hungry, and it was a way of existing that had helped me come to America in the first place, made it possible for me to survive the uprooting.

I was reminded of Enid Blyton while reading an essay written by one of my brothers, himself a poet and an eminent journalist in Sri Lanka, entitled "On the Books We Read and Those That Read Us," in which he speaks about his daughters and their love for this same children's author. Musing on the experience of particular books, he writes, "If 'book' is metaphor, then the world is made of answers to any question you can think of. There are pages in flowers, in fragrance, in root. The soil and the sky are leaves of a novel. The cloud is a line of poetry and so too its edge, its blur with sky, its rendering in song, music score, on canvas and its etching in memory and the etch itself."

So, too, the absence of a book: its own question, its own answer. Now, as I sit here writing this, I gaze at the books that line the shelves before me. The topmost shelves are filed with favorites like *Sula* and *Tar Baby* by Toni Morrison, Colum McCann's *Apeirogon*, Rohinton Mistry's *A Fine Balance*, V. S. Naipaul's *A Room for Mr. Biswas*, essays by Zadie Smith and Ursula K. Le Guin, Abraham Varghese's *Cutting for Stone*, Lynn Freed's *Home Ground*, Ursula Hegi's *Stones from the River,* every bit of criticism by James Woods, every edition of *Freeman's* edited by my beloved brother, John Freeman. Other shelves are filled with the books written by my friends, ordered again by my favorites. Among them are Jesmyn Ward's *Salvage the*

Bones, Paul Yoon's *Once The Shore*, Josh Weil's *The New Valley*, Frances de Pontes Peebles's *The Seamstress*, and all of Jamaica Kincaid's oeuvre. There are shelves filled up with the books of poetry that I cannot resist: collections by Mahmoud Darwish, Rabindranath Tagore, Evan Boland, Terrance Hayes, Heather McHugh, Brigit Pegeen Kelly, Wislawa Szymborska, Stanley Kunitz, Camille T. Dungy, Anne Carson...

There is no room now on my shelf for *The Wonderful Wishing Chair*. That book and dozens of others by Blyton sit on the bookshelves that dominate my daughters' rooms. I leave it to them to discover an ailing deep within their hearts, some lack that will drive them to discoveries, to adventures, to mishaps, to irreparable remorse, to life. Over the years I have made peace with my American life where food, shelter, and clothing are so easily mine. I have discovered a new craving, perfect and insatiable: for more words, for more books, for the heady and blissful company of writers. My last waking thoughts are, once more, of flight, of other rooms, other lives. From repeating the stories that Blyton told in my own attempts at short fiction as a child, in this world where everything is simultaneously possible and lost, I have grown to spin my own.

2.
Silk

I first read Alessandro Baricco's *Silk* in 1998 in its English translation by Guido Waldman. The book—a tale of travel, passion, and mysterious, silent communication—resonated with me immediately.

I had just returned to the United States after my graduate studies in Sri Lanka, and I was struck by the elegance of a story that appealed to my Sri Lankan heart—one raised on the bittersweet joy of not having what one desired. Not only had Baricco made that sorrow palpable, he had done it in fewer than one hundred pages.

Fifteen years later, I read the book again. A great deal had changed. I had grown up and out of the heady romance of my new American life and come to understand that in leaving home, I had lost more than I had ever been willing to let go. My trips back to Sri Lanka had become an effort to gather into my arms the things that were no longer part of my daily life and the regrets that I could never articulate to a family that celebrated my seeming success.

Far from the country that mattered so much to me, I created homes for myself among books and writers. I lived in an imaginary world of far-away loves that threatened the life I had chosen—even the hearts that I now minded as the mother of three daughters. My own writing had begun to echo with longing. This time, as I read, my mind lingered not over the intricacies of the plot, but over the message of a book based on the premise of love that is never consummated, yet is wholly shared.

In Baricco's novella, a Frenchman, Hervé Joncour, makes a difficult journey from his village and through Siberia to Japan to obtain silkworms from one of its islands. During his first visit, he is invited to stay with a man who is referred to as the "master of all that the world contrived to carry off the island." There he meets a woman who is either his host's captive spouse, mistress, or lover—it is never clear.

His interactions with this woman are entirely wordless. In all but two instances, they take place in the presence of the man with whom she shares her life, fraught with the danger that their secret passion for each other will be discovered and Joncour will be put to death. In the single written exchange between them, the girl to whom he has never spoken writes to him thus: "Come back, or I shall die." And with those words, Joncour is transformed into a man who will sacrifice his life to do no more than see his beloved again.

Baricco's language is exquisitely phrased. It was easy to accompany Joncour on his difficult travels and luxuriate in the sensuousness that awaits at the end of his journey. As I read, I could see exotic birds trapped in an aviary as a gift to a beloved and the heady luxury of his host's house. Above all, I could feel the intoxicating chemistry between two lovers who hold each other in plain sight of the world, though their bodies remain forever separate. A glance takes the place of a kiss. A cup of tea sipped from the same place on its rim stands in for an embrace.

Baricco has set down a story enshrined in the acceptance that nothing will change, there can be no reversal, no comfort in the certainty that the wish made will one day be fulfilled. In reading the book again, I came to understand that during my first read, I had been so preoccupied with where I was that I was blind to the journeys I could take with my mind. If bliss can be found in the mere existence of another reality, a country or a lover, distance eventually becomes immaterial.

It is a particular triumph to pull off writing the truest love story of them all, as Baricco has done, the one where though life is lonely and loss is guaranteed, the heart, that oft-neglected center of life, still manages to find its peace.

3.
One Book to Rule Them All
Jamaica Kincaid's *See Now Then*

In the spring of 2013, in preparation for a Master/Class conversation I would be doing with Jamaica Kincaid for the PEN World Voices Festival in April of that year, I spent a week reading all the books she had ever written, beginning with *At the Bottom of the River* (1983), on through her nonfiction, covering the death of her brother (*My Brother*, 1997), and her sojourn into the Himalayas in search of flowers (*Among Flowers*, 2005), all the way to her latest novel, *See Now Then* (2013). It was quite something to walk beside a writerly mind unfolding over the course of three decades. I could see the evolution of her technique and the echoes of themes touched on in the earliest books, as well as the unfolding of a life glimpsed in small flashes as the myriad useful and malleable details of a life were strewn among the fictions.

I found something fresh and educational in every single one of them, whether it was the precise explanation of colonialism and argument against the neo-colonialism of the tourist industry (*A Small Place*, 1988), the exploitation of national resources and the renaming (and thereby claiming ownership) of native plants (*My Garden Book*, 2001), or the complex depths of the mother-daughter relationship that permeates almost all of her work, but most importantly the novels *Annie John* (1985) and *The Autobiography of My Mother* (1995). But the one I loved the best was *See Now Then*.

If we go by the analysis offered up by the Grand Old Lady of LitCrit, *The New York Times Book Review*, we could conclude, as Dwight Garner did, that this latest book was an act of revenge against a husband who left the author for a younger, more easily digested, and therefore infinitely more palatable version of womanhood. True, the novel echoes the dissolution of Kincaid's marriage to the composer Allen Shawn, who happens to be the son of the man she admits to having admired the most throughout her life, the one for whom she wrote everything she did, the late long-time editor of *The New Yorker*, William Shawn. And, true, the Mrs. Sweet of the book, the one who tends so diligently to the needs of her children and husband, is an author, someone whose work about "her goddamn mother" and her "stupid little island" are direct references to Elaine Richardson's (better known as Jamaica Kincaid's) own mother, and the Antigua of Elaine's birth, the taproot of her imagination.

So what?

Authors are notoriously relentless at culling the gems from the minutiae of their lives. There is a reason why such awkward laughter is generated by the t-shirt embroidered with these words: *careful, or you'll end up in my novel.* We all do it. Yet *See Now Then* is not simply a recounting of the entanglement, disappointment, betrayal, and quiescence that are the four corners of the institution of marriage, though it does that with great facility. I read it as a brilliant unpicking of the intricate tapestry of time, the time that it takes to get from one place to another, from being single and full of promise to being discarded and ridiculed, and all the dances in between: the sultry samba of innocence, the salsa tempo of dreams, the slow tango of motherhood, the quickstep of parenthood, and the graceful sway of bowing off a stage from which one has been effectively, if impolitely, excused. It is about marriage, and it is about everything else.

Most books that revolve around the end of a relationship concentrate on the present. There is the customary "how could she?" or "why did he?" but these are not questions that the author can hope to answer, nor do they usually result in enhancing the mind of the questioner. Not in Kincaid's novel. "See now then," her novel begins, placing Mrs. Sweet at a window overlooking the garden, from which vantage she can see and unsee what she had previously believed she had seen (i.e. known) at the time (i.e., then) about her life. "Now and then," she begins again, in an early segue back and forth in time: "Now and then, Mrs. Sweet said to herself, though this was done only in her mind's eye, as she stood at the window, unmindful of the rage and hatred and utter disdain that her beloved Mr. Sweet nurtured in his small breast for her now and then, seeing it as it presented itself, a series of tableaus."

If there is bitterness, it is cloaked in the dark and intelligent humor of a writer who understands that life, as Molière put it, really is a comedy for those who think. And Jamaica Kincaid is a thinker. Consider this: Mrs. Sweet enlists the tried and true method to earn vast sums of money—cash crops and the exploitation of menial labor—in order to make a hundred lyres and procure one hundred musicians with the skill to play those lyres, and even construct a music hall in which to place these people, just so Mr. Sweet could indulge in the performance of his fantasies, but each time Mr. Sweet shies away from the event. There is, obviously, no such event, but it is a hilarious stand-in for the extent to which we all go, whether married or not, in our personal and public lives to enable the happiness of people—to "make the impossible demand, possible"—whose happiness truly depends solely upon being able to reverse time so that their paths and ours never cross.

Kincaid has been hailed as the queen of the endless sentence, worlds of meaning and multiple story threads coming together seamlessly, or only with the aid of a carefully placed comma. In *See Now Then*, the skill displayed in her short story "Girl" (her first short fiction to appear in *The New Yorker*, in 1978, which consists of 650 words without periods, and only one punctuation, a question mark) comes into its own. Long paragraphs running into pages at times give us both history and context, a life lived, and a life coming undone, choices made and regrets felt. These pages are filled with convoluted sentences and thoughts that echo the colossal mess of our minds, the way we as writers and human beings speak to ourselves, narrating our own lives and imagining the narration of others around us, spinning one yarn after another until it is quite impossible to distinguish where the story begins or ends. More than that, the experiences of a lifetime—leaving home, the loving estrangement between mothers and daughters, life in these United States, the damning lies that are told to each other routinely by Americans more invested in politeness than honesty, the business of receiving the "pity and scorn" of people who don't look like we do, the desire to be more than we were born to be, the pursuit of art in a world often hostile to the arts, all things that are examined in one or more of her previous books—are brought together and held up to the light of retrospection in *See Now Then*.

I have read this book numerous times now, and would willingly sit down and read it again in a heartbeat. Few writers display courage and wit in their writing as persistently as Jamaica Kincaid has done. Fewer still can be openly self-critical, and just as outspoken about the injustices of our time (both within family, for women, and outside, for nations) as she can. Rarely are female writers willing (or allowed) to dismantle the institutions of motherhood and marriage, and the way each can cripple the mind and life of a woman of talent and intelligence—indeed, I can only imagine the rave review this same book would have garnered were it written by a man—and I have deep admiration for the way Kincaid has made this meditation about something more than the facts themselves.

I have many favorite books and writers, those who demonstrate the inherent worth of good characters no matter when they are introduced into the narrative (Rohinton Mistry), those who wed social commentary with gripping, forward-moving prose (Chang-rae Lee, Ursula Hegi, Jesmyn Ward), and those who can touch on all of these things while spinning a wonderful tale (José Saramago, Francesca Marciano, Abraham Verghese), but what Jamaica Kincaid does in *See Now Then* is to hold a mirror up to all our illusions—about writing, and about life—and she does so with inimitable craft and language. Whenever I read it, I enter and leave the world of her novel as myself, gathering clarity of sight, as well as the gift so vital to mitigating that harsh insight: humor.

4.
Extraordinary Rendition
May, 2015. Jerusalem, Palestine

How does one write about this place? Every sentence is open to dispute. Every place name objected to by someone. Every barely stated fact seems familiar already, at once tiresome and necessary. Whatever is written is examined not only for what it includes but for what it leaves out: have we acknowledged the horror of the Holocaust? The perfidy of the Palestinian Authority? The callousness of Hamas? Under these conditions, the dispossessed—I will leave aside all caveats and plainly state that the Palestinians are the dispossessed—have to spend their entire lives negotiating what should not be matters for negotiation at all: freedom of movement, the right to self-determination, equal protection under the law. —Teju Cole

Over Christmas and New Year of 2008, Israeli bombs were dropped on Gaza, killing 1,417 people, 313 of them children. On a long-distance phone call, after he had read a piece I had written in *The Huffington Post* about having decided not to attend the inauguration of a president I had spent more than two years campaigning for, my father asked me this question: What are American writers saying about this? A lifelong advocate for global social justice who had never needed a reminder that we are always either participant or perpetrator, my father spoke on into my silence. There were American writers, he said, who had written about the Vietnam War. Then, he added, "It was your publisher who brought out that book. Can't you get them to do the same for a volume of writing about Palestine?"

What can and cannot be done in America is a question that carries enormous hope on the part of people who do not live here, and a corresponding despondency on the part of those who do. I could have gone into an explanation of it, but I, raised by such a father, in a family where what needed to be done was what we focussed on, never the obstacles to that work, knew better than to make excuses. I hung up the phone, marveling at the fact that my father would not only know about such a collection of writing, but that he would possess a copy of it, now long out of print in its nation of origin, stored in his tropical home where there were routine massacres of white ants who marched forth to devour his books, and I set about seeing what was possible.

The publication he was referring to had august origins. In 1937, writer and activist Nancy Cunard and W. H. Auden had posed a singular question to 200 authors: "Are you for, or against, the legal government and people of Republican Spain? Are you for, or against, Franco and Fascism? For it is impossible any longer to take no side." A total of 147 authors responded, including Samuel Beckett, Evelyn Waugh, H.G. Wells, Ezra Pound, and T. S. Eliot. The writing that resulted was published as *Authors Take Sides on the Spanish War* (Left Review, 1937).

Thirty years later, in 1967, building on that tradition, as they put it in their opening remarks, editors at Simon & Schuster undertook a similar exercise regarding Vietnam, and asked a different question: "Are you for, or against, U.S. intervention in Vietnam? How, in your opinion, should the conflict be resolved?" The responses resulted in the collection *Authors Take Sides on Vietnam* (Peter Owen, 1967). The 160 writers in the collection include James Baldwin, Nelson Algren, Simone de Beauvoir, Allen Ginsberg, Doris Lessing, William Burroughs, Graham Greene, Italo Calvino, Robert Graves, Harold Pinter, John Updike, James Michener, Marianne Moore, and Arthur Miller.

Forty-three years after that, I believed like my father did that surely we might ask ourselves a similar question about Palestine. Along with poet Matthew Siegel, with whom I had disagreed bitterly and publicly, I began a Facebook page urging other writers to join us in speaking about Israel and Palestine. It seemed long overdue that our generation of writers, people who understood the power of the written word, face our responsibility to add our voices to a vital conversation. Yet despite much wringing of hands, and the horrific news out of Gaza that ticked across social media, nobody joined. I wrote to publishers asking if they might be willing to carry out such a project. There was no response. For four years the project stalled, the Facebook Page remained silent.

In 2014, I asked again for a simple show of hands. Who might speak for Palestine?

The impetus to ask a group of writers to set their names down beside their own reflections on the ongoing assault on the thin and shifting borders of Palestine, and the people who are confined to that tenuous landscape, became impossible to set aside in the face of the 2014 assault on Gaza, an assault in which Israel claimed it hit 5,226 targets within the 139 square miles that constitute Gaza, and one which killed 2,104 Palestinians, including 495 children, injured 10,224, many critically, and displaced 475,000 people.[50] In the face of such numbers, and the fact that we, as Americans, willingly or not, fund the perpetration of such violence through our taxes, but more so by our silence, I felt that we needed to confront the reality that Cunard articulated in 1937: it is impossible any longer to take no side.

Against the backdrop of what had transpired, it would have been easy enough to gather a group of people who could give us facts and figures, history and conjecture, attack and defense. Yet the 2,402 square miles of Palestine, and the 3.9 million people who live within its fragmented territories, occupy a larger moral and ethical space, particularly for American writers, one which is critical to the way we look at the world into which we release all our artistic endeavors. We need, as artists, to be able to hear the beat of that larger world, to provide in its hour of need some perspective that can move toward a recognition of the fact that our hands, too, are stained—if we remain silent—with the blood of others.

We are fond of identifying ourselves with victims during certain historical moments: We were all Americans (during 9/11); we were all from Newtown (in the aftermath of that shooting); we were all Trayvon Martin/Michael Brown/Eric Garner and, now, George Floyd and Breonna Taylor; we all rose and fell with the Berlin Wall, with Nelson Mandela, and the cathedral of Notre Dame in Paris. Yet we are rarely inclined to commit our art to documenting how, exactly, this comes to be. How does, in this case, the struggle in Palestine belong to us all? What makes us identify with people and a cause that is geographically remote but pulses with an intimacy that belies that distance? How does the giving and receiving of help sharpen our resolve on other fronts, and strengthen our bonds, and what forms can that solidarity and empathy take? Is it direct and literal, or oblique and fragmentary?

---

[50] "Is the Fighting Over?" BBC News, August 26th, 2014.
[51] Johnson, Sara Eliza. "Poetry & Inhumanity: Anti-War Art: Nearly Impossible?" *The Best American Poetry*, August 19th, 2014.

In an article titled "Poetry & Inhumanity: Anti-War Art: Nearly Impossible?"[51] Sara Eliza Johnson takes issue with an article by Noah Belatsky, "Anti-War Art: Nearly Impossible," which was written in the context of the July attack on Gaza by the Israeli Defense Forces.[52] Belatsky concludes that such art is almost impossible, that the prettifying (through narrative, aesthetic inference, etc.) drive of the artist distances the consumer, and renders the art itself irrelevant in terms of it having any impact on the machinery of war. Johnson, on the other hand, argues for writers, poets in particular, to consider their response to state-sanctioned violence that extends from police brutality (Ferguson) to the subsidizing of terror in other nations (Iraq, Iran, and Palestine). To support her argument for art that removes the space we often leave between ourselves and the misery and horror experienced by "others," she points to Thomas Hirschhom's "The Incommensurable Banner," a visual art installation that depicts photographs of dead victims of numerous wars, a piece that serves to create discomfort, to nag at our conscience, to observe that this dead body is, in fact, not us, but that we are deeply culpable in its existence.[53] That discomfort is a useful way to describe the space that the writers in this collection were asked to occupy.

The spirit behind the anthology I edited, *Extraordinary Rendition: (American) Writers on Palestine*, and to which this essay, in a different form, served as the preface, was that it would first compel us to set our names down beside each other as writers willing to remove the barrier between the story we hear and/or are told, and ourselves. Secondly, that it would permit the creation of a new way of thinking about how we, as writers and readers, might raise our voices against the seeming inevitability of war, and a culture of dispossession and invasion that has been allowed to remain unquestioned for too long. How they chose to engage with Palestine—which, as is beautifully captured in the novel *Apeirogon*, the most recent book by Colum McCann, is both the heart and conscience of the world—varied with each writer whose work appeared in the anthology.

I once wrote that we jump off the ledges of our fear because we know a net exists, and the only way to know it does is to participate in its

---

[52] Berlatsky, Noah. "Anti-War Art: Nearly Impossible." *The Atlantic*, July 29th, 2014.
[53] Premiering at the 2008 Brighton Photo Biennial, "The Incommensurable Banner" depicts photographs of wars waged in our names, particularly in Iraq, Afghanistan, and the Middle East.

creation. As a literary citizen of the world, it is necessary to acknowledge the way in which the private conduct of our lives can move toward and, with time, bring to fruition the public work that becomes our legacy. The overview that follows of the writing that was included will serve, I hope, as a reminder of that reality, as evidence that critical voices amplified my own, and that, in the words of the architect Olafur Eliasson, "you do not have to be the same in order to share the space." In this case the space of kinship and devotion to a more enlightened, far more compassionate reading of our common history.

*

A poet and a novelist, Roger Reeves and Colum McCann, open the collection. Both writers use the concept of flight to release sorrow like kites into the air, setting it free from the mundanity and ultimate uselessness of known facts. Reeves uses the brilliant conceit of a lynched Black man disintegrating and floating over the world, hovering over Gaza, and onward, to look at what links a thirty-year-old African American man to the massacres taking place in Palestine. McCann responds with a story written when he was just twenty-five years old. It is a tale that uses a Hebrew myth heard in a Baptist Church in Texas to speak about the violence in Ireland—with its divergent loyalties of the past, one side with Palestine, the other with Israel—but whose narrator's burden could be held equally by a young man in Derry or an old man in Gaza. Both the poem and the story reveal the place where our skill at harnessing our words to our imagination gives us writers the ability to hold multiple realities, central to all of which is grief, in our hands.

The late Chana Bloch's pilot, who not merely dismisses but refuses to acknowledge the destruction he has caused, is made human again at the end of Ramola Dharmaraj's story about the death of five daughters, even as Ravokovich's dead Arab is brought to life in those same girls in the seconds before they are incinerated. Dwayne Betts grapples with the vacuum that takes the place of news about Palestine, and sets the stage for Ed Pavlic's unfolding of the layers of journalistic subterfuge that surround our understanding of what occurs in a country we rarely name. Nate Brown's participation in the erasure of the fact of a nation, is mirrored in Phillip

B. William's memory of being called an Indian, the solidarity he then feels with the Pakistani who also disavowed the same label, each claiming their own identity: I am Black, I am Pakistani, and each insisting on the right to self-define.

Writers as varied in their aesthetic as Rickey Laurentiis, Lawrence Joseph, Kiese Laymon, Farid Matuk, and Naomi Shihab Nye take up the call to Americans to understand that our national myopia regarding an institutionalized history of violence against our own from Ferguson to New York City is bound tightly to our dismissal of the violence that unfolds in the streets of Gaza.

Peter Mountford, availing himself of all possible facts, feels both impotence and the futility of righteous rage, the "circle dancing" of an "us" which can safely leave a "them" outside. The call and response to his dilemma harkens back to Roger Reeves's opening statement as well as forward to Leslie Jamieson, who uses the deadly intertwining of the drug war in Mexico, which provides the backdrop to a literary conference, to embrace both ignorance and speech, as well as to Duranya Freeman's nineteen-year-old bravery, and her resolution that the only political stupidity is to remain silent in the face of injustice.

The question of the right to speak is also taken up by Tomas Morin, as he reflects on how we engage with electoral politics, and then move on from the policies that are formulated without our consent and lead to perpetrations of violence we do not condone and cannot abide, but do. Morin's supermarket in suburban America takes shape again in a tunnel in Gaza described by Matt Bell, who spends endless hours on YouTube, watching the construction of these defiances.

Tess Gallagher picks up several threads, her ladybugs saving children from a burning house echoing Ramola Dharmaraj and foreshadowing Nathalie Handal, and her assertion that all soldiers should mind doll buggies is at the heart of what is advocated by all these writers; the Trojan Horse of her imagination pushes against the walls snaking through Arizona and Gaza, scattering populations from Tijuana to Tel Aviv, a purer innocence setting us all free.

Children abound in this collection. Cristina Garcia's longing for the name of each broken child is answered by Kafah Bachari's story of Lala, a girl in a red-riding-hood coat wandering through the rubble of Gaza.

Unwittingly, the self-immolation of an Orthodox boy in David Gorin's poem evokes four children on a beach, Mohammad, Ismail, Zakariya, and Ahed Bakr, children who are mourned in many of these pieces, and held up as a call to see more closely, as Kim Jensen urges, and to reject the glib rhetoric of false parity, as Susan Muaddi Daraj decides to do.[54] America's own fallen angel, the one unmourned by her nation, Rachel Corrie, returns to life and to death in the words of those like Schumacher who served as she did, and in those who remember her in their poetry, as Phil Termen does, as a daughter, and as America's conscience.[55]

Central to this anthology is, of course, the question of whether the language of poets and writers can transform what seems intractable, and it is articulated by Askold Melnyczuk, and Jane Hirshfield, answered repeatedly by the voices of what I prefer to call sight rather than witness (for witness presumes an equal partnership in what has been suffered, whereas sight acknowledges the luxury of distance and safe passage). That sight, whether imagined or real, is heard in Fanny Howe's scant few lines which, mirror the little that is left and the magnitude of the loss, and Claire Messud's narrative, which moves through impotent dreams and wakeful nightmares. Imprisonment for the crime of creating art itself is revealed in the farcical trial observed by Ammiel Alcalay, and picked up and arrayed in the poetry of Philip Metres and Steve Willey.

It is answered also in how language delineates the negotiation of space, a theme that runs through several pieces. Alan Shapiro's reflection on the reconstruction of physical history and the memorializing of violence moves into Ahdaf Souef's description of the erasure of a culture in Silwan, homes and personal stories dismantled through artifice and cunning. Kafah Bachari's Uncle Hashem's meager dwelling with its view of the sea could very well be the home in Deir Kafa where Michael Collier's Mohamed looks out on the Mediterranean, where the sea and sky are one.

Tom Sleigh's critical insistence on the necessity of acknowledging not merely grievance but grief is illustrated in his poem "A Wedding in Cana, Lebanon 2007," and in the words of several writers speaking as both

---

[54] Greenwald, Glenn. "NBC News Pulls Veteran Reporter from Gaza After Witnessing Israeli Attack on Children." *The Intercept,* July 17th, 2014.

[55] Mackey, Robert, "Witness to Rachel Corrie's Death Responds to Israeli Court Ruling Absolving Soldier." *The New York Times,* August 28th, 2012.

observers and victims. If there is mourning for what ails us, what has befallen people who are not us, but are us, it is voiced also in the numbered notes of the artist and writer, Robert Shetterly, who has been commissioned to draw art on the wall that imprisons Palestinians, in the poetry of lament and ardor of Nathalie Handal, writing from Gaza as the bombs were dropped around her in July of 2014, and in the body of Dina Omar's brother, buried in foreign soil, and the bit of earth her Israeli friend brings back from the home to which she herself cannot return, the brown dust of Palestine that she presses onto her brother's grave in West Covina, California.

This is not an anthology of agreement but rather of resolve. An effort by writers to utilize the tool that we have been gifted, that of the imagination, to embrace ambiguity and uncertainty, to see color in a place where color has itself been outlawed in favor of the stark dichotomies that dissolve empathy, the blacks and the whites of intractability. Aquifers water the trees of settlers in Kazim Ali's diary, but the meaning of those trees, in planting, in uprooting, and in movement, is voiced as sorrow by Alice Rothchild. Caryl Churchill's play "Seven Jewish Children: A Play About Gaza" evokes the opposite response in the minds of two Jewish writers, a poet and a novelist, Jason Schneiderman and William Sutcliffe, respectively, and yet both arrive at a similar conclusion that acknowledges helplessness and the quest to understand. In the Israeli town of Sderot, Kazim Ali writes of a sculptor welding together a menorah created from the fallen rockets from Gaza, while inside Gaza, Robert Shetterly and Kazim Ali observe children collecting spent gas canisters to use as toys, or to line their meager gardens.

This is, above all, a conversation, for we are bound by our words, which inform the way we move through the news of our world, and what we choose to do with that information. We tunnel, collectively, diligently, holding ourselves accountable for what we do and do not know, searching for "the marker that may push through to another side." A side no less safe, or fraught, but new nonetheless. A place where the "informed compassion" called for in Susan Muaddi Daraj's essay is given body in Sarah Schulman's call to action, and her insistence that the point of solidarity is to be effective.

It made sense to append to this collection a summary of findings by the Russell Tribunal, a convening of an international people's tribunal on Palestine. It is included as a way of supporting other efforts such as ours, those made by ordinary citizens, predominantly writers, who refuse to absolve themselves of the duty to take action on matters that are pertinent to the humanity with which we are concerned in our art.

Included also as an appendix is Marlene Dumas's note for her exhibit "Against the Wall," from which the cover for the collection is taken. Dumas broke from her usual style to paint the series to visualize the significance and dissonance of the wall that hems in the people of Palestine, and she details the reason for this shift in her note. Interestingly, both the title of Robert Shetterly's work and hers juxtapose the wall of faith and goodwill with the wall of ideology and hatred, and both invoke the Palestinian poet Mahmoud Darwish. The photograph that she gifted to us, "Wall Weeping," was chosen for the way it reflects the sinew and muscle of this collection of writing, in which we acknowledge the existence of a wall, the realities that it attempts to conceal, the people pressed up against it with nowhere to go, and those who also raise their hands, not in surrender but with deliberate intent, to disintegrate its false boundaries.

This anthology includes three writers who have no affiliations of residency or citizenship with the United States, though their work is well-known in this country, and they have each traveled within the United States and are familiar with an American audience. They are Ahdaf Soueif, William Sutcliffe, and Steve Willey. I solicited their prose and poetry because they provided a perspective that enhanced the anthology as a whole, while not altering the parameters that I had set since, like the anthologies that preceded this one, my task was to ask a group of writers whose country was involved in the violence being perpetrated but who may not naturally be inclined to write about that to do so. There is ample work to fill many volumes with the poetry and prose of many other contemporary writers beyond the borders of America, particularly Palestinian writers such as Mourid Barghouti, Adania Shibli, Sahar Khalifa, Najwan Darwish, Suad Amiry, Raja Shehadeh, and Mahmoud Shukair, to name a few, who write movingly and with passion about Palestine. Anthologizing those voices in a single volume is a vital undertaking and one that I hope will be taken on by someone with a far more intimate and deeper knowledge of that work than that which I possess.

In choosing which pieces should be included, I erred on the side of engagement rather than dictate. There are only two exceptions to this: Janne Teller's submission, which reminds us of the importance of history,

"I Wish I Had Words," and the closing poem in the anthology, Steve Willey's, "Postscript," which urges and challenges us this way:

> *Say Free Palestine*
> *It starts in your mouth*
> *It ends in the streets*
> *Say Free Free Palestine*
> *Say its been good writing to you*
> *Say it clear as hell*
> *And then say it again*
> *Free Free Palestine*
> *Go on I know these words are in you.*

I chose these two pieces because, in a milieu where violence is perpetrated through the affirmation of theories of creation and promise written or divined from our personal sacred texts, we must surely make room for the known and empirical truths of war and occupation. Further, this writing that we have collectively committed to print and the public eye constitutes the freeing of our own voices, our own new visibility, as well as an invitation to our fellow writers who, too, hold these words within their conscience.

While some writers, usually the most secure in their careers, expressed fear of backlash from an unnamed and unseen "them," many more were open to persuasion, to be nudged away from safe places or a sense of helplessness. Tomas Q. Morin was one such writer, who went back and forth through stages of attempting, giving up, and rallying again, and whose poem, "Extraordinary Rendition," has given the collection its name. It is a title that honors the worth and work of each of these writers who took the time to read through a long editorial statement, and chose to come forward to offer up work that they themselves frequently felt was flawed, or insufficient, or did not "fit." I look at this work now, set one beside the other, and note only this: that each writer's work speaks both fearlessly and flawlessly of a specific moment or revelation, but that taken together, they speak with equal power of a larger whole, one which demonstrates that our writerly preoccupations arc inevitably toward justice.

5.
Our Security Is, By Definition, Indivisible

On June 27th, 2018, upon hearing news that the United States Supreme Court would uphold a travel ban that turned into law the prejudicial treatment of people from certain countries, my seventeen-year-old middle daughter, a young activist in her own right, burst into tears. "What is the point of this country," she asked, "what is the point of all this power and wealth if you can't be good?" It was a simple and all-encompassing question.

My daughters are of a generation that has grown up with the world in their sights. Their connections are trans-continental even as the forces of profit and greed arrayed against them are similarly global. Their minds and their hearts move unfettered past borders even as borders are being drawn and fortified by an older generation accustomed to, and reliant on, the creation and sustenance of fear. This new generation does not wait for permission to act, for the right kinds of support structures to be erected, in order to ask for change and seek solutions to the things that ail us. The teenagers from the Parkland massacre who brought 800,000 people to DC to advocate for the de-weaponization of civic life in America on March 24th, 2018, had been galvanized by deep personal tragedy, but their activism harkened beyond Marjory Stoneman Douglas High School. Their call to action persuaded more than 800 groups to join them in cities from Portland, Oregon, to Denver, Colorado, to Washington, DC, from London to Rome to Tokyo. That same spirit runs through an anthology that I edited in the wake of the 2016 election, for the American Friends Service Committee, *Indivisible: Global Leaders on Shared Security* (2018).

Collectively, the young people in the anthology have overcome bullet wounds, lived as refugees, built reconciliation efforts around empathetic dialogue, advocated for young girls and women, and risen to prominence in their communities and on the world stage, all while refusing the false dichotomies of a zero-sum game that have resulted in short-sighted policies and wars that have dislocated their lives. They are powerful reminders that youth embody the promise and hope of all our survival in a manner unparalleled in human history, and are very much a part of a globally connected, culturally sensitive, and innovative solution.

That way of thinking is echoed by their elders who also wrote for the collection, from Archbishop Desmond Tutu to international peace activist Dr. Maria J. Stephens and New Zealand's Prime Minister Jacinda Ardern (who made sure that her piece was in order even as she readied herself to go on maternity leave for the birth of her first child). Each of them reminds us of the foundational principles of peace-building: open, difficult conversations, underlined by the presumption of goodwill, and a commitment to enduring relationships. More than that, they demonstrated that, to give of oneself to uplifting humanity is to commit to it no matter the setbacks, as evidenced by the life's work of President Carter, whose essays are also part of the anthology.

As I read their essays, I came to realize that though their efforts take place in venues far removed from each other, and seem to address different realities, their responses are to social dislocations and a state of insecurity caused, often deliberately, by identical ideologies of exclusion and stunted notions of power. Indeed, each of them address their respective set of circumstances, culturally or nationally proscribed, with the same intention to create a world where resources are shared, and no one human being's worth is elevated above any other's. It is exhilarating to contemplate what profound change can happen when they—by which I mean we—come together in recognition of that fact.

Like the people of the fictional, morally bankrupt town of Omelas in the Ursula K. Le Guin short story "The Ones Who Walk Away from Omelas," these activists recognize that a status quo that disfranchises people, impoverishes others, and subjects still more to unimaginable cruelty cannot be allowed to go unchallenged. At the heart of all our joys and all our failings is the fact that we are ruled by our definitions, including our ability to clearly define the problems we face in the same way that those who walked away from Omelas understood that acquiescing would mean validating unconscionable injustice. Security in the end does not come at the cost of losing our own humanity, rather, it stems from ensuring that the good we seek belongs to everyone.

Many years ago, I opened my nearly 350-page undergraduate thesis on the inequalities that are written into the prerequisites for receiving aid from politically motivated funding agencies such as USAID and the IMF with a quote from my father, Gamini Seneviratne, a poet and civil-servant who has dedicated his life to the wellbeing and self-sufficiency of my island country of Sri Lanka: *the sky does not become less private because other people share it.* Parallel to that worldview was that of my late mother, Indrani Seneviratne's underlying words of wisdom. A teacher and guide to hundreds of young people who grew up to achieve much thanks to her mentorship, her courage, and her example, she reminded us frequently that each human being was some mother's child. If we witnessed someone wasting their life away in the grip of addiction or dedicating themselves to violence, she would say, *Their mother did not intend that for him.* That way of seeing the world and its resources, on the part of my father, and being gentle and generous in our dealings with each person we met, on the part of my mother, bookended our upbringing, my brothers' and mine, leading us all to dedicate our lives to issues of social justice. We recognized at a very young age that we were rich in the ways that mattered, and that the wealth of our various capabilities should be given in the service of uplifting the lives of others less fortunate.

Likewise, these writers who are and are not my brothers nor me, covered peace-building work in the countries of South Sudan, Myanmar, North and South Korea, Palestine, Uganda, Zimbabwe, Northern Ireland, China, Sri Lanka, Colombia, Guatemala, the Central African Republic, Jamaica, Algeria, the United States, France, the United Kingdom, and Japan, among others. With a remarkable and passionate unity of purpose, they related the power of holding on to faith in human good. A common thread unites us all, and binds a generation in their eighties and nineties with those in their twenties. It is a heartening reminder that the solution to what ails us has always been present.

What Is Feminism?

My idea of feminism is defined primarily by the culture in which I was raised, in Sri Lanka, one that accords all but immortal power to women and demands everything it is possible to give to a community, to family, to life, in return. It is a duality that often confuses the visitor, but is clear as daylight to natives. Our pop songs speak of the gift of daughters, of how a home with a dozen sons remains dark without the light that is brought to it by a daughter. In the long-ago tradition of our matriarchal society, women owned property, not men, and I enjoyed learning of the practice whereby a man would work on a woman's land for a season, and if she liked him she could choose to keep him. Girls have equal access to our system of free education from grade one through university and are heavily represented at all levels of government and in the private sector. Female head of state? I grew up with one, the first in the world. I do not know, to this day, whether she could make a mean coconut sambol; her cooking skills were never in question, never a banner headline in any newspaper before, during, or after her period of public service. As a nation we called her "Mother," but what kind of a mother she was to her own children we did not know, nor did we ask. Suffice to say that both her son and her daughter rose to political power—her daughter, for better or worse, to become the first president of Sri Lanka.

Within that larger context I also learned to love femininity, to value the long hair and hip-sway-head-held-straight walk of the women around me. I admired and emulated the homemade potions and remedies that produced smooth skin and soft lips, and though I never learned to sew, I developed a keen appreciation for the grace of colorful textures and impeccably cut clothes, as well as the elegance of high-heeled shoes. I absorbed, from my mother, the sensory pleasure of holding jewelry in my palms, feeling the weight of pendants and earrings passed down through generations, the delight of glittery necklaces—bought for a song from traveling saleswomen—held up to my neck. With each act, with each such moment, I learned to transform myself into a tangible presence of beauty, the kind that might, one day, walk into any room and be able to attract the adoration of not only men but, more importantly, women. It stood to reason that this dressing up, this preening, learned, built, and measured in the presence of women, would bring with it a deep love for women, even as it attracted the attention of men.

How hard it was, then, to discover, as a newly arrived freshman in college, that America had a different set of rules for women, ones that forced a choice upon me that I did not wish to make. In my undergraduate classes I struggled to make sense of texts that placed men in opposition to women while in the social sphere women were placed in constant competition with other women. Why did my highly paid professor of economics at my highly competitive liberal arts college speak with such disdain to the women in his class? Why were girls who dressed well referred to in such derogatory terms? I grew older here, in this country, learning to refer to Title IX and nod wisely when my activist friends condemned other women as identifying with the male worldview. I called on my Sri Lankan interiority to do my job, to win the things I needed—money, power, discretion—from American men who enjoyed calling me "honey" and "babe," terms that never threatened my sense of self, my confidence, or my stature among them. And I projected the American me that I knew was called for with men who treated me as a human being only, my femininity out of sight.

We are accustomed, in this other country of my dual citizenship, to bemoaning the lack of freedom in faraway places; even in an essay for the same series on feminism for which I pen this now, Jane Smiley writes about the problems faced in "many cultures" where solidarity trumps individual will, unlike here in America where personal interpretation of feminism is a triumph for individualism.[56] I see an abyss in such a reading of our common world, one where we are each poised to free fall, alone, into a sharp-edged pit of joylessness. I, too, envision a world where women—and men—are spared the horror of rage, violence, and condemnation, partic-ularly within the intimate setting of home, but I understand that this is the reality for many women and men in this vast land where we genuflect before the altar of individuation, as it is in my country of birth, where our first resort and our last is always communal. Our successes, my American

---

[56] This essay responds to the *Virginia Quarterly Review* series in which a diverse range of women writers discuss their definition, idea, or experience of feminism. Jane Smiley's piece for the series appeared on October 16th, 2012.

sisters' and mine, are better for the fact that they complement each other. It has been said before, but it merits being said again: we rise and we fall together, and a deeper appreciation for the ways in which we navigate our common world is something I value far more than any notion that one or the other of us is privy to the "right" way to celebrate the multitudinous blessings of our gender.

As I reflect upon one of the cornerstones of my own activism—how the world beholds and what the world holds for girls and women—I am conscious, most of all, of the example I set for my own three daughters, the oldest of whom is now laying the groundwork to, perhaps, take on elected office, on the brink of setting off to make mistakes and celebrate triumphs of her own. A straight-A student and an athlete with medals adorning all the corners of her room, she was the beneficiary of the hard work of American feminists who ensured that she learned in classrooms but also ran and swam at a college of her choice. She and her sisters are also the beneficiaries of Sri Lankan women who have taught them to inhabit any space—outdoors or within buildings, public or private—as though it were built specially for them, nothing denied them, nothing to diminish their worth. Their worth that includes the beauty that comes from a way of being among and with other women, an inner self-definition that has nothing to do with political ideologies.

Worth It

L'Oréal may have a $2.3 billion advertising budget, but it stole its slogan from my mother. Long before I arrived in America all the way from Sri Lanka to attend college with nothing less than her belief in my potential and my two suitcases stuffed with puff-sleeved dresses, tooth-brushes, toothpaste, gardenia talc, and ballpoint pens—things she didn't believe America could provide for me—my mother had engraved an aph-orism into my brain: *buy pretty things for yourself because you are worth it*. Or, the unplugged version: always buy beautiful things, and buy them for yourself *first*. Before you buy anything for your husband, your friends, or even—and this last was inconceivable to contemplate in a culture such as ours—before you buy anything for your children.

Her life was testament—she often demonstrated, and I dutifully observed—to the fact that doing otherwise had been the biggest mistake of her life. Bigger even than falling in love with a radical communist whose notion of a good time was reading Marx and leading an uprising against the Official Languages Act of Sri Lanka (passed, 95 to 5), bigger than becoming pregnant before her marriage to her thwarted revolutionary, bigger than letting her shame distance her from her high-caste relatives, bigger than being too afraid to let her own oldest son apply to American colleges in the mid-eighties, though she had already been sidelining as a guidance counselor for a decade, one whose legion of students she managed to place in the finest colleges across America, earning a special award from Harvard University for her work. Nothing could compare, though it certainly explained the setbacks in her life better than the fact that she did not buy herself a new sari and a pair of shoes with every paycheck. It was advice imparted to her by her own mother who had, herself, given up school to marry at the age of nineteen, who expended her intellect in serving on the board of the Catholic convent she had attended and in running the estate she brought with her as dowry.

In an effort to inculcate in me a love of—some may call it an addiction to—beautiful things with which to clothe myself, my mother spent money not on herself but on me. As a schoolteacher, she earned two hundred and fifty rupees a month for most of her life, a sum that had increased to nine hundred and sixty ($5.51) by the time she retired, after twenty-five years of service. Except during the years of austerity the country went through during the reign of the world's first female head of state, Mrs. Sirimavo Bandaranaike, when there was nothing pretty to be seen in the shop windows, let alone purchased, my mother made it her business to locate and buy lengths of fabric that she kept in a suitcase on top of her almirah. She participated in a system referred to as a *seettu*, a forced savings program that her fellow teachers dreamed up whereby they all contributed a hundred rupees each month to a fund that then went, each month, to one or the other of them, the kind of informal system of support that makes Western banks tear their hair out in despair. When it was her turn to collect, she bought finery for me, even though, by the prevailing standards at the time, I was utterly devoid of any of the redeeming feminine charms of the milieu: I was extremely thin, flat-chested, dark-skinned, short-haired, quick-tempered, opinionated, and, in general, a boy without the boy package.

And yet. There I was, encouraged to look at the fabric and design my own clothes, almost all of which she approved of and which she then turned into wearable creations by hiring the best tailors she could find. The dresses I designed for my skinny boy body veered between strapless, tight-fitting numbers that she once exclaimed made me look like *a spaghetti wrapped around a noodle* (victuals that were beyond the realm of her salary) and flowing fairytale dresses I modeled on the gowns worn by Princess Diana. Yes, I dreamed big. I was going to stand prettily and at ease in the center: between road-tart and royalty.

It was also my conservative mother, who never wore so much as a swipe of lipstick, who placed a giant checkmark next to my spending my entire post-high-school salary of seven hundred and fifty rupees (and a little extra borrowed from her) on a single New Year's Eve designer party dress in yellow silk. I cringe, a little, recalling my appearance at the dance, where my beau at the time—I realize only in retrospect—was knocked off his feet not by my beauty but, rather, from reeling at the glare of my canary in a coal mine presentation (or, I should say, the coal mine decked in canary feather presentation).

What I was learning along the way was that there was nothing wrong in wanting to possess something I considered beautiful, no matter what was considered fashionable; I loved the feel and shine of that yellow silk. And when my father had the opportunity to go to Italy in the course of his work for the government and he asked me, the only girl in the family, what I might like, I replied, "Patent leather pumps with four-inch heels." He wore out his own sandals walking the length and breadth of Rome being told by one scornful shopkeeper after another that four-inch patent leather pumps were no longer in style until he was able to find the last pair in existence and brought it home for me. They did not fit me, and so I sold those shoes and, once more, borrowed a little extra from my mother to buy a different pair, one that matched, exactly, the color of a dress that I had designed and sewn out of a length of fabric that my mother had bought for me at Harvard Square where, once more, she thought nothing of spending $69 (five thousand four hundred and fifty-one rupees at the rate of exchange at the time), most of the money she had brought from Sri Lanka when she arrived to attend my brother's graduation, on an extravagance for me. I wore that dress and those shoes to the graduation of my boyfriend—later husband—from the college we both attended.

That boyfriend tried to temper the message my mother engraved on my heart; in America perhaps this was a necessary antidote. After all, unlike in Sri Lanka where money is a fluid commodity, borrowed and shared and going where it is needed, here I am reminded daily that money is finite, and "more" comes with steep interest from banks. When I was dazzled by the *tchochkahs* at Kmart as we were checking out one day, early in our romance, my boyfriend asked me "to just consider how many hours you have to work in the library at $3.25 an hour in order to buy that." It was a grim reality that I had to face. I had a full scholarship to college, but everything "extra" I had to earn with the three jobs I held on campus throughout my time there—one at the library, one at the gym, one at the science building where I had to feed and water (though I also picked up and caressed, holding each against my chest in commiseration, my Buddhist upbringing so at conflict with the entire business) hamsters shipped in for experiment and eventual slaughter.

I took stock and I adapted. I discovered The Salvation Army. Each fortnight when I collected my check, I gathered my best friend, Josh Kennedy (son of the poet X. J. Kennedy), and had him accompany me to the local store, where I shopped for clothes. At the annual dance I sallied forth in a lace-trimmed, ankle-length creation that cost 50 cents. The boyfriend, at this point my fiancé, he who was not on a scholarship, said, with some amazement, "You look nicer than all the girls in their fancy dresses." And that comment served to ice the cake of my fantasy, the fantasy in which I would manage glamor by hook or by crook.

I have a closet in which I can still see some of the dresses I once designed, the cut-lawn top, the Guippio lace-edged blouse that I wore to my thesis defense with the factory-reject deep green paisley skirt, the outfit I wore each time I met one of my future in-laws ("the good girl suit," as my once fiancé, then husband called it). I still have those green shoes my mother found to match my green dress. And I have hundreds, yes, hundreds, of other items. Shoes, dresses, skirts, pants, jackets, scarves, and jewelry that remind me of what sits at the core of my anti-consumerist, left-wing activist self: the knowledge that beauty is 99 percent belief, 1 percent standard, the proof that there is no funk, no setback, no ridicule that can erase the bliss of knowing that I can put myself together faster than most people can relieve a full bladder. And that at the end of it I can look pretty damned good on a song.

I don't have a lot of discretionary income. By the rules of American sanity, I have none. I do not have six months of salary saved "in case of," I do not have cash diligently socked away for a retirement I may never live to enjoy, I may not be able to pay for college for my three daughters, I cannot afford to shop at Anthropologie or Free People or even Macy's, and most of what people go to buy as bargains at T.J. Maxx are out of the reach of my unique-looking purse. What I do have is eBay and consignment stores and a keen eye for knowing that how I carry myself makes my fashion current. What I do have is a daily boost of happiness as I walk past my beautiful possessions on my way to the shower or on my way to bed. What I do have is the incredible joy of watching my daughters come shopping among my purchases (and the double joy of knowing that every purchase I make will be happily worn by one or the other of them, or, more frequently still, by each of them in turn). What I do have is the uplifting thrill of knowing that my girls are slowly absorbing that old message passed down from my grandmother to my mother, neither of whom were able to live the truth, that we earn money not to save for the future but to live today, that all money is mad money, it is just a matter of where you choose to indulge your madness.

I did not grow up to be a high-profile policy maker fighting for justice at the United Nations. I did not grow up to be the high-profile human rights lawyer I always wanted to be. I do not live in an artsy community in Park Slope or SoHo, inhabiting a loft and being called by NPR for my opinion on this and that. There are half a dozen talents that I know lie dormant in my unfulfilled other life, the one that author Cheryl Strayed described in one of her Dear Sugar columns as *the ship that did not carry us*, and on more than one occasion I have described myself as a MacBook Pro operating at 2 percent capacity. But for everything that I have not done, for every disappointment that I have ever faced, for every loss that I have endured, including (and more devastating than any other) the death of my mother, I have a life in which I feed my soul with the artifice of adornment.

Somewhere out there, my mother is delighted each time I shut my eyes and quote her as I make a purchase that has nothing to do with anybody but myself: the clothes, the heels, the bangles, the lotion, the better shampoo, the fancy haircut. Somewhere out there she is whispering in my ear the priceless gift she gave me: you are worth it.

Dear Natalie Gyte: I Hope You Dance

In an article titled "Why I Won't Support One Billion Rising," Natalie Gyte, who leads the Women's Resource Center, an umbrella organization of women's charities, argued quite persuasively against the efforts of Eve Ensler (author of *The Vagina Monologues*) to raise awareness about violence against women on Valentine's Day by urging people to gather in flash mobs and at organized events to dance. Dancing, in this reading, was a way to rise up above the desperation that kept many women trapped in difficult situations. According to Gyte, however, Ensler's effort undermined the work of ordinary activists because it did not address the patriarchal system that underlay much of the violence that is perpetrated against women, it included men, and it was too sexy—though she didn't use that term—and, therefore, media-worthy.

I disagree with almost everything in this piece. I believe firmly in the rights of girls and women to fulfill their ambitions, but I protest equally firmly the notion that the achievement of those ambitions should come at the cost of the peace, safety, and security that women have valued for centuries, or the dismissal of what a majority of women embrace: a feminine aesthetic, a female essence, intangible but no less critical to what we bring to the discussion.

Gyte berates the movement for including men. She condemns Stella Casey thus for stating that violence is not limited to gender, that it affects society as a whole: "Really, Stella? Really?" Yes, really, Natalie, really. Violence is a societal issue. And so long as we keep pretending that it isn't, nothing is going to change. And to speak of violence perpetrated against women by a male hierarchy, as Gyte does, but claim that we must exclude men from the conversation is like arguing that the priesthood is fornicating with little choir boys but we can end the problem by just focusing on the little boys and leaving the priests out!

Gyte explains that two activists—one "beautiful and radiant" Congolese, and one Iranian (presumably ugly and drab?)—question the idea that White middle-class women (who are in effect the upper class in the global scheme) should tell them what to do. They are right, of course. But might we remember that in that regard, they should also question, then, the cultural hegemony of White women who do what Gyte does. Fact is, they probably do.

Non-White women have questioned for decades the privilege assumed by people like Gloria Steinem, the one percent of the feminist movement to which Gyte also belongs by virtue of her hue and class. And yet we have chosen to march beside them, holding the wheat and letting the chaff blow away in the wind, as best we can, because we champion the better intention over the lesser negligence.

To skewer a fellow activist who has, by Gyte's own admission, done admirable work for choosing to fight this particular battle on several fronts is to confirm the divisive stereotype of women attacking other women. It makes me cringe for us all. And it reminds me of another fierce woman warrior, Audre Lorde, whose words have been the foundation of every bit of political work I have ever undertaken. The words that concluded my undergraduate thesis on the brutal and insidious political, cultural, and economic hegemony of the West (the very one that Gyte and the two activists above decry) are still the words that guide me now: "There is no such thing as a single-issue struggle because we do not live single-issue lives."

Finally, Gyte's harangue against the joy inherent in this effort reminds me of nothing more than the beautiful exchange between Jesus Christ and Judas Iscariot in the musical *Jesus Christ Superstar*. Judas berates Mary Magdalene for buying myrrh for Jesus because that money could have raised "300 silver pieces or more," and that "people who are hungry, people who are starving matter more than your feet and head." The reply from Jesus is priceless. It reminds us of the fact that it is Judas who condescends to Mary (dismissed by him as a mere prostitute), and that it is he who betrays Jesus, never mind the poor and struggling, never mind the myrrh and silver.

There is something vital and affirming that is lost to us as a collective of men and women when we decide that any expression of joy undermines the sorrows that plague us. And so I come, as I have done before, to these lines from Jack Gilbert in his poem "A Brief for the Defense"[57] from the collection *Refusing Heaven.*

---

[57] Gilbert, Jack. "A Brief for the Defense," from *Refusing Heaven*, Knopf, Reprint Edition, 2007.

We must risk delight. We can do without pleasure,
but not delight. Not enjoyment. We must have
the stubbornness to accept our gladness in the ruthless
furnace of this world. To make injustice the only
measure of our attention is to praise the Devil.
If the locomotive of the Lord runs us down,
we should give thanks that the end had magnitude.
We must admit there will be music despite everything.

Joy is allowed. Seriously. And dance is all-inclusive. It transcends gender and class, culture and color. It is the great unifier. The revolution begs you, if not on every other day then at least on this day, when you get the chance to sit it out or dance, to choose to dance.

#MeToo Is Not Enough

We have officially entered the era of vigilante justice via social media, that magic portal that triggers the Gorgon head that can turn our most intrepid warriors into stone. We have placed our faith on the bleak and frequently uninformed oversight of like, share, and RT buttons, have devoured the grist of websites that, bewilderingly, pride themselves on anonymity, and have gorged ourselves on whisper campaigns. We have merrily perverted the intent of Title VII and the intersection between Title IX and the Clery Act. Our marching orders require a single "ism." Consider the fallout within the academy: faculty and administrators of color, as well as those ever-useful pariahs, (Old) White Men, from Berkley to BU reeling before accusations of various harassments, the most outrageous of which seem to be sexual. America has gathered its crucifixes, lit its pyres, and found an umbrella large enough for the weird dichotomies of its culture, both relentlessly prurient and zealously puritanical.

Women, we're told, are at long last in charge of something, taking to the streets (with due permission, down prearranged routes, in impeccably orderly fashion), taking selfies in millinery decorated with pink feline motifs, posting photographs and umbrage on social media.

What is missing in this nation that upholds the rights of the individual above the good of the community is identity. American women seem to have a peculiar aversion to self-identification when they make allegations, preferring to hide behind swaths of proxy fighters primed to chest pound on their behalf. Much of their rage is reserved for those whose patronage these women may have already benefited from over decades as adults during which they, like the anonymous "Grace," lacked the ability to say "I'd prefer to wait for a glass of white wine at dinner" when she didn't like the cabernet being served to her by her particular Aziz Ansari.

The tawdry protections of anonymity are brandished because, we are told, they shield us from persecution, as alleged by the fifteen unnamed women who brought charges against three named professors at Dartmouth. In other words, those women are willing to come forward to allege misconduct in a system that is, supposedly, weighted against them, but not willing to fight the system itself. They will ask for the resignation of these men, but essentially concede, helplessly, that if they were found out, they would not be offered fair treatment by the "numerous grant-proposal review boards, and academic organizations" on which these professors and their friends serve, and which could "influence their professional futures." As if we do not live in a world where nothing is secret. As if we still inhabit a universe of carrier pigeons.

It is worth our while to imagine the change that could occur when we are willing to identify ourselves as having had our rights and decencies violated, to fight that battle in broad daylight, to be willing to *continue* the fight long after the battle is won, if indeed victory is found in our favor. That would mean, in this case, that should these women be penalized for their effort to win redress, they would be willing to bring the full force of the country's laws to bear upon that next line of attack. Anything short of that is cowardice and opportunism. It is a way of protecting oneself and one's own career, hiding behind a mask while claiming a front-row seat on the latest bandwagon and making grandiose claims regarding the takedown of the patriarchy.

Right now, there is very little recognizable as powerful or just in the hashtag movement du jour. For their part, universities have become too cozy with posterior-saving statements that do little to address allegations but everything to protect against lawsuits in which they might be listed as respondents. A "climate" is noted, an adversary is assessed, and the one most likely to be burned on the stake of public opinion is ushered out the door. Something has been done, but it doesn't *quite* resemble justice.

Our academic institutions were created to interrogate our views, trends, histories, predilections, pronouncements, and trajectories. That would mean, for a start, two things. One, that all accusations be announced in public and without anonymity, for if the charges are true and serious, then the victim ought to have no fear of holding her own during an investigation. Secondly, that both those who bring such charges and those within the academy who are accused of wrongdoing, *no matter their status*, be afforded the administrative and financial support of the university in order to defend their respective positions, support that can be recuperated if the case is dismissed or the defendant is found guilty.

I am an American woman, who was raised in a culture—in Sri Lanka—where women have been seen, heard, and voted into the highest office in the land. We claimed both our voices and our names with pride no matter which side of an equation we found ourselves on, defense or prosecution. Even branded with my American subcategories (foreigner, person of color), I refuse to be bullied by forces far greater than me. I insist, with a fervor that is perhaps particular to immigrants, we who are more inclined to believe in the dream, less assured of its existence, that I am afforded the right to defend myself or those around me. I refuse to disengage from the foundation of the laws that govern this nation, innocent until proven guilty; mine is not one lone voice crying out in the wilderness, but one that gathers the full range of its pitch from the law itself.

If my American sisters wish to press those laws into service, they must first be able to say their own names out loud. If the Greek chorus of our peers wants to join in their hallelujahs then so be it, but they should be recognized for the fickle, often misinformed group that they are. They are not the answer. We are.

Ru(Th)less

My name is not my name. It started at birth. I was drawn tight in the Caucasian chalk circle of my parents' love, trapped between the inner terror of recognition and the larger force of aspiration.

"She is everything that is precious," my mother said, dispatching my father to enter my name into public record a few days after I arrived.

In Sri Lanka, where I was born, there is no hurry to name a baby. Many things need to happen before that weighty burden can be placed upon a newborn: an astrologer has to be consulted, a horoscope drawn, the most auspicious *akshara*—loosely translated as "sound," but more like "utterance"—has to be revealed (in my case, "ru"), and only then can the parents begin to examine the choices offered by extended family and friends, never mind their own.

Everything that is precious is what she saw me as, the longed-for daughter and her youngest, in a culture that adores daughters and spoils the last born.

"Ruani," she said. "That's her name."

My father returned brandishing a birth certificate that bore the name that he felt better described the red-faced tyrant who had come into the world screaming her presence and her determination to thrive: Rushitha, i.e., the angry one. And though I must have continued to deserve this terrible announcement of a personality that never has, never will shy away from a battle that must be fought, at the witching hour on the last day possible, the forty-second after my birth, my mother prevailed and I became something to be cherished again, not a creature to be withstood.

Aside: Across town on that same September 8th, my mother's best friend also gave birth to a daughter, a youngest after three sons. Preethi, a woman who hailed from Colombo's high society even as her university roommate, Indrani, my mother, had been raised in the quiet habits of the high caste rural landowners, had decided that, should she give birth to a girl, Ruvani would be her name. Instead, when her sons met their sister, she changed her mind and named her Rushira, only a letter removed from the name my father had chosen for me.

My name had been changed, but my father had managed, being the one present at the court on the day he went to alter the name, to have a say over one thing. He spelled it with the hard "v" and an "e": Ruveni. Which evoked not the softness my mother had hoped for but the hardness of the name of the first queen of my country, she who was descended from the raksha (devils), Kuveni. Indeed, that was a name that my second older brother would throw at me in the midst of a fight. "You are just like her! You are not Ruveni, you are Kuveni! Kuveni! Kuveni!" A second crossed-out notarized amendment to the birth certificate was not possible, and my parents had run out of time, and so there I remained, named but not quite, intended, but not entirely.

Aside: Just short of two years before these events, my father had, in defiance of my mother, named my older brother Manabharana, placing the weighty history of the King of Southern Sri Lanka upon his newborn second son. Back he went, on the last day possible, to return my mother's name for my brother to him: Malinda. My brother has gone on to embody both the quality of gentleness associated with the Greek meaning of his changed name and the aspirations contained in the one my father gave him; at one point he even ran for president of my country with the hope of unifying numerous warring factions as their common candidate.

I had an addition to that name, one born of my mother's adamance that I grow up in possession of a certain set of graces; she gave me part of her mother's name. My grandmother had been named for Kisa Gothami, whose story is one of the first that every Buddhist child learns: a woman whose baby dies goes to the Buddha to ask him for medicine to cure her son of his "sickness" and bring him back to life. *Go bring me mustard seeds from a house that has suffered no loss,* he says. Elated, she goes in search of the seeds, but of course, there is no such house. She returns to the Buddha having reconciled herself to this fact of human life, that it must end, that everyone must suffer loss. It might seem morbid to give such a name to an oldest daughter, but Sri Lankans rarely separate joy from sorrow or shield the young from the particulars of aging or death. These too, like birth and childhood, are integral to the conduct of life. So there was my grandmother, carrying the name of Kisa Gothami, and there I was, two generations later, being anointed with the same name.

If I'd had the chance, I'd have preferred the first half of that name for its sweetness, but instead I was given—thanks to the way my horoscope was cast—the second, Gothami, with its hard, guttural start. Still, I claimed ownership of it all, good and bad, even at the age of five, yelling my correction into the microphone held by a teacher at the convent I attended. I had won second prize in the basket race. A race that consisted of running with a basket my mother had decorated in yellow crepe paper, picking up items—also similarly decorated—along the way, before getting to the finish line. The Tamil teacher had mispronounced this middle name (what kind of child finds it necessary to give even the middle name at the finish line for a second prize? I step forward with pride. I own my relentlessness).

"Gothambe," she intoned.

"My name is not Gothambe! My name is Ruvani *Gothami* Pieris-Seneviratne!" I said, my irate voice echoing through the loudspeakers, much to my mother's consternation and my older brothers' delight.

"Are you Gothambe?" that second-oldest brother began to say.

Actually, quick clarification, just so we are clear. My full name was longer than that. In its entirety, it recalls the "house" to which my father belonged, what is called the "ge" name. *Ge* (pronounced "gay") means house. Malawana Nissanka Raalahaamilaa*ge* Ruveni Gothami Pieris-Seneviratne. Mercifully, at that young age, I wasn't aware of the prefix of heritage, or else I'm sure I'd have rattled it all off for the entire school to hear.

I grew into a teenager, mostly muddling through with my unfit name. Once I began to write more, particularly when I wrote for the cricket magazine that my mother edited, a magazine at a boys' school in which I had no business appearing, I hid behind initials: R.S. The nuns didn't know that I was, essentially, "hobnobbing" with boys, but they kicked me out for a host of other irreverences, none of which could elicit the remorse they demanded of me. Repentance had never been my strong suit anyway. I became "Ruv" at the new school, a school given to these kinds of affectations, a tendency toward emulating the tiny "Sues" and "Jills" of Europe and America, of distancing self from the "Vathsalas" and the "Subhashinis" of our own nation.

I made peace, in essence, for a while, but eventually I grew bored. Ruvani, which I spelled the way my mother had wanted it spelled, at least for a time, was not the right name for me, I felt, my parents' tussle coming to fruition in my own head. I looked around me, casting a wide net for a new name. I was not Ruvani. I was…Meneka.

Meneka Gandhi, daughter-in-law of Indira Gandhi, was on my radar; her beauty and political life combined with the ostracism of the Gandhi family were the kind of things, I felt, that women of courage and substance had to withstand. I considered myself to be an aspiring woman-of-courage-and-substance. I pronounced this name "Mer-nay-car," instead of the common sounding of it, "May-ner-kah."

This phase coincided with my mother packing me off to Western Australia, where my father was on a postgraduate scholarship because, according to her hysterical phone call to him, "I can't cope with her!" I don't remember that I was difficult in any way, it was only that I had grown up, taken my advanced level examinations, had entered university to study law but was unable to attend because of unrest in the country that kept institutions of higher education in a constant state of closure, and I had boyfriends. I think it was the boyfriends that did it.

I got to Perth and assumed a new identity as I talked my way into classes I was only able to audit without credit. I was now Meneka Pieris. Short and sweet, one name nobody had given me and half of my surname. Inside I must still have been Rushitha, for I remained feisty and ceaselessly innovative, shaping my life on my own terms. I secured a prized job on campus, I wrote for the campus literary publication (and won a prize for a poem, "Paul," that I wrote for a quiet classmate who went to America and killed himself, prize money I used partly to buy a Paddington Bear that I had stepped in to caress every day at the college bookstore on my way to work, clearly a foreign child, still, underneath the bravado). I devoured my lectures and read my texts with zeal. I also managed to find time to write love poems to a particular professor in whose tutorial I had insisted on being placed.

"There's a long waiting list, and there are many other tutorials you could be in. Why do you need to be in mine?" he asked, blue eyes intent under Mr. Spock eyebrows. His eyes were the blue of ice, not of sparkle.

I could hold the gaze. The truth didn't frighten me: "Because I want to be." It was he who looked away.

Two days later in seminar, he said, "Good news, Meneka. I made room for you in my tutorial."

Of course he did.

I aced all my classes as Meneka, writing long papers that combined the rigor of a Sri Lankan education with the resources of a foreign university, like a strong body bouncing high off a well-constructed trampoline.

"Someone is leaving poems under my door," he said one day in class. "They're quite good. I wonder who is writing them."

The theater had always been a background to my life, with my mother producing and directing everything from Shakespeare to O'Neill. My face donned the innocence that is so often assumed of South Asian women as I looked serenely back. Poems? Who knew?

"Well, hello, Ruveni Gothami Pieris-Seneviratne," said that same blue-eyed professor one morning at the end of the year when I went to collect a recommendation he had written for my future applications to American colleges and universities. "So here I was, writing this recommendation for Meneka Pieris, and I went to file it and found that this is not your name."

"It's the name I felt fit me," I said.

"Well, I can't put a false name on a recommendation, so you are going to have to take back your legal name."

I didn't hear from him for twenty-five years. The internet reconnected us. My writing had popped up at him from the pages of the UK *Guardian* one Sunday morning. My books had found him in Australia. I confessed to having written those poems. Time remedies youthful infatuations and closes the gaps of age and experience. We were equals who could laugh about these things.

The difficulties of finding a name I wanted to belong to became compounded in America. Americans are blessed with the ability to pronounce Kopczynski, but cannot manage Ruvani. Ru-vaaa-ni, I heard them say. Again and again and again. I spelled it differently: Ruani, hoping that losing the 'v' would help. Ru-aaah-ni, they said, convinced they had got it right. I wrote it out this way: Ru+er+knee. Oh! Ru-errr-knee, they said, yelling the first syllable, dragging out the second, making me sound like an epithet and a problem. Ru, I said, finally. Just call me Ru. Ru was, and is, an endearment, the kind of diminutive that finally coated my name tender. When people met me and said "Ru," I felt favorably disposed toward them, far from the aggrieved rage that gripped me when they butchered the whole name. Still, many of my liberal American friends continue to inquire, "Tell me how your name is pronounced, write it out. I want to say your whole name."

"Not a good idea," I want to say. "There's a side to me that finds it relatively easy to scorch people, and even if you don't see it, it will still burn me. Mispronouncing my name will not be a good thing for either of us."

I can't say those words. So I say, "Ru is fine. Ru is enough."

The effort to help myself in my American life, however, stops short at bureaucracies. "Can you decide, Ru, what it is you want to be called and how you want to spell your name?" Mark, my American ex-husband, once said to me, exasperated. He could make this sound simple, sailing free with his happy, uncomplicated nomenclature (though *his* father misspelled his middle name, Alan, and made it Allan).

"Your ticket says Ruvani [Ruvaaani] but your driver's license says Ruveni [Ruvayni]," they tell me at the most inconvenient times, like when I've rushed up late for a flight. "Go back to the desk and have them reissue your ticket."

"How am I listed for taxes?" I ask Mark.

"Ruvani Seneviratne Freeman."

"And my passport says Ruvani Seneviratne Freeman. Should be enough, no?"

He sighs.

He gets to sigh, this psychology and religion double major having, guitar playing, tarot car reading, semester abroad to study Sinhala and Buddhism guy who baffled me with his request that I take his name in marriage. It wasn't a big deal to me. None of my names had felt right enough, and though I wanted to hold on to the surname, the only part that I felt grounded me, it would have been silly to triple barrel myself, to become Ruvani Gothami Pieris-Seneviratne-Freeman. I became Ruvani Seneviratne Freeman. Sometimes Ruvani Gothami Seneviratne Freeman. To become, to all intents and purposes, Ru Freeman, seemed inevitable. A decision made on a whim.

And yet, easy as that had been, when it was time to decide how to write my name on the covers of my books, I wanted to go back to the culture and family that had shaped how I conceived those stories, what stories mattered to me. Other considerations took hold. Would people be able to find my book under my name? Seneviratne? For Americans who seem to trip over even "Ru" (I am constantly Ruth. Like Ruth without the "th," I have said a hundred times or more; I use RuThless as a handle on social media sometimes), Seneviratne would be insurmountable. Further, the obsessive streak in me that craved order disliked the imbalance of the three parts as it would be written, for Seneviratne was too strong a name to follow the coy coo of that Ru. I remained Ru Freeman.

It is a decision that has taken away two things: my embodiment of the diversity that America loves to say it loves, especially in the literary world, and the easy connection to home. Many are the friends who, upon publication, red-flag their book covers with the silent half of a foreign-born parent's last name as it becomes, suddenly, thrillingly exotic. As for me, most Sri Lankans read to the end of my books before realizing that I am Sri Lankan. The glamor-shot author pictures do not help, for, it seems, with each succeeding shoot I become an air-brushed perfection that is more Caucasian than South Asian, and I have to pay out-of-pocket sometimes to request that a photographer, please, for the love of god, give me back my own skin tone!

Much has been lost.

Still, if I could redo it, I'd probably take this same road now. Versions of a name that was never quite my name shaped like the indented stones I like to collect along cold beaches, holding the memory of past magnitude, the scarred brunt of journeys, but also an essence of self. What remains is that original sound that set me up to become what I have become: invaluable to some, necessary to certain people and causes, a fire burning that can provide warmth when heat is called for, purifying flames when ending is what must be achieved. I was not Ruvani entirely, nor Rushitha entirely. I am Ru. It is disposition more than name. I write it this way: ru.

In All Things, Absent

In an article titled "Estrangement" in the summer 2008 issue of *AARP: The Magazine*, Jamaica Kinkaid articulates her attempt to come to terms with the fact that she stopped speaking to her mother three years before her death.

Her effort, however, is not full of regret but incomprehension that she misses her mother, incomprehension that she does not wish to be buried next to her, and also that she does not know if she wishes her own children be buried beside her someday. She ends with the words "I do not know, I do not know."

The loss of my mother fills my life with a similar unknowing. My mother was, as her favorite student described her during his heartfelt and perfect eulogy, difficult. And it was her difficulties that my brothers and I, as adults, responded to, not her ease. I learned to dismiss every concern she brought up, about my brothers, their wives, her grandchildren, me, my life, my father, and her health. Her own regrets and sorrow were so deep that I feared that I, too, would fall into that bottomless well and never come up for air, or that my affirmation of those sentiments might seal her forever in that tomb of despair. Had I been listening harder, perhaps, I might have heard the mothering behind what she said, might have assumed, rather, the role that she wanted of me, of a gentle and caring child, of the never-grown-up companion I had once been, of being again the girl whose goal in life had been to wear her clothes and do what she did for a living, teaching English Literature and Classics to armies of devoted boys.

Instead, I was the opposite of her. I prided myself in taking no shit from anybody. I was flamboyant where she was conservative, boisterous where she was quiet, and I forswore the undying affection of schoolboys and replaced it with the fickle attention of grown men. I frolicked in the man's world that had circumscribed her life, and I laughed when she spoke of devotion, consistency, and simplicity, never letting on that in act, though not in word, I was all those things. Whereas she had waited, as refined women of her time did, to have her appearance or clothes or work admired by other people, I paid myself compliments. I wrote about politics when all she cared about was the pride felt in seeing her children's bylines. During all my shenanigans, I recall seeing both delight and fear in my mother's eyes.

She seemed to both love the cloak of freedom that I had flung so seemingly easily around myself and fear for my life. I was not a good woman, I was not a good wife. Somewhere down the line, my husband was bound to leave me. Somewhere down the line, I would need something besides flair and flourish, and did I have those other, inner resources? I did, I do, but I was not going to let her see those aspects of myself that were so similar to the strengths she possessed. All I would say in response to her "He might leave you" was "And if he does I won't spend my life running after some man who doesn't want me."

In more ways than one, I was trying to define for my mother a life that I wanted her to live. I wanted her to be more like the person I was playing for her. I wanted to rub away the timidity that overcame her whenever she boarded an airplane to America, the kind of thing that would lead airport officials to fling her bags around and deny her compensation for lost luggage and that I could secure on her behalf with no greater skill than a simple steady glare that would leave her full of awe at powers she believed I had, powers she was glad I had, in this strange, unfriendly, place, but whose acquisition she regretted, for, as far as she could tell—and she did tell it!—they had exacted the price of tenderness. I wanted to nullify all of her regrets and fears, to drag her into the future where everything was impossibly hard and yet also possible and full of loveliness. I wanted to put makeup on her face, I wanted her to wear the beautiful clothes she owned but never put on, falling back constantly on her worn saris, the old skirt, the tattered nightdress.

But I held that tattered nightdress to my face when I returned home for her funeral and breathed in not what it showed to the world—its faded, overused fabric—but the sweet perfume it had earned for itself and still held. My mother's life was full of a doing with which mine could never compare. She had no time for the kind of self-creation at which I had become so adept; she was too busy making a living, staving off hopelessness, and, more than everything else, helping the people who came looking for her in a ceaseless stream. People who did not care that she wore no makeup, that she traveled in buses and scooter-taxis in a country where such travel is perilous even for the young and healthy, that she sometimes opened the door to them with a smile, sometimes—quite often—with scathing, unfiltered criticism, did not care that her home was an uncertain refuge where sometimes the gate was padlocked and the phone unanswered and nobody could find her, or that she was awash in eccentricities that led her to scream for Brand's Essence of Chicken as though it was a cure certified by the pantheon of multi-origin Gods whom she worshiped, drive her children out of her house "to go live anywhere," or to hang a sign on one of her precious plants with the following statement: *We are very poor and we have no money for your religious festivities. If you have any money to spare, please leave some here—Happy Vesak, Happy Christmas, Happy Ramazan, Happy Deevali!* That spirit perfumed her clothes, her hair, her life. It did not make everybody admire her—indeed, many people (most specially her students) were terrified of incurring her wrath—but it made them love her unabashedly. It made them write to her and come and visit her carrying the cakes and sweets she was not supposed to eat, willing to forgive her moods. That spirit frayed her clothes, splashed them with mud, ripped at their seams.

Over the course of the two days before she died, my mother had hauled a chair to be mended (so the set could be given to my oldest brother), cleaned her house, given her sister money for an operation, called up all her friends, all her relatives, all her favorite students, and all of our friends, and, of course, secured for herself a bottle of Brand's Essence of Chicken. She had given away much of her wardrobe of beautiful, unspoiled saris and dresses, and most of her vast collection of perfumes. Whatever precious jewelry had not already been given away had been robbed. On the day she died, unbeknownst to any of us, she was so weak she had to ask the woman who worked for her now and again to boil water for her and bathe her. On that day, after that bath, she used whatever strength she had left to sit down with one of her students to help her with a college application, an application that has since secured a place for that student at an Ivy League school. She climbed into a car carrying two saris she wanted to give to the servant of the friend who came to pick her up and spent most of the journey laughing. She suffered a heart attack right as she was trying to field a telephone call from another student's tennis coach. She left mid-thought, mid-act, mid-goodness.

I can tell myself a variety of things to stave off the grief that I feel. I can say my brothers were there, their wives were there, she was not alone. I can accept what other people say to me, that a mother does not remember the disappointments, but rather the good times. I can say that she knew, she knew, that though I did not write and did not call, my inner conversations were always with her, that every time I stood before a crowd, or walked down a street or performed some good work or signed a book, or sang to my daughters, what I felt was her presence, her glad acknowledgement that yes, heaven be praised, he had not left me yet, I was still the most beautiful person in the room, the smartest one, the best, in all things the best. In her absence I will never again be that "best" that she saw whenever she looked at me. In a crowd full of women, in my mother's eyes, I was always more than any of them. On a shelf full of books, mine were better. My words were articulated more clearly, my clothing was more stylish, my deeds were greater, my husband was perfect, my children flawless. I can tell myself stories, but they are as useless as my wearing the cardigan that I had bought for her during her last visit, as futile as my attempt to fill it up with her, to feel her around me.

What I remember, now, are not all the things that I did not affirm in my mother, all the things that I wished she hadn't done or said, but the things she did do. What I remember is that she brought me music, theater, literature, language, a sense of humor, confidence, strength, joy, and a model of motherhood that runs in my veins as naturally as my blood.

I remember that she found it funny when I placed 38th in a class of 40 students and asked flippantly if I had failed math too, as we walked hand in hand away from the convent I attended. What I remember is that when I was expelled from that convent for an array of irreverences but subsequently invited back, my mother—though she screamed at me in private and threatened to cut off my hair, which, she said, was the source of all my problems—dismissed the offer from the nuns and enrolled me in a "school more suited to [her] daughter's spirit, intelligence, and interests." What I remember is that she paid for piano lessons when we did not yet own a piano, swallowing her pride and letting us go next door to practice. I remember her voice pouring song after song into all of us, bringing Ireland, England, and America to us through lyrics and melodies, and that those songs still take the edge off the acts of governments that were also discussed in the house. I remember that she polished the floors of our house on her hands and knees with coconut refuse and kerosene and now and then with polish, that she planted every blade of grass in the garden and pruned her lawn and hedges with handheld shears that left blisters on her piano-playing fingers and that out of the arid earth that surrounded our city home, she could make flowers bloom. I remember that she gave me a girl-only space in a house that held so many permanent and transient visitors, and that it contained a dressing table, a fan, an almirah, a bed, a table, a bookcase, and the silk bedspreads that had once been gifted to her, and that all of these things made my room magical in a time when magic rarely translated into concrete evidence. I remember that she listened to me read, that when I asked her if she was sleeping, the answer even when it took a while for her to say it was, always, a comforting "no, of course I'm not sleeping!" I remember that she encouraged me to wear my hair short and climb our roof and play French Cricket and run faster than the boys and, also, to steal guavas and skip school to attend cricket matches…

And I remember that she spent a teacher's salary on buying bolts of fabric that she stored in a suitcase, beautiful cloth waiting to be turned into dresses by the best of seamstresses according to designs I sketched in ballpoint pen. I remember that except for there being no compromising on decency and modesty, she put no restrictions on the clothes I chose to put on, literally and metaphorically. She stood by and let me be everything that she was not. I wish I had done the same for her.

Not long ago, just before I left for a residency where I finished writing my second novel, completing it on the first anniversary of my mother's death, I went to listen to Jamaica Kincaid read and speak at Bryn Mawr College. She read from new work, from a story that is told from the perspective of two children who scorn their mother for writing and writing about her own mother, her country of birth, the work that would become *See Now Then*. Her answers to the questions posed afterward continued to reflect that conflict. But when I went to introduce myself to her and mentioned that I had used her words to guide me through this new lifetime of grief, she reached out and held my hand. "Oh, my dear," she said, gazing deep into my eyes, "now you are truly an orphan. It doesn't matter, it doesn't matter that your father is here with you, when your mother is gone, you are orphaned."

There are things for which we are never prepared. Childbirth is one of them. The loss of a mother is another. It has been said that, as human beings, there are only three or so significant decisions that we make: whom we marry, whether or not to have children, where we choose to work and live. Each of these decisions narrows the world a little further, concentrating our attention on the work involved in succeeding at any of this. But the death of a mother, I have discovered, unravels those decisions and the accompanying work. It has set me adrift in a place where nothing at all makes sense, where there are no anchors or guarantees, where even the statement "you are going to be taller than me," uttered to a daughter at the bus stop, comes with a shadow sentence that tells me, even if I don't say it aloud, that I can make no promises: of the return of the bus, of the greeting at the door, of years in which she might grow into a height that exceeds my own. I can only promise that there will be regret and that the world will, one day, become dislocated for them as it has become for me. But it is a promise I cannot articulate; it waits for them as it did for me.

Her absence is present in how and whom I teach. Whether my classes are about race, class, conflict, or love, the common thread is compassion. For our inevitable losses, our inevitable griefs.

Glory

A few days ago, all these many years into my adulthood, I posted the following on Facebook, to a chorus of commiserating murmurs:

> Haircut. i.e. Morning during which I writhe in agony wondering if I even need a haircut, wanting a change, resisting a change, picking out a different hairstyle, printing out those different hairstyles, and then working myself up into such a state that I plonk on the chair and state emphatically that I LOVE MY LONG HAIR, and coming away after paying a ton of money for a nice chat, shampoo, and 1/2 an inch off the ends. What is wrong with me people? What is WRONG with me?

I went for the said haircut, and returned to upload a photograph that shows me largely unchanged, albeit slightly buffed.

My obsession with hair is partly cultural (Sri Lankan culture values thick, long hair), and partly personal (the emphasis people placed on my hair as I grew into my teenaged years). We inherited great hair genes, my brothers and I, with sweeping locks that seem not to age. My oldest brother grows his down to his waist and, when pressured by my mother to cut it, when she was still alive, would invoke Samson, and my other older brother, a die-hard socialist who sets aside large parts of his salary to help strangers and friends, sees no contrary tendency in purchasing product for his hair.

When I was a very young child there was never a fuss made about my hair. As a single-digit child, I was marched off to the barber along with the boys, and once famously received sideburns because the barber could not distinguish my skinny boy body from that of my brothers and assumed I was a third son. But once I turned thirteen and my mother decided it was time for me to *begin to look like a girl*, people outside the house began to express admiration for my hair.

Whether it was because the quality of my hair was somehow exceptional in a country whose women almost invariably had long hair, or whether it was because there was not much else by way of female assets that were notable enough to mention, it was my hair that people spoke about.

Within the extended family, my paternal grandmother, who was never very fond of me (an antipathy carried over from her feelings about my mother) would sometimes stroke my head and bemoan the fact that my hair was not good enough. *No curls*, she'd say, dejectedly, pronouncing it "kay-rels," the part I latched on to so I could make a joke of a comment that stung. But she was the exception. At school, in the days before things turned sour between us, my classmates would cajole me to audition for the new advertisements that were being broadcast on TV (TV itself had just arrived in Sri Lanka, gifted by the Japanese, along with Japanese television sets) for a shampoo we'd never heard of: Sunsilk. Other friends begged to spend recess, which we called intervals, playing with my hair, undoing my ponytails and braids and running their fingers repeatedly through the hair that seemed to weigh more than my head. The nuns at the convent I attended—those reliable killjoys—insisted on tight braids that hid the beauty of our hair, but I took pleasure in ripping out the rubber bands and practicing a bouncy swagger that swung my waist-length ponytail from side to side as I walked. It stood to reason then that I was soon expelled from that school and left without a backward glance.

From the convent I was moved to a fancy private girls' school, where I was admitted not on my own merit but on account of my mother's fame as a renowned teacher of English literature. It was a school established by the more insidious Christian missionaries, who were smart enough to cloak their god-given right to spread goodwill among us Buddhists in laissez-faire derring-do. These girls laughed at the slogan by which I had been ruled at the convent: *Simplicity Is the Keynote of a Familian.* Here, there was no prescribed length for our uniforms, and hair could be managed any way we pleased. It was not an easy transition. These were young girls with notions of fashion and a lot of money. Hair dryers were the norm. I didn't possess one (my family did not possess many electrical gadgets, not even a radio). I improvised. There was a single table fan that was placed in my bedroom, since I was the only girl in the family—a title I bore with great pride. I used this fan to dry my hair, pulling out long sections and holding them in front of the fan until the mass of it fell straight down my back. I hadn't known it then because I didn't grow into it until I was an adult, but I had what was an amalgamation of my mother's and father's hair. Hair that when wet and left to dry displayed the *kay-rels* of my now-deceased grandmother's heart, when combed out would fall in waves, and within a day would turn straight. I didn't need hairstyles because my hair styled itself.

Fast forward to the year of our Lord 2005. I was rooming with another writer, Nina McConigley, at the Bread Loaf Writers' Conference, and I witnessed something I had never seen being used before: a flat iron. Like most Sri Lankans, I don't wash my hair every day, almost never blow-dry it, use only oils for styling, and do even that rarely and sparingly.

"What is that?"

"A flat iron."

"What does it do?"

"It straightens your hair," she said, then proceeded to demonstrate on a few strands of my hair.

What smooth sleekness! What miracles! Here was a chance to augment the versatility of my hair. I could, I figured, wash it and let it be curly on one day, wavy the next, straight the third, and a sheet of glass the fourth! Nina gave me various tips on purchasing one of these contraptions and, indeed, when I returned home, I bought one. I hardly used it over the next few years while I *eked out my existence,* as I put it, *on the sidelines of history,* writing articles and stories and eventually a book. The flat iron only came into its own during a second book tour, and only because I had been shown—while being primped for my author photograph—the use of a curler. A curler, it seemed, could only work on my untamable hair if I first flat-ironed parts of it. And though my preference is still to let my hair just be, I confess that I've played with this a few times, enough to feel I have some skills I could hand off.

Not long ago, I was visiting editor-turned-agent Anjali Singh, and happened to sit down with her older daughter to read her a goodnight story. In the book we read was a woman who was using curlers in her hair. She didn't know what they were, and I explained, conjuring up an image of high fashion all with the use of some plastic curlers, as she listened. Oh, I could just feel the yearning in her little girl body, a yearning that took me back to my own girlhood. Anjali, forgive me, I couldn't resist:

"But," I told her, "nowadays there are electric curlers, you just roll up your hair"—and I rolled up my hair to show her—"and when you take it out, you have pretty curls."

She nestled up to me with adoration in her eyes. "Do you own one?" she asked.

"Uh-huh," I said, "and your mom, if you ask her, she'll probably be able to get one for you."

Yes, as a kid I had not only drunk but wholeheartedly believed the Kool-Aid my mother fed me, referring repeatedly to hair as "a woman's crowning glory." The biggest lie I ever told my mother revolved around my hair (I claimed that there was a free styling offered by the hairdresser when I needed to go to a very important party at the age of fifteen); her biggest outrage at my oldest brother came when he accompanied me to that same hairstylist (for his own hair), and encouraged me to ask for a Farrah Fawcett number that destroyed both the highly prized length and quantity of my hair; and the one time I ran away from home it was because, after having been temporarily expelled from the convent (the nuns could get creative with their punishments, the more guilt-inducing the better), she swore that all my misbehavior stemmed from my obsession with my *bloody hair!* and marched off to fetch a pair of scissors so she could hack it off herself. I remember sitting on the floor under my table, as instructed by her, figuring out how long it might take her to find a pair of scissors in our chaotic house where nothing was where it was supposed to be and where most rudimentary tools simply did not exist, and realizing that there was nothing for it but to run away. And so I did, running barefoot through the streets, taking my precious hair with me.

It wasn't hard to believe in the drama of hair, given that my grandmother, my mother, and my mother's sisters all had beautiful manes that grazed the backs of their knees. My grandmother, cast in the role of Asokamala as a young girl, the female lead in the most famous love story of Sri Lankan history who wooed the young heir to the throne to give up his entire inheritance (Wallis Simpson had nothing on her), was forced to cut off some of the hair that pooled on the floor as she sat up in a tree! My mother's combing and braiding of her own hair was mesmerizing to behold, the way her plait moved as she walked. I was not yet a woman like they clearly were, but I swore I'd acquire whatever glory was being handed out through this mane with which I had been thusly blessed. I learned to organize my clothing around my hair—whatever looked best with whatever my hair happened to be doing, that was what I would put on. It never failed to work its magic, and I sailed through everything—from finding and losing boyfriends, surviving two schools where, for reasons I cannot go into, I spent a year being ostracized by my entire class (not even my hair could win me their affection, though, in my wicked and adaptive way, I took pride in the fact that their envy was still intact), defending my undergraduate honors thesis, teaching dance, and all the way to black-tie galas in NYC, feeling not simply passable but utterly magnificent.

It was those words spoken by my mother about the importance of my hair that made it feel like the most natural thing in the world for me to spend most of my student-job wages on Pantene while my fellow internationals on our snow-filled campus in Maine purchased Suave.

"How could you spend so much on shampoo?!" my friend from Marshfield, Massachusetts, asked me, the first time we were driven to Kmart to acquire supplies.

"Because it's my hair!" I said, fully expecting this to suffice as explanation and dismissal.

But this hair was not just my hair, it was my badge of courage, my shield, my vice, my tiara, and my salvation all rolled into one. In the fall of 2004, I made a series of decisions that left me living once more in Maine, with no job and no money to call my own. I had moved with the intention to write, but this was practically impossible while going through the ups and downs of pregnancies and childbirth and the unforeseeable difficulties of raising three very young children among, as I liked to point out regularly to my Caucasian husband, *all these White people!* But more than the fact that I could not write, I felt the weight of being useless in the world.

I have nothing to give, I mused one day, sitting at the dining table while three small people sat before their afternoon snacks and regarded my sad face. I was wrapping my hair around my fingers as I said this, and in the silence that follows such utterances made in the presence of children who can neither understand nor help, it came to me that I did have one thing I could give: my hair. I had not cut my hair short since I was thirteen years old. All my haircuts were mere trims. All my haircuts since would remain trims. But for a glorious afternoon in the midst of such despair, I felt wealthy. This hair that had always been my luxury, I could and I would cut off and do something useful with it, something that had nothing to do with personal vanity, albeit it surely had something to do with a certain vanity of the spirit that seeks to impress itself in some way upon the world. My husband approached the task with the enthusiasm he brings to kitchen renovation projects. I doubt he understood the enormity of the moment, but he participated fully in getting it done precisely and according to the instructions from Locks of Love. Bands at the top and the bottom, and a clip that took off much more than a foot of hair.

Of course, the aftermath was predictable. I went to the hairdresser to get it styled into something other than the jagged mess I now had and came back with a beehive. (The only woman of color in the whole magazine wore a beehive, so I guess that stylist assumed that would suit me too.) I said nothing but came home sobbing. I tried to rinse it out, to pull it down from its high perch, to no avail. I tied a scarf around it and went about looking like a Russian peasant for a few days. And then I decided that this was no way to behave in front of three impressionable girls. *It's just hair*, I told myself, *it'll grow*. And though it hurt like hell to have my oldest daughter say, as I climbed into her bunk bed to kiss her goodnight, *you don't look like my mother*, indeed, it did grow back.

Most of the time the things we do shape our children more than the things we say. Following the advice of my mother, who was channeling her own ancestors, I made sure to shave the heads of each of my three daughters before they turned one, the ritual most likely to guarantee the development of gorgeous hair. *You have to do it before they speak their first word*, my mother told me, *otherwise the shock of it will delay their speech*. There they sat, each in her turn, one minute like every other floppy five-month-old, the next their features sharply in focus beneath their shining, tender pols. I am not convinced that the inability to articulate their feelings about the change meant they weren't horrified. To this day, they behave as I do in the lead-up to and the aftermath of a haircut, displaying in exact sequence intense self-evaluation, courage, excitement, pleasure, and dismay over the most trivial of changes. All except the rebel youngest.

I listen sympathetically. I murmur soothing words. I know I'm raising girls who will grow into women who will carry around a talisman that can morph on the turn of a dime into weapon or cloak, wrap or jeweled ornament, comfort or strength. I can see them walking through life nursing private anxieties but exuding a certain joie de vivre, their heartstrings linked invisibly to each strand of their beautiful hair. The older ones buy their clothes, like I usually do, on consignment, eBay, or end-of-season sales, and the youngest simply inherits. But from the age of nine, each of them has visited real hairdressers. I can't afford Mason-Pearson boar bristle hairbrushes, but the ones I buy them are the best I can find for what I can afford. The two swimmers and runners have shampoo that protects against chlorine and sun damage, the one with the fine, blond-streaked locks gets hair treatments.

When I take them home to Sri Lanka, and in the sadness of my mother's absence, my father sometimes sits them down and rubs large quantities of coconut oil into their heads as they sit wrinkling their noses. I disregard their baleful glares. I smile, remembering such moments in my own childhood. Yes, I cursed and swore (silently), but I knew that those hands held powerful intention. Sometimes here, in my American life, I massage wishes into my daughter's lives, holding each lush and unique mass, each fistful of dark and light hair in my palms, rubbing potions into one, rinsing foam off another, braiding and twisting, ceaselessly caressing not their heads but their innermost selves. I do these things and I see them growing up, leaving me, having babies. I see them shaving heads, brushing hair, rubbing oils, passing on this same, easeful message of self-love.

Why I Travel

I am a reluctant immigrant, someone who, like thousands of others, only came to the United States for a specific purpose—in my case, a college degree—and who, for a multitude of reasons that are wholly personal, ended up never being able to go home. The question that plays on my mind most of the time is: Why am I so far away from home? But perhaps that is also the answer to the question of travel, that it is a search for a home for our heart of hearts, which, after all, is what all stories are about.

In a feature in *Poets and Writers* titled "The Importance of Place: Where Writers Write and Why,"[58] Alexandra Enders details the spatial preferences of writers ranging from Conrad Aiken to William Maxwell, from Katherine Ann Porter to Rachel Cline, and from the writers who needed certain objects in their specific room (Robert Graves) to those who craved the noise of cafés (Jean-Paul Sartre and Simone de Beauvoir), to those who loved libraries (Melville, Cather, Woolf, Eliot, and Shaw). Mixed in with those kinds of writers are the ones who can write in the middle of things, writers like Jane Austen, Isabelle Allende, Richard Bausch, and Eudora Welty, who have all written without the need for sacred spaces, for imposed silences.

Many writers enjoy their solitude, their quiet retirement into cabins and homes of their making. I do, too, when it is time to write earnestly and at length, but it is not something I require on a daily basis. It is travel that stimulates my writing, travel that results in the engagement I crave with the world in which I live so that I may write something worthy of its attention.

It has been rare to find those writers for whom travel is—as it is for me—a critical element to their writing lives; Enders mentions the poet Tom Sleigh, among a scant few others. I was therefore doubly intrigued by the intense initial interest in the Amtrak Writing Residency, which spoke to a possibility of a yearning in many more writers for writing on the run. The train, with its endless taking on and emptying of passengers, its many small dramas (the best take place in the Quiet Car, where umbrage-ready

---

[58] Enders, Alexandra. "The Importance of Place: Where Writers Write and Why." *Poets & Writers*, March/April, 2008.

individuals abound), and its constantly changing views—not to mention its extremely spotty WiFi connections—offers those so inclined many opportunities to write. I've ridden the Amtrak sleeper car between Philadelphia and Chicago, LA and Seattle, and can attest that very few trips that I have taken compare to those in terms of the stories I collected along the way from observing and then talking with strangers stranded across from me in the dining car.

Any kind of travel can lead to those discoveries that fuel my writing, even the sometimes-arduous book tour. In the streets of Milwaukee, I heard the story of the late and second romance of a writer I'd not seen in years. I keep returning to that moment now, in the way we writers poke around a small evidence of truth that could be converted to bolster fiction; I think of the way he spoke, the fear and joy apparent, and I imagine his new love, his grown son, these people I do not know. That same writer introduced me to the Milwaukee Art Museum's Burke Brise Soleil, the 217-foot-long "wings" that open and close over the building. It is a spectacle that I knew would surface in a story, if not as itself, then as an echo, and indeed it has, in a short story titled "Tomorrow I Will Knock on My Own Front Door." In Atlanta, Georgia, in between the flights bookending my twenty-four-hour visit, I went over to the Ebenezer Baptist Church and found myself in the middle of a Men's Day where I heard the hall reverberating with the voice of John Hope Bryant holding up the importance of action over pontification, and declaring that PhDs don't have anything on PhDos! I gathered story seedlings all morning long, offered up in the warm smiles and handshakes, in the averted glance and bent heads, in the light reflecting off the blue infinity pool at the King Center. In Seattle I lost the blight of my East Coast focus and thereby discovered a whole new American city that I had not known existed. A city where on any given day multiple venues fill up with audiences for readings, where some of my favorite artists first performed, and where sits the best bookstore in the whole country, Elliott Bay Book Company.

This wander-thirst that I experience is not limited to travel within the US. I have, when asked and, more importantly, funded, agreed to go to other countries. Canada may not count as "real" travel, but it is an entirely different feeling beyond that well-managed border, beginning, in one case, with signs in French when crossing into Quebec. India (Sri Lanka's

"Canada," in terms of proximity) was a place I'd only ever flown over, a land associated with invasion and geopolitical dominance, until I went to Rajasthan for the Jaipur Literary Festival. There, between glittering palaces and scooter-taxi rides through slums, between listening to Jhumpa Lahiri and Xialu Goa discussing the global novel, and acres of poverty so harsh that I had to shut my eyes on the train in which I was traveling, I learned of booksellers and translators and young schoolboys who ride hundreds of miles and sleep at the railway station just so they could be at this same festival. I signed a blank notebook for a young volunteer, a stunningly beautiful girl I'd noticed every time I came and went from the hotel, who gave it to me, saying, "Write anything for me." This, after she had just told me about her approaching the end of her days at the university there, about the marriage arranged for her, the one she would agree to because it was not right to cause grief to one's parents. These are not sources of inspiration that can be generated at my desk, they are wells that must be dug by going out on location.

At a conference in Seattle, I listened to the poet Nathalie Handal—whose voice, Yusef Komunyakaa once wrote, "luxuriates in crossing necessary borders"—speak of her writing and how it has been influenced by the many places in which she has traveled and lived, as well as the languages she speaks. Affecting a French accent, her cadence lifted a little tightly and off the ground, then switching to the rolling "r" of Spanish she turned earthy and lush, and in Arabic she was full of heart and fire. This is what travel, and the "language" of it, does: it permeates the stories we have to tell and informs our truths, giving them both context and the freedom to roam. I travel *precisely* because it takes me away from the familiarity of my surroundings. I travel to gather the ingredients that I reach for when I write: threads and colors, spices and aromas, sorrows and delights, landscapes and architecture, the voices of old women and young men, the laughter and tears of children, the sound of crows and songbirds.

This Brown, This Green

I agree to write an essay because I think that whatever it is that Google Earth can show me cannot compare to the images in my mind. I imagine that the imprecision of a program that captures only what it can discern as physical demarcations will be a poor substitute for the alterations made on topography by a culture such as mine.

I download and I click. I am right: this address, 601/2 Havelock Road, Colombo 06, Sri Lanka, appears only as an anonymous rooftop set into a landscape that is mostly brown. The mud-colored streets sided by dull, taupe homes and shops, a few splotches of withered green to calm the eye, and that is it. No yellow-tinged araliya, no purple bougainvillea, no orange-fruited thambili trees, and none of the myriad hues of green that are the first thing you notice about the country as you glide in off the Indian Ocean, cross the empty beaches, and land on the 270-by-150-mile island that holds my home. The landmark that heralds the turnoff to the dead-end street of my child-hood, however, is clearly represented, with its blue roof and rows of white cars for sale, just as it is in the instructions we now give on-call taxi drivers as they hurtle down the one-way road that accesses this lane down which I once lived, and which now lives on in my second novel as the titular Sal Mal Lane. What the trader demolished in order to sell cars for roadways that can barely carry them—the batik shop run by the bow-legged widow, Mrs. Wettasinghe, the hut she had gifted an old, impoverished couple, Lucas and Alice, these homes and their inhabitants—exist only in that novel.

My home sits at the heart of that book, and I used a novelist's sleight of hand to censor the small and large deprivations, both material and emotional, and imbue the Herath family with the best of what my own family once shared: the philosophical, music-making oldest son, the boy wordsmith who came after, the only girl who was both boon and bane, the distracted teacher, the mostly absent civil servant, and the open-door pol-icy that brought all manner of misfits into our rooms and onto our sparse couches and hard cement floors over the years. I brought to life the people who had passed on down that lane and gave them stories they had never lived. It was all true, and it was all imaginary.

The life that unfolded in reality more closely resembles the hues of the bleak map that I look at now. Our lives were difficult in fundamental ways: food was there or it was not, we did not ask; I went to school often on tea and nothing else, and many were the days when my lunch was so unpalatable that I would use a trick of the mind to eat it: this is my last meal, I'd say to myself, my last meal in prison, I'd add, turning what was distasteful into something delicious. In this way I learned to love pumpkin curry and the green-leaved *malluns* I loathed. In this way I learned to lead lives beyond the one I had in that house, in stations both higher than might have been expected of a skinny, hot-headed, boy-girl, and much lower than were hoped for me by my parents.

Some of those dreams took place up on the roof that is what marks my house on Google Earth. Climbing the roof was the kind of excitement that was permissible only because my mother had once been a girl who—like me—had been a dark-skinned daredevil who could outrun the boys and climb higher than any of them. I'd shimmy up the steep slopes even as my older brothers watched from the flatter surfaces beneath, and from its peak I'd talk about what I could see from such heights. The whereabouts of Aunty Mallika, who lived next door and routinely yelled at us, the exact ripeness of the fruit on the guava trees next door and the specific strength of the roots of the ivy that separated that guava tree from us, the means I would use to scale it, whether Uncle Gomez (who owned all the homes down the street) was setting off on some errand or not, and what that might mean for all manner of shenanigans we could get up to at the far end of the lane that abutted his house. Mostly, I liked going there alone, a diary in hand, to hide under the one bit of shade that could be found where the asbestos of the new roof reached beneath the red tiles of the old one, or crouch in the overhang of the Sal Mal tree that belonged to the people behind our house.

The roof is barely visible now on Google Maps, buried as it is beneath the reach of that very tree, the tree that caused years of discord between its owners and my family. Its branches were heavy and laden with flowers that rained down into the drains and gutters of our home, and its foliage blocked the sun enough to provide a welcome shade, yes, but also made it impossible to dry clothes on the lines that sagged in deep fatigue between the sour biling tree and the posts in our own backyard. Its tangled jack-in-the-beanstalk vines were the stuff of dreams for us children, but it seemed to represent something more ominous than waiting giants for our parents. My mother could be found ordering some hired day-laborer to wrench the gnarled tendrils down, or setting fire to papers infested with termites in great bonfires that singed the greenery above, and my father would rail with the best of them at *those bastards* who had so little sense of neighborly duty that our distress would not occur to them.

And yet. There was the matter of the ever forty-year-old, ever bare-bodied son of those neighbors, the one whom we kids feared, the one who was visible in the half-lit interiors of his house when I climbed up on the wall between our homes, my feet placed just so between the sharp shards of glass embedded into the concrete, and peered in. Their house was more decrepit then than ours now is, and the sooty walls of the kitchen in which he usually hovered were only made worse by the equally filthy cook who cackled and shooed me from within. What they did all day, he, his parents, this cook, I don't know. We called him the Knouer's Son, and I worried that he, tall as he was, could see me showering, that he was watching our house, that he had designs on my person or my brothers. He, like his parents' tree, occupied a great space in my life. I don't know, now, where he went, or his family, I only see, when I climb up on the roof, that there is a landscaped garden that laps against a beautiful house. And the only thing that remains of that time is the Sal Mal tree.

I take up that battle on my father's behalf, asking not for the felling of the tree but for the pruning of the branches that hang over our house. I find a man who scales the tree that is covered in large stinging red ants, and cuts them down, and I find common ground with the new owner, who agrees to pay for the poor man's labors. My sister-in-law quips that it is must surely be the power of the visiting American that can so easily dissolve all of our previous acrimony. Perhaps, I think, it is only the American way of asking for what one wants in such matters, over the Sri Lankan way of expecting what is right to come to pass, that makes the difference. I am grateful for the sunlight that now pours into the backyard, but I mourn the loss of the shade and beauty of this sacred tree, the tree that gave my book its name.

Such contradictions are what my family is made of. On this visit, my father, who has done his bit to keep his granddaughters off his leaking, broken, unsafe roof, even as I urge them on, asks for their help to bring down the harvest from his plantain tree, which holds the long stem full of combs over the low asbestos covering over the back of the house. I watch four of his many granddaughters, aged eleven to fourteen, wrestle with the long flat leaves, the pliant yet bulky trunk of the banana tree, the milky insides that spurt and stain their shirts. I watch my brother's friend, who had been summoned to fix my father's computer, climb this same roof in his khaki pants, polo shirt, and dress shoes, and join them in the tussle. Nobody complains.

How can an aerial photograph tell us anything of real value?

*

There were wars waged here, in this house and in this neighborhood. Carols, and Buddhist and Hindu prayers, were uttered in times of peace in houses that were burned to the ground in a single day that carved a permanent scar on the conscience of a nation. Here, my mother's raging brother was once tied to his bed at the back of the house during an ugly, hopeless night, the same place where Old Mr. Sylvester, an invalid, was carried in on his bed during the anti-Tamil riots of 1983 that left part of his house in ashes. Here my oldest brother lit incense, dreamed of a career in music, sang *bhajans*, played U2 chords on his borrowed guitar and Mozart on the handed-down piano, and never seemed to be touched by the harsh winds of disenchantment that blew through the house. Here also my second older brother flung furniture around and wrote love poetry to a succession of girls, declaring an equal, everlasting devotion to each one of them. The half-wall in the verandah over which that brother tripped and nearly lost his life was the same one on which I sat in the light of a full moon, all of seventeen, and experienced a kiss that asked not for the body but for the soul itself.

The space allocated for a garage once housed my father's Citroën, a heap of junk that he prized, and which ran perhaps twice in its lifetime before it was sold, a sale and removal I remember watching as it transformed my father's features, a dream of a sort being hauled up and taken away. That 15-by-10-foot garage was turned into a kitchen and a living room by my American husband and me, a setup that rivaled the functionality of Ikea's small-space designs in a quintessentially Sri Lankan way, with space for a half-blond baby, for entertaining strangers from Poland to America, *and* a shrine to the Buddha with a lamp lit each night and no fear of fires that could ignite our cane and wood furniture or the paper accoutrements of graduate students. That garage emptied when I left, taking my parents' first grandchild with me, and returned to the decay it had embraced when my father's car had been hauled off. It became my oldest brother's mad sanctuary when he could neither bring himself to divorce his first wife, whom he loved, nor marry the second, with whom he was in love. Somewhere into one of its corners my mother tucked the wedding albums and framed wedding photographs, the memorabilia of my other brother's first marriage, items she could not convince herself to discard with the same alacrity with which he had released his vows. In that garage, simmering piles of papers and books piled high up each wall, my brothers sat, one at each end of the room, cigarette smoke thick in the air, while I watched them pass pages of my first four hundred and sixty-seven page novel to each other, reading through the night, one declaring the book was useless, the other asking for permission to finish before commenting; a book I never published.

Around the corner from our street, by the bridge, there was a checkpoint that grew from a hut with a single policeman to a monstrosity that filled with armed soldiers. There were soldiers in the house next door, and informants down the streets; death threats arrived at my parents' home, my brother was jailed, we fled, and we returned. From this house my parents heard that their second son was contesting an election in the north where the war was raging, suicide bombers were being groomed for destruction, and the roadways were jeweled with land mines. In this house my parents heard that their oldest son was missing in the tsunami and, later, that he had survived. Year after year, their children, we, brought them news both devastating and joyful: the end of marriages, the discovery of cancer, accolades around the writing we had all learned to do as a way of surviving the earthquakes of our childhood, the birth of granddaughters. In that house my mother nurtured thousands of students, turning American colleges and universities from Pomona to Princeton into household names.

This was a home where people were as likely to be driven out as they were to be welcomed, often the same people. The mother who gave me every last cent she had was also the same one who smashed her fist against the door to the apartment I'd carved for myself out of her house; a glassless rectangle marks the spot. Yet what it recalls is not so much her hurt at the time, but the fact that it began to serve the function of passing gifts, written messages, telephone calls, and voices through from one side to the other. These were the ways in which we learned that nothing was permanent: the sometimes ostracized, other times included, the threatened and those who found solace, we all served some good at some point. Many things were broken, and yet in our broken state we found ways to be deserving of love, and to love. There were strengths, but in far greater measure there were frailties in this house, in this neighborhood, in the country itself. And though we could never do the same for ourselves, we had no choice but to forgive someone every single day.

*

I gaze and I gaze at the photograph that Google Earth provides. In it I can find nothing but rudimentary information about a place devoid of meaning. It reminds me of our addiction to access, our insatiable need to collect information rather than knowledge, our preference for the quickly summoned explanation—who cares who provides it, or with what intent— over an immersion in a place. This is how we read the news from other places, this is how we skim the world, thinking that all there is to know can be known from our desks, couches, tables. We believe that if we tap into a fad (neem for the face, jade eggs for our vaginas, yoga for our spirits, etc.), we have experienced a culture. We click "like" on a Facebook photograph and think we know a place. We imagine that following a Twitter feed makes us understand both personal and national revolutions, and the bitter sorrow of a failed aftermath.

But Google Earth cannot show you the split slat underneath the insufficient cushions on the hard couches my mother bought with her few funds. It cannot tell you that she strove to match the vomit green of those cushions to the cream and green curtains unevenly hemmed with the help of her aging eyes. It cannot tell you that I take those cushions and use them to extend the breadth of the double bed that my father had built for my six-foot husband, when we were first married, so that it can accommodate the tangle of the butterscotch bodies of my three daughters, and their mother, as we sleep at night under a mosquito net in the one room with a functioning fan. It cannot tell you that for a girl like me who grew up with only the cool cement floor as relief from Colombo's interminable heat, this arrangement is a luxury. It cannot tell you that each night before I fall asleep, I imagine my mother's joy at this innovation, at the sheer usefulness of her cushions. It cannot tell you that she lived and died believing that the elegant and beautiful life she had imagined for herself, in a home that did not resemble this one, would one day be hers. It cannot tell you that I was witness to the things that haunted her, and the things that undid her, and that I understand her grief in a time when she is not here for me to tell of that awakening.

Google Earth shows you a dark roof in a crowded brown landscape. We do not live there.

Sight

It takes seven hours to cross a few hundred yards into Occupied Palestine. We are the last ones left in the empty waiting room tiled so smooth it turns my mind to dance. Someone finds music on his iPhone and I stand up, defying the odds.

In Ramallah we sit under a slivered new moon, a venue so open it holds everybody and no late arrival disturbs. Our readers speak of Guantánamo and Palestine. A child peers down over a high wall, holding his father's safe-keeping hand, listening.

There is an American-city edge to the bar we sit in, late. Arak, licoriced, slightly sweet, intoxication growing within, undetected, like the place itself. "Fever" plays on the sound system, chosen by a man who designs t-shirts. I buy one for $20, black, its red declaration that *I am a citizen of the earth, though I have no country.*

A Palestinian friend says, *Ramallah has three bars, but we Bethlehemites can pretend we aren't occupied.* Enigma: Bethlehem lies broken into pieces like candied brittle. We have learned to navigate shards.

Time is made of elasticity and imagination. Will I ever forget dancing to "Rock Around the Clock" in the waiting rooms of the Allenby Bridge Crossing, risking everything for an act of defiance? That, instead of speaking of hunger and fear, we spoke of how my seventy-year-old dance partner did not want to dance without proper heels in front of the handsome older man in our group?

O Palestine. How quickly we learned to wrest joy out of denial. How swift, this transformation from righteous indignation to acknowledging the euphoria of the allowable moment.

*

In Qalandiya, between steel bars, funneled like consumer products off to the next destination for packaging and barcodes, we suppress everything except our laughter at the discombobulated voice floating down from the manacled watchtower: *No pictures! I saw one picture!* I hand out mints on the other side and celebrate us, we who have taken more than two hundred pictures in that crossing.

Armed soldiers idle outside the oldest library in Jerusalem, where the Khalidi family patriarch speaks proudly of his ancestors. He omits nothing.

Inside the Church of the Holy Sepulcher we place palms over the stone where Jesus is said to have been embalmed. Around us doors, crosses, an extravagance of windows above beckoning stone paths.

At night the effulgence of this sacred place descends. The pink and yellow walls rise up, containing.

*

In the old city of al-Khalil/Hebron, the occupation is relentlessly evident. New plaques on renamed streets announce fictions that permit desecration. Checkpoints are as ordinary as red lights. We examine this new normal: to require a permit for any journey; to have your home demolished and then be forced to pay the demolisher to remove the debris; to rebuild, then, in anticipation of demolition, take a hammer to your own roof and salvage what's possible; to circumnavigate along a wall for seven miles to make a half-mile trip; to have filth thrown on your head as you walk down romantic cobbled streets where in any European town bright cafés would spring up.

Safe passage means quiescence. So you take pictures: of vine leaves in bunches, pickled vegetables; children jostling to see themselves on your camera; the curved road of shuttered shops with their pretty green and blue doors—now sealed with chains, wrought-iron balconies in disrepair; four American teenagers on a "birthright" trip, sipping soda and laughing on the porch that once belonged to a Palestinian, while soldiers patrol, and settlers with machine guns drive too fast or pace the silent roads.

The call to prayer rises over the heads of soldiers and barricades, cuts through checkpoints, fills every trench and barrel, slips through the bars of rusty gates and coils of barbed wire that are supposed to block and exclude, wraps around the rubble and ruins of pale pink rock, collects each shard of glass in its embrace.

You think of God.

*

Hebron. Fifteen hundred soldiers guard four hundred illegal settlers. Watchtowers point in four directions above Palestinian homes, the noses of rifles cocked. Water barrels on Palestinians' roofs are riddled from the guns of settlers. Ahead, a road carves through the home of a Palestinian family. *We did not destroy it*, the soldiers say, *see, it is still intact.*

Everywhere, the twenty-five-foot-high wall stretches, hooded in sharp angles over roads, bridges, tunnels. I imagine setting fire at one end. Like an incendiary Andy Goldsworthy installation of land art, I want to watch its 650 kilometers implode in orderly flames. The leftover ash would settle into the earth, releasing us to grieve.

*

The stage in Haifa is set up like an open-air political podium, bare and stark. A rostrum and mike. Beyond it, an amphitheater. A table on the side with food and drink. A young woman sings ballads in Arabic, which are always about love, longing, home, and freedom. I listen in translation: *The stab of daggers is better than the rule of the treacherous.*

Despite missing pages, a replacement translator, and lights so blinding I cannot see the words before me, I read of recognizable things: family and revolution. We make the best of whatever remains.

*

There is a comic madness to the term "present absentee," coined to define 335,204 Palestinians who live in what is called Israel but not in their original homes, which have been confiscated. If numbers are measured by Israeli textbooks—whose maps even omit Gaza and the West Bank—that number would be five million. Palestinians return the favor: they pretend not to see the settlers and soldiers, denying the oppressor his validity.

There are ghosts who walk among ghosts here, and we are visitors wading through the thicknesses of fiercely held history.

Like this: The Hilton Hotel rises above Palestinian graves in the Abd Al-Nabi Cemetery in Jaffa, and the Wadi Hunayn mosque in Ramle is now a synagogue. Israel's Museum of Tolerance is being built over Palestine's Mamilla Cemetery. Those claiming there were no people on a barren land preserve the home of the Abu Kahli family in Sheik Mawanis; it is the club-house for the faculty at Tel Aviv University.

On the bus someone recalls meeting Arafat, how much regard she had for an unsophisticated man who, despite his failures, gave his life to Palestine.

*

The mountains en route to Nablus are deformed by settlements that fall and fall and fall into verdant valleys. Palestinians exist in the crevices left to them, and yet, around the most basic shelters, flowers and plants are cultivated. Color wrested from thin air.

At the souk in the old city we buy z'atar, star anise, saffron, olive soap. In a thin perfumery, I stop. The owner and I smell essences and talk of books, life, his young child. His private collection of bottles, tiny and ex-pensive, he refuses to sell, but, before I leave, he applies a dot of his favorite, a white musk, on my wrist. It lasts all day and through the night.

Every shop is like this, a portal into a world where nothing hostile awaits. Every turn reveals slopes climbing into other realms in these intimate centers of town that recall communal life. Cars creep down stairways built shallow, resilient enough to carry more than they were meant to.

A man gifts me a keffiyeh for my father. He makes me photograph his name and address. *Remember me*, he says.

Our evening program is in a space decorated with small Palestinian flags and traffic lights. Birds interrupt the first reader, and at one point we stop for the *adhan*. Around us fat felines wander, but, on the way back through streets surfeit with secrets, I see a skinny cat leaping over a high roof, sure-footed against the skies.

*

In Nablus the wheels of cars break the quiet as though they are fleeing, tires squealing.

Late, I look for cardboard to protect the maps I've been carrying on and off our bus, visual proof of a brutal occupation whose specificities may escape my memory and voice. AJ, the hostel receptionist, finds construction paper, twine. During the second Intifada, AJ, trapped in Ramallah, forfeited his education to work in film and media until the company could no longer make payroll after a year of Israel seizing tax revenues belonging to Palestinians. Movies from ISIS have begun to be released, and we talk about the cost involved in producing such things. They are similar to Israeli propaganda films, he tells me. Has anybody followed the money?

Social media changed perceptions of America, he says. *The hashtags showed American advocacy for Palestine, people marching. Things will change.*

Outside, gunshots. He translates the rhythms: a family member returned from jail…mourning the dead.

On Facebook, a friend request from a boy in Gaza: *Welcome to my country. You will be changed forever.*

*

Palestine is desiccated by settlements.

The first outpost is the Orange mobile tower on a hillside. Mobile homes follow, often spaced across some distance. The government deems that roads are necessary to connect these homes. Then that the roads must be protected from Palestinians. In these incremental ways land is annexed.

Al Walaja is being split to connect Gilo—the oldest, largest settlement—to West Jerusalem. Israel's wall will confiscate the last green space left in Bethlehem District and prevent farmers from accessing their land.

The Israeli government is intent on forcing Palestinians into the service sector; the settlers' sprawl effectively carries out government policy. Forced unemployment in the West Bank means 100,000 Palestinians withstand the misery of checkpoints every day, starting as early as two a.m. to labor in Israel.

The word "settlement" evokes temporariness. The permanence of these structures devastates.

*

The Catholic university in Bethlehem observes the call to prayer on Friday. In its gardens, memorials to students killed by the Israelis.

Our readings cover the Nakba, American life, the Egyptian revolution, Palestine, Grenada, Guyana, London. The discussion after is electric.

At a falafel joint in Bethlehem, I talk with students who travel from Dheisheh refugee camp. Our conversation is easy: clothes, boyfriends, families, what led each to choose to wear the hijab, their preferred breakfast—hummus made by their mothers—their future, the possibility of attending Bard University, how to take a better selfie.

Later, a taxi driver defies the law and races us to the church of a newly canonized nun—the first Palestinian—at the Carmelite convent. We are six, perched on laps, sometimes breaking into hysterical laughter along with the driver, giddiness born of getting away with bad behavior, other times solemn as we pass memorial after memorial to the war dead.

At the market, a young boy stops me from paying for a purchase in Jordanian dinars, the sixth most valuable currency in the world, ranked far above the Israeli shekels I'd thought I carried. He disappears with my money and returns with the right currency.

The Church of the Nativity, being renovated by the Palestinian Authority, contains the spot where Jesus is said to have been born. I kneel and pray for the believers in my life.

*

Aida, the largest of fifty-nine camps, contains people from 41 of the 543 villages depopulated by Israel in 1948, 61 percent below the age of twenty-four. Its graffiti on the apartheid wall exemplifies the Palestinian concept of *sumoud*—steadfastness, perseverance. One says: "Ferguson, Palestine." A half backbend is required to see the top. The beauty of the movement juxtaposes with the unassailable atrocity of this wall, its existence stains the life and spirit I celebrate in dance. I weep.

Unlike the elegance of old Palestinian architecture, camps are rudimentary. There, beauty was visible, though the occupation wove through with the virulence of weeds, choking life out of orchards, homes, people. Here, survival dictates everything. What were originally tents became sheds became rubble became brick became homes.

From the roof of the Alrowwad Cultural Center, we see the wall jag around three sides of a single home that has resisted demolition, imprisoning it in a sharp U that reminds me of Hebrew script. Inside the center, a nineteen-year-old boy dances like his very life could take flight. A fourteen-year-old girl sings "We Shall Overcome," and my heart clenches. I hear the anthem "Mawtini": *Will I see you in your eminence? Reaching to the stars. My homeland, my homeland.* Her voice around the Arabic is lush with longing.

*

The al-Aqsa Mosque stands in the most disfigured and militarized holy ground in the world, the approach barred by a checkpoint barbellate with ordnance. To reach the mosque, Palestinians must first pass settlers coming to celebrate *mitzvahs* amid raucous singing and drums, the guards joining them in dance, guns and fists in the air. After that, more security and through a long, caged tunnel lined with riot gear. There is no escape.

Inside, Palestinian women take turns to sit in a circle and read audibly from the Qur'an. A group of settlers comes threateningly close, and the women raise their voices: *God is great!* Palestinian guards tell the settlers they must leave. The threat of tragedy and political disaster is the norm; all that the Palestinians can do is attempt to avoid it.

It is beautiful here. Pale walls built in time long past, the skill apparent in the details, the sheer scale. It is hard not to compare monument to monstrosity, that other wall that grinds itself into the earth.

A Palestinian man sweeps the long, narrow, labyrinthine floors of the checkpoint.

*

The climb through Ramallah's hills leads through furrowed fields, grooved like the outside of walnuts. The trees are small, the spacing between each enough to allow travel, the leaves silvery in the light. Along each path there are shrubs: nettles, pungent farrow, the blood of Jesus (a dark pink flower that is the last to die), thyme, sage, other herbs. We climb on unsteady rocks all the way to *qasr* used by the farmers during the harvests. It is made of the creamy peach rock that I associate with this country. Stairs ascend to the open roof from the cool interior with its uneven floor. I imagine weathered men and women working here, their children running wild, unwatched for a day.

The light falls yellow-gold as we leave, gilding the thin grasses.

*

Our closing event is at the Sakakini Center in Ramallah. There is a chill in the air, and we shiver as we sit in the gardens. The last reading begins with lines from Darwish. At dinner I walk a bartender through making me a drink I've come to know, rum enfolded in Sambuca and Yellow Chartreuse. They call it "Palestine Libre."

Everything but the Ranch

You know what work is—if you're
old enough to read this you know what
work is, although you may not do it

from "What Work Is," by Philip Levine

There's a light that is particular to the Chihuahuan desert of West Texas, to which the town of Marfa belongs, that has less to do with color than it has to do with magnitude and scope. The skies out here remind me of the telescopic nature of sight, that our point of interaction—the cones inside and the rods outside the macula, the retina that gathers detail and color—is both infinitesimal and so vast that it is beyond our human comprehension. My time with the Aufdengarten men and their group of cowboys is similarly beyond the known world, both mine and theirs.

Perhaps it is the peculiar demographics of this town that first lead Ellery Aufdengarten, a man of deep American conservative values, and a woman like me, deeply rooted in the socialist culture of my native country of Sri Lanka, to practice civility. Marfa's population, evenly split between men and women, is predominantly Hispanic, but its next largest population—Caucasian—lags by a mere four hundred odd souls, and a significant part of its economy is sustained by cowboys and artists. In addition, with the nearest airport and major services three hours away, it stands to reason that neighborliness and goodwill must take precedence over the big city indulgences of self: isolation and self-reliance.

I meet Ellery Aufdengarten at an airstream parked at the end of the 40,000-acre Eppenauer Ranch outside the 1.6 square mile area of the main town. A destination for large-imprint movies such as *No Country for Old Men*, *There Will be Blood*, and, a long time ago, *Giant*, this area is full of the pull of the West, resting at ease between mythology and legend. As we stand seemingly contained by a sky both far and near, its scale so expansive that it appears to touch down on all sides of us, it is easy to see why.

*

Our host, Toronto-based Scottish photographer Bob Anderson, introduces us over cocktails. I smile at being referred to as yet another writer who wants to meet a cowboy. Ellery, who has stopped by on his way home after a long day of work at the ranch, bows his head and raises his hat, and the graciousness of the gesture, so unfamiliar to someone who has spent her adult life in American cities, disarms me. I slip easily into the feminine modus operandi that has been carved into my soul along with those egalitarian values. *I'm like them*, I say, *just more beautiful*, and reach out my hand.

At this point I have only been in Marfa for a few days, but I am already lost to the ethereal pull of its charm. I have risen each of those nights to step outside and place the stars among the constellations, and risen again to watch the sunrise. I have walked for miles each evening to accompany the sunset, knowing that such skies ought to be attended. Above my head, the sky imprints with variations of forms to which I want to attach meaning: open-mouthed indigo alligators, a shoal of goldfish at play, the rust orange resplendence of the palms of gods holding shut the blue-peach skin of the sky. It is that sky that bring me my first inkling that what moves a man like Ellery to tend to his life is precisely that which moves me, though we use different dialects of faith to describe the phenomenon.

Ellery gestures to take in a sky that has flushed deep into its swirling reds in a frenzy of pleasure. "This is why we pray," he tells me. "How can you not be grateful for this?"

We talk then about church, which he attends each Sunday. On some days he dozes off during the sermon—understandable, for an outdoors man—but he goes anyway. The ritual has less to do with the fervor of his religious beliefs than it has to do with common decency, the kind that requires gratitude for whatever is made possible. What he feels about God is between him and God, he says, and I am reminded of the far steadier ground on which the truly faithful stand, which has always rung truer to me than the showcase religiosity of those whose public vehemence has little to do with the tenets of their beliefs.

Showing up is a big deal in the Aufdengarten family, and not just on one's own behalf at church. For decades, the family has worked the Fletcher Ranch outside Marfa, partway down toward the famous Pinto Canyon

Road, with Ellery taking over from his father-in-law, Hayes Mitchell (who had been running operations since the 1950s), in 2010, and not one day since has been an off day.

For the past sixteen years, Ellery and his sons, Mitchell and Gerald, have kept the ranch working, an integral part of a system of codependence that binds ranchers across this remote corner of West Texas. If it takes a village to raise a child, it takes every other ranch to keep any one of them functioning. No one family can survive alone. Though they may conceivably be able to do the basic hard work of sustaining a working ranch, the matter of fixing fences, maintaining waterholes, tending livestock and treating a herd, mending equipment, and so forth, everything from routine roundups of cattle that roam across hundreds of acres of land to fighting natural disasters requires the open-hearted assistance of fellow cowboys, and in the giving and receiving of help, few if any questions are asked. Each rancher can anticipate and provide what another needs, secure in the knowledge that the giving is always reciprocal.

A few mornings before I leave Marfa, I join the family on a spring cattle roundup, where a herd is brought together to be branded, earmarked, weaned, and sometimes sorted for ownership or cut for shipment. My four a.m. alarm still does not have me ready in time to make it to the Fletcher Ranch, so I miss the excitement of readying the work horses, with their quiet but determined mien, and gathering the equipment for the work ahead. The tack—saddlecloths and, in this case, the western saddles that provide a secure seat for long hours of work with its rawhide saddle-tree and deep stirrups, bridles, split reins, a horn for holding the lariat, etc.— has already been loaded along with the beasts, and the convoy only needs a quick stop for fuel before heading to the ranch. In the quiet cold morning, I marvel at the alert energy of the men around me who have traveled from nearby Fort Worth to as far away as New Mexico.

Roundup is a quick word for the long hours that must be put in to effect it. This morning, the Aufdengarten men are there to help the owner of the Penitas Ranch gather the cattle on his ranch, which spills over acreage that is lush with grasslands and stripes of native trees and shrubs, ponderosa pines, oak, and piñon. At the last rise before the path runs out, the men stop and release the horses from the calico trailers used to transport them. I get down and watch as Ellery and the owner of the ranch cut a circle for each other, demarcating the area of land that each of the cowboys will take. I imagine that were these men looking not for cattle but for human beings, the calm they exude would be terrifying; they have the air of people long accustomed to their tasks, secure in their deep familiarity with the land and the knowledge that they are successful at accomplishing what they set out to do. As the pickup I'd been in bumped over what seemed an uncertain path and I looked out over the sweep of land still clothed in the darkness of a barely lightening dawn, I had wondered where the cattle might be and, more importantly, how on earth they might be corralled. The thought returns again as I follow the line of sight that Ellery seems to be pointing to.

Ellery's younger son, Gery, confirms once more the codependence required to work a ranch: "Gathering a pasture is like casting a net for fish. Your cowboys are the net."

And indeed, that's just how it is. The men peel off, their heads under wide-brimmed Stetsons and their legs around sturdy horses, silhouetted like figures from a moviemaker's impression of the West. For a long moment, I wonder what it would be like to ride with them, to follow where they might lead onto land that holds no markers for the layperson but that the cowboys read like a map.

For the next few hours there is nothing for me to do but wait. Gery's fiancée Jordayn Platt and I ride back together with Bob, and I am happy to interrupt our girl-talk about wedding dresses and college and surprise her by singing along to the old country music that is playing on the radio station. It's surreal to be listening now to the songs that I grew up with, when I lived among people who accept suffering and heartbreak as a natural part of life, thriving on the pathos of American lyrics, sung, often, in Southern accents.

"It's a good time to take a nap," Jordayn tells me when we finally return to the corrals to which the cattle will be brought. Then she gestures with a practical air to the brush. "Also, if you need to use the bathroom, this would be your chance to do it before the boys get back."

I sit in Bob's car and write while he naps. Jodayn sleeps for a little while, then perches at the edge of her truck to watch the cowboys return, first one appearing on the far horizon, then another, assembling at last as though by prior arrangement; their cattle obedient and in order before them, they're resigned to riding out at the next roundup to gather "remnants," those animals they missed. In the dry and present heat of the late morning, the men have shed their jackets and now toil, with only a break for cold water, wearing button-down shirts, bandanas, worn leather chaps over crisp blue jeans seamed smooth on the insides, and cowboy boots. I silently admire people who honor the worth of their work by dressing up in their best to perform it, heedless of the grime and dust.

There is a brief pause, and then the men separate again into a semicircle, driving the cattle before them. I get a closer look at the horses now. These are mostly American Quarter Horses, known more routinely as stock horses, a breed particular to Texas that traces its bloodstock to Mustang and Iberian horse ancestry, with some influence from the East Coast Arabians. The horses are divided among those that are lighter and can do the work of cutting (separating groups of cattle) and the heavier ones that are able to hold a larger adult animal on a rope. Despite the degree of chaos around them, the horses remain calm, responsive to their riders, and seemingly able to anticipate the rush of panicked calves and heifers.

There is a mesmerizing rhythm to what follows after the animals are brought into the main holding pen, as the cattle are "cut" into their separate groups, the mothers away from their calves, until each set is processed. I feel myself tense as I hear and feel the disturbance among the separated pairs, each mother lowing in distress, the calves jostling each other in certain panic and adding their own cries. Still, I continue to perch on the wood-topped surface of the rear of the pens, and after a while I am caught up in the choreography of the cowboys at their work and the synchronicity of their movements, more acutely aware of how vital it must be to have a well-trained horse to aid in this work.

I, like most people with some knowledge, however romanticized, of the American West, associate the dance of a lasso with cowboys, but this is the first time I have actually seen one used in the course of a day's work. In their hands, the 35–40 foot ropes—whether made of agave fiber or hemp—tipped with a *hondo* that can tighten quickly around an ankle or make slow circles in the air, unite grace with menace as they effortlessly pick a single animal among the many shoving against the barriers to reel in. During all the hours of watching, I don't catch a single miss or a single rope tangle with any but the particular animal for whom it is destined. One by one, vaccines are administered and ears are tagged. Each animal is brought down with a neatly applied lariat, the rope spinning above each cowboy's head in hypnotic patterns before it stretches to loop the intended hoof. There are a few calls made that I cannot decipher as the cowboys cajole the animals, and there is hardly any conversation between the men, yet communication takes place. Whatever hurt must be inflicted—whether tagging or injecting, or castrating the males destined to become steers, or all three—is done with alacrity; there is the briefest of intervals between the time an animal is brought down to the time he or she is released from a three-person hold (two to keep it steady, a third to do what must be done).

Jordayn has been helping the men all morning, handing out the castrating bander, or emasculator, to one or the other of them, and filling up and administering vaccinations, and she is, like they are, covered in the red dust of West Texas. But at lunch time, the men ease themselves into whatever shaded perch they can find, and Jordayn manages the food that has been brought up by Ellery's son-in-law, a restaurateur in Marfa; it's a modern innovation and a departure from the chuck wagon, complete with on-site cook, that once accompanied roundup. I join her, useful for the first time all day, and feel the precise pleasure of being in a place where gender roles are accepted in fundamental ways—women as caregivers, men as receivers of that care—a notion that sits easy with a girl raised in a South Asian culture that places women on an exalted plane where what is expected is both professional public competence as well as private nurture and grace. I relish too, therefore, the way Jordayn returns to work with them afterward, this time to process a calf for the first time. It yields my favorite tableaux of that day: Jordayn walking away from the calf, her palms held out and slick with blood, as Gery, managing his own animal, looks on and another one of the men fetches her a cloth. Learning on a ranch is by doing, not by textbook, and though her first stab is not as clean and swift as the men, it is a moment that both she and the calf survive.

Out here, there is no separation of human need from human act. If cattle are to be raised to be turned into meat, then this is the visceral muscularity of what must precede it. Watching the cowboys for close on eight hours should function as the final blow when added to the things that have given me pause over the years about consuming beef—*Eating Animals* by Jonathan Safran Foer, for instance, the Mick Jackson documentary about Dr. Temple Grandin—but it does not. There's too much that is intentional here. One by one, they drop the severed testicles into a bucket placed beside the tool truck, the contents to be cooked later. It reminds me once more of home. A place where, though we did not eat meat very often, when we did do so, no part of it was ever wasted. My father, a great cook, and my paternal grandmother served what is known as sweet-bread there, Rocky Mountain oysters here, and brain and oxtail and tongue with as much panache as they did any other part of a bovine. What I feel, then, is not disgust but a greater regard for the men who, though they may go away for education and training, stay so close to the earth, their lifestyle wedded to the land, their work itself dependent upon the vagaries of the natural world, with no way of glossing over the realities of human desire.

There is a confluence of beauty that attends the town of Marfa: the most silent place in the United States (Big Bend); the largest spring-fed outdoor pool (Balmorhea); the most powerful observatory in the country (McDonald) which trains its many eyes upon a firmament of such clarity that the storm raging on Saturn and the craters on the moon draw close enough to pierce the heart. But there is a rare human beauty that lies at its very center and that, if you hang around long enough, reveals itself: a live-and-let-live atmosphere that brings ranchers to poetry readings, writers to ranches, and both alongside the native Mexican population to the same dive bar in town where the pool table makes music at one end and local bands perform at the other. Out on the cattle ranch that day, I feel the stir-rings of hope for wider-reaching beauty, the possibility of common ground with the people who are, on the outside, most unlike myself.

In a country whose politicians have mastered the strategy perfected first by the Assyrians and most famously named by Julius Caesar—*divida et impera*—Marfa remains an exception to the rules of conquering through division. My time there, and my association with the Aufdengartens, re-minds me that even in America, as elsewhere, we citizens contain the spec-trum, and that the choice to claim a single hue (in our case, the red or blue political stripe) is nothing more than the same defensive mechanism that prompts less evolved creatures to tinge only a single color of alarm.

There is a rancher's term that is used to describe the cattle that have not been gathered and remain untouched by the cowboys: mavericks. Mavericks, unhandled and alone, become more difficult to manage as they age. In a sense, we—the cowboys and I—as representatives of our kind could bear the same classification. Without exposure to each other's way of life, the raison d'être for each of us remains invisible to the other. Over the course of that day, though, we bridge the vast divide. What I see isn't ideology or politics or religious differences, but good people unencumbered by the pretensions permissible for those whose work is removed by screens and desks and glass towers from those who are affected by it. I do not know what they think of me, but whatever it is, they are faultlessly gracious.

When I return to my house in Marfa that night, I write a draft of a poem I title "Song for the Cowboys." Much later, with Bob's help, I create a broadside set with one of my photographs from that day that I send to them, along with a letter of thanks. Ellery writes back this way: *I'll cherish this forever. You understand our way life. You are always welcome here. Please come back.* *

When I post the photographs of my time with the cowboys on social media, I do not post those that show the cattle hog-tied, lassoed, or being reeled and separated, offspring from parents, or later reunited. I know that my friends on the other side of the political spectrum would throw the razored spears of their contempt upon the practice, say hurtful things. Some things are untranslatable. I feel fiercely protective of the people I have come to refer to as "my cowboys." To understand human beings, their real worth, you have to walk among them for a while. It was a privilege to do so with the Aufdengarten family and their friends. I hope my side of this equation would, in our vastly different world, if put to the same test of intimate observation of a single day in our lives, pass with the same flying colors.

* In the years since this essay was written, the Aufdengartens, lifelong Republicans who had intended to sit the election out if Bernie Sanders had been the democratic candidate, turned out instead and voted en bloc for Donald Trump. We argue with strained but fierce civility on each other's Facebook walls on occasion about immigration, border walls, foreign aid, and wars. I send them the series of books by Yorkshire veterinarian James Herriot that take their titles from the Anglican hymn "All Things Bright and Beautiful." I take my family to visit them, and they spend the day delighting my daughters with a display of their skill with herding, diagnosing and treating cattle, and tending to the ranch land before Gery drives them

to the highest point on the land, the place where he used to go hang out with his best friends as a teenager. He doesn't talk much, but he smiles often, watching my daughters. It seems enough that we are there, seeing what he sees. Every now and again I see a "like" from one of them on a post that I have made about politics or family life. Every now and again I see a post on one of their walls where they include everyone in the country in their prayers. The art projects of my middle daughter, Hasadri, incorporate the West Texas landscape and Ellery's family. *How can an East Coast mixed-race girl feel kinship with White West Texan cowboys?* she asks in the text accompanying her photography and film. How do White West Texas cowboys write this way to an immigrant like me? *How can Jordayn and I think of bringing children into such a divided country?* or *Jordayn is going to London for a friend's wedding, please would you pray for her safe return?* When Ellery passed away during COVID in July 2020, Gery wrote to me saying they couldn't have many people at his service, but that they wanted to display the poem I wrote as consolation. It isn't change, but I call it progress.

Playing the Game

I was sitting in a café in Seattle, on the Pacific West Coast of the United States, when I was asked if I would write something for a national newspaper back in Sri Lanka. The request made me smile, and my companion, Rick Simonson of Elliott Bay Books, who knew my work and my family, asked me what the email I was reading was about. I tried to explain. *The Royal-Thomian,* I said, *you know, the cricket match that causes so many problems for the Herath family in my novel.* He nodded, oh that. But I knew that whatever I had written in that book was insufficient to convey the magnitude of what I meant. *Big match*, I said, then added, *blue and gold*, condensing into simple dichotomies a lifetime of histories stacked like the striated layers of sedimented rocks: each barely visible, but the whole staggering in its wealth of experiences.

But what did those couplets mean to someone who had never witnessed a game of cricket, let alone *this* game of cricket? I talked for a long time, my mind leaping from moment to moment, to a time of two-day matches, to the grand Centennial when the game went to three days, a move that caused an extra problem for my mother, who had studiously written fake excuse letters to the nuns at Holy Family Convent for me year after year because, good god almighty, what else would a Seneviratne girl do but attend the big match?

I talked about how I lived for those two, then three, days and had written for the big match souvenir, so called because there was no other souvenir that was valued more highly than that printed book, under the pseudonym "RS & SP," how I was the only girl to have ever written for that particular bastion of boyhood. I spoke of how I made tea—and considered it a holy duty—to be served to the cricketers who sat around our dining table, helping my mother craft her limericks about the players each year. How clever I had thought she was, how the banner-headers under which she placed the reserves—for instance, "they also serve who only stand and wait" (Milton)—had taught me that those who hold up, who wait to step in, are just as vital as those who are anointed, that observation is how we learn to play the game. I talked about how much time I had spent at Wesley Press and Felix Printers with her, and how that was where I first learned to inhale the aphrodisiacal scent of words on paper, a habit I have not lost and that my daughters have inherited, their own eyes shut as they begin reading by first breathing in the scent of a book. In those establishments, nestled between shanties and studios in Maradana, I had kept vigil with her and her small army of boys, way past midnight on school nights, creasing papers, checking for typos, and hauling stacks of finished copies under great secrecy into the locked trunks of various cars.

I talked about how the first pair of blue jeans I'd ever owned was bought with hard-saved money on the morning before a big match, and that they came with a creamy yellow blouse that together mimicked the best colors in the world. And about the silk of the two matching blue shirts my brothers wore when they were still too young for the boys' tent, the golden chariots on them, and how when the game broke for tea, they were lofted high on the shoulders of the older boys, carried like flags. How one of those shirts, made for a very small boy, has somehow made it through every move and still sits among my grown-up clothes in my American closet.

I talked about the cycle parade, where the boys from both schools pour into the streets on bicycles and in cars and trucks to sing their anthems and songs through the city, no police escort needed to stop traffic. About the year in which my friend, Tharindra Dharmasiri, and I had cajoled our respective mothers to take us to watch it pass by (for years I'd stood and watched, though I'd have given anything to climb up on the back of an open-air lorry!), and how by the time we got to our perfect spot, the parade had already left. How hard they had laughed, holding their sides, our mothers, these two teachers from my most beloved school, while Tharindra and I stood there in tears, gazing forlornly at the empty road, and how much worse were the empty days between this missed parade and the next, a year away.

I talked about what it felt like as I grew older and learned the thrill of wearing the Royal shield for a while on a loaned hat from a prefect, how that could still not compare to the joy of holding my first flag, and how both taken together were not enough to still the yearning in my heart to storm the field during the lunch and the tea intervals and most especially when a century was reached by one of ours, and that no ticker-tape American parade can compare to the glory of a well-matched pair of batsman being escorted off the field in a messy honor guard of euphoric young and old boys to the sound of the onomatopoeically named *pappata-pappam* band.

Royal College, and everything it was, had provided all the heartbreak and silver linings of my childhood, its deep blue the heaven on which I pinned all my stars, its gold the gilding of my adolescence.

I reached into my fiction, proving the point I make repeatedly to audiences, that all fiction is nonfiction. Devi, who stormed the green to field balls before the game in my novel? That girl was me, long ago: a determined, bone-skinny, dark-skinned dervish of a thing, hair cropped short like my brothers', hell-bent on being not just a boy, but a Royalist. I could imagine that to someone who has seen me do the female thing with aplomb, from lipstick to ball gowns to sky-high heels, the notion of a wild spirit whose deepest pleasure came from lifting high not the white and blue of my own school, Holy Family Convent, but the blue and gold of Royal, was a hard sell. I could see on his face that although he was listening, he could not reconcile the gracious woman who now stands before audiences and uses soothing accents and a musical voice to charm, with the fervorful girl who thought nothing of screaming *blue-black-and-blue-for-ne-ver!* over the voices of the Thomians and belting out *Disce aut Discede*, as if it were a motto she could abide by, as if she'd never failed to learn and been asked to depart.

And my character Nihil, what of him? He, too, was a part of me. That colors cap that Ranjan Madugalle let him wear for a while? That cap was given not to my brothers but to me by Ranjan during the 99th Battle of the Blues, because I was the daughter of his beloved teacher, and he was a beautiful human being even then, a gentleman who signed autographs while keeping a sedate distance from the grown-up girls who clamored to be noticed by him but would invite a little one like I was then to sit with the first eleven. A gracious young man who took the time to send me a Christmas card when I had sent one to him, this hero of mine from the time he had first walked out on that field at the age of fifteen.

Ranjan helped me write the scenes on cricket in the book. He didn't just help me by telling me how things work in the mind of a cricketer, he went back in time to the day on which he played his first big match. He spoke about what it had felt like to him, the field, the walk to the pitch, the walk back, how he learned what he did, how he moved from being overwhelmed to being at ease, and how ease more than anything else is what makes a good batsman great. In many ways, decades later, he echoed that sweet gesture from 1979: he beckoned me to join him and sit for a while in exalted company. He let me be a Royalist.

If at the center of my novel was a cricket-mad boy and his adoring sister, then the course of their lives surely had to pivot on a moment in time when their deepest pleasures were being reached for, and their most secret fears confirmed. And so it was. The day of the big match dawned, Devi broke the rules made for girls, and everything changed.

When I fell silent, I realized that I was not at the Oval, not at the SSC, that there were no brothers of all ages, no *baila*, no flagpoles hitting a *takarang* roof, no police, no *ice palams*, no baskets of food or Elephant House lunches in brown paper bags. For an hour or so everything had come back to me, more than all else my mother, around whom the college had swirled, and never more so than during those exhilarating days of March. I had remembered that the impulse that had made me get up from my seat, break through the simple barricades, and run onto a field where I was not supposed to go was the one that had been nurtured all those years when I sat on the sidelines and cheered for my team. It had taught me to see the world as being without boundaries, to see myself as deserving, to take my place wherever I felt I wanted to be.

I had been asked to write something for the big match, and in doing so I had been reminded of something I had let slip away: that I, too, had learned of books and men and learned to play the game.

Je Suis et Je Ne Suis Pas Charlie Hebdo

I come from a family of gadflies who never shrank from being contrary, and annoying the powers that be, if such was called for. We have, in whole or part, lost jobs, resigned jobs, taken jobs, been slandered in public fora, been incarcerated, and received death threats for our points of view. And we are all writers. While we have cautioned each other to, maybe, "tone it down," "be careful," "watch your back," or "trust nobody," we have each steadfastly refused to take this advice.

The notion that ten writers and two bodyguards could be shot to death during an editorial meeting does not sit well with someone like me. I do not believe that murdering people, even those whom we consider to be foolish, lacking in judgement, and irrelevant to sustainable human progress (people who aren't dissimilar to Fred Phelps and those within the Westboro Baptist Church), is a fair response to the incitement caused by their use of pen, pencils, and paper.

I joined my fellow writers in signing PEN America's condemnation of the attack on *Charlie Hebdo*. I did so even though I was dismayed by the refusal of PEN America to make any statement about the conditions forced upon writers in Palestine as they live under the yoke of occupation. I did so even though I disagreed with one part of the statement, because in the end, I agreed wholeheartedly with the idea that a punishment, or revenge, or any other human response, ought to be equal to the crime or offense.

This is the sentence with which I disagree: *The right to satirize, to question, to expose, to mock, even when offensive to some, is a bulwark of a free society.*

I do not pray to the god of the French, and of many Americans, whose devotees value a "free society" over human decency. I do not support the American Civil Liberties Union (ACLU) because I do not believe that the right to free speech on the part of one person overrides the right to grief and mourning on the part of another. The Westboro Baptist Church is simply wrong. And so was the ACLU for supporting it. (Its sudden epiphany in the wake of the 2016 presidential election and retraction of its support for that organization is not an act of integrity but rather a confirmation of the decades of irrationality and unsophistication on the part of one of liberal America's favorites, which helped bring a tyrant into the White House.) The French Republic is founded on the guiding principle of *laïcité* ("freedom of conscience"), an idea that has seen an effective separation of church and state. But look at that word: conscience. Conscience = a set of ethical and moral principles that controls or inhibits the actions or thoughts of an individual. As such, our conscience, whether it prompts us to attend church or mosque, or whether it urges us to stay away from such places of worship, defines our religion. France is no less dogmatic about its religion of "free speech" than is Catholicism about the Ten Commandments or Islam about its One God.

As I followed coverage of the event, I became steadily unhappier with the American take on the attack, even on the more center-leaning programs, such as *The Rachel Maddow Show*. Yes, the attack was vile, yes, nobody should be murdered for drawing cartoons, but no, thousands of people of the Muslim faith aren't religious fundamentalists and zealots for marching in nations around the world, peacefully protesting the denigration of their faith. And no, seriously, no, lampooning your own politicians and dress designers is not the same as expressing obscenities about someone else's religion.

We define what is considered criminal based on our own set of ideas, whatever our own culture has taught us to believe. Thousands of Muslims were outraged by the way *Charlie Hebdo* portrayed their faith and their God, and they were justified in their rage. Thousands in France and abroad were equally angered by the outrage of the Muslims, and they, too, were justified in their rage. Each had offended the others' religion. The protests that followed the satirical cartoons of the Prophet Mohammed in *Charlie Hebdo* in 2012 were an appropriate response. Intelligent people (both Muslim and otherwise) should have taken it further and exerted other pressures (diplomatic, cultural, economic) in order to mitigate the fallout from the offense, had they felt it necessary to do so. Instead, one side picked up weapons, the other side claimed that "l'Amour plus fort que la haine"[59] but really practiced the opposite.

It is tasteless to speak ill of the dead, but the anti-Muslim cartoons that made *Charlie Hebdo* infamous were similarly tasteless. They were designed

---

[59] Sorkin, Amy Davidson. "The Attack on Charlie Hebdo." *The New Yorker*, January 7th, 2015.

to harass, not educate. They were, in essence, cowardly, and masturbatory. No more elegant than men getting off on exposing themselves to children in public playgrounds. They were unnecessary and made no contribution to civil society, to cultural understanding, or to a collective human good. Cartoonist Stéphane Charbonnier incurred a great deal of hatred in his four years as editor-in-chief. And if he had not been killed so mercilessly, I would still be hard-pressed to imagine those four years as having been lived with genuine purpose. As the saying goes, we are put upon this earth to see each other through, not to see through each other.

Charbonnier made it a goal in life to purloin the freedom of the press to report, and misused that freedom to ridicule, malign, and nourish antagonism in a flammable world. I wish that the response on the part of the French to the bafflement and subsequent anger of so many Muslims had not been euphoria and condescension. I wish it had simply been an equally forceful ridiculing of an editorial vision that ran counter to creating a better, more peaceful world. I wish that goodwill and decency, not to be equated with censorship, had been considered an option.

I sit here in the long years after, considering something both complex and simple. I wish for a world that understands that concession wins more ground than mockery. But I also wish that all of those people, including Stéphane Charbonnier, had been given the time to do something different with their lives. Because the right to journey through life, to evolve, to realize the potential to do good in the world, is sacred. The pen truly is mightier than the sword. I wish for a better world, one in which people recognize and harness the power of that fact.

Fearlessness
The Creative Writer's Role in the Age of _____

In post 11/8/16 America, the citizenry became more aware, more active, more willing to submit themselves to self-examination. Yet while the world of journals both print (*Freeman's*) and online (*Guernica*, *Lit Hub*, *Electric Literature*), already at the forefront, have increased their commitment to the exploration of socio-political realities in their literature, and while even the usually slow-moving publishing world has stepped up its game, throwing a fair portion of its customary caution to the winds in an effort to slip anchor and sail toward the future, creative writing programs have refused to budge. And they have refused to budge in two significant ways: in their rote pedagogical practice, which remains insular, and in the criteria they use to select new faculty that emphasize paper qualifications that favor a certain demographic over skills and experiences that define others.

The preoccupations of a changing demographic, the churn of their concerns and the eloquences with which they articulate them, have remained, to all intents and purposes, the subject of a voyeuristic and oddly self-conscious glance on the part of English departments from coast to coast: a course on the literatures of__, a faculty member who looks the part but cannot speak the now tender, now razor-edged languages of the outsider—displacement and refuge, the largesse born of impoverishment, the brutality and beauty of communal embrace, to name a few—and most departments seem to believe that they have filled the vacuum. It is as though the inclusion of voices that are not merely global in thought but so in deed, or that straddle multiple realities while still attempting to walk the path of linearity required of them, might bastardize a pureness of literary form and inquiry.

In a recent article for *The New York Times*, Pulitzer Prize–winning author Viet Nguyen described the hidebound thus:

> The identity behind the workshop's origins is invisible.
> Like all privileges, this identity is unmarked until it is thrown
> into relief against that which is marked, visible and outspoken,

which is to say me and others like me. We, the barbarians at the gate, the descendants of Caliban, the ones who have no choice but to speak in the language we have—we come bearing the experiences and ideas the workshop suppresses. We come from the Communist countries America bombed during the Cold War, or where it sponsored counter-Communist efforts. We come from the lands America occupied, invaded or colonized. We come as refugees and immigrants, documented and undocumented. We come from the ghettos, barrios, reservations and borders of America where there are no workshops. We come from the bedrooms and the kitchens of the American home, where we were supposed to stay, and stay silent. We come speaking languages other than English. We come from the margins, where English is broken. We come with financial aid and loans and families that do not understand what "creative writing" is. We come from communities we do not wish to renounce in the name of our individualism. We come wanting to do more than just sell our stories to white audiences. And we come with the desire not just to show, but to tell.[60]

Nguyen's argument is not against the model of the workshop, per se, but the notion of the sanctity of its origins and the absoluteness of its conduct. I have taught now for several years in a variety of settings, small and large universities whose students are drawn from the vast and rural American landscape, and distinguished urban institutions whose students range from the very wealthy to the not so much, each displaying their own prejudices. In each of these, no matter the class, my approach has been not to prioritize the dissection of prose—and sometimes poetry—to shape a voice, but to treat the preexisting conditions of desire and intent behind those voices as they speak of the world to which their stories are addressed. That first, always.

The choice to teach in this way might be considered unorthodox. Surely, line edits on a particular piece of writing would be more useful. Perhaps it is. But of what use is a well-written bit of prose if it is devoid of substance? The most artfully written sentence cannot make up for what is missing in content and what does not, in some way, move humankind forward. If there is no emotional truth to what is being set down on paper, there is nothing that can be done to salvage it from the dustbin of history in which it surely belongs.

Here's an example: I was once required to critique a piece of nonfic-

---

[60] Nguyen, Việt Thanh. *The New York Times*, April 26th, 2017.

tion written by an undergraduate at a highly competitive liberal arts college in New England whose intention was to write about her experiences studying human rights over the course of three months of travel in Nepal, Jordan, and Chile. The piece I read concentrated on her month in Jordan, during which she was supposed to master "the human rights issues, histories, and current politics" not only of Jordan, but of its surrounding nations of Palestine, Syria, Iraq, and Israel.

I submit to you that my role in that classroom, as her professor, is not to perpetuate the myopia and the idiocy of the American program directors who obviously feel that the long histories and complex cultures of other nations can be imbibed—with, say, a vial of arak or a cup of Arabic coffee—by young people whose only comprehensive reference to their own country comes in a seventh grade assignment to match the fifty states to their capitals. No. My role in that classroom is to direct her gaze at the baggage she is being asked to carry with her through the world, the kind that cannot be hauled into the underbelly of her transport and picked up later, the kind that will blight her vision for the rest of her life. To give her, in other words, an entry point to her essay that is far more useful in this world than the *my god!* of the drivel that might otherwise ensue.

We must be willing and able to recognize that what we are called upon to do in our classrooms goes beyond polite discussions of craft. And this is particularly true today, for we are at long last agreed on the moral contours of our socio-political landscape. We are all equally un-blinkered: looking at an age of consternation, panic, hysteria, blaming, myopia, fear, all of which can be encapsulated under the concept of ignorance. We are a nation of ignorance, and by this I do not mean every soul on this great stolen land, but rather that we combine—with our silences and our inactions and our cowardice—to make of ourselves a nation's worth of ignorance where the meek walk sans compass or light cursing both the stars and the dark, yet lack the will to exert our energies toward demonstrating a more thoughtful, relevant, and courageous conduct of life, in our minds, in our deeds, in our words, and most particularly in our classrooms. It isn't as difficult as we have been persuaded to believe it is.

Around this same time in 2008, I was listening to news of Israeli forces bombing Gaza, leaving 1,417 people, 313 of them children, dead, when my father called me from Sri Lanka, wanting to know what American writers were saying about all of this. He suggested that I ask my own publisher to bring out a collection of writing about this issue, for once, in a braver time, there had been a collection of American writers who had written about Vietnam. It would have been easy to say "but my potential prospects for employment..." or "but my potential *New York Times* book reviews..." There is always a way to imagine that servility and playing by the rules will somehow propel us to great fame. But, as we have learned from the great tale of David and Goliath, one does not beat Goliath by accepting his rules of engagement, which have been designed to serve him. So sixty-five other writers and I chose not to.

There are no excuses to be made. There never have been. And this will, this determination to address with our art and with our teaching and with our very life, every single day, this world and its injustices alongside its beauty is not something to be learned, it is something to be recognized as a privilege. For privilege itself accords us that responsibility. I wasn't born here, you might say, I was raised differently. Yet in America, among its poorest and its darkest, there is a similar innate recognition of what we are here to do, that what is morally repugnant must be referred to as such, must be countered with all our might.

No, I could not wait for anointment, for someone to say, "All hail Ru, she must be the one to take this on, and here's the golden circular embossed stamp to place on your book covers, and here's your byline in the *NYT* so that fear will no longer grip the cockles of your heart. Go forth and preach, sister!" And no, we others couldn't wait, unlike, say, the ACLU, for a bottom-feeder to occupy the White House before we could have our come-to-Jesus moment and realize that, hey, no, it's not okay to disrupt a fellow human being's moment of mourning and burial, as the Westboro Baptist Church did regularly, doggedly defended by the ACLU, which was in turn roundly applauded and funded by many of us. No, we others cannot wait until the correct number of congressional aides have answered the requisite number of tallied phone calls to protest the murder of another Black child, another man with a turban, another woman in a hijab.

This might be our burden, but it is also our gift. And it is called fearlessness. And if we cannot teach fearlessness in the creative writing classroom, the classroom where, above all other classrooms, we learn to imagine and we learn to articulate not only what is but what can be forged into being, what the hell else is there to teach? If we cannot hire and defend the people who can and will take on that work, who have a lifetime of preparation to do that work, in our creative writing departments, at what unconscionable price do we protect an evil that flourishes in plain sight? For your solutions are everywhere: we are your mostly female, mostly of color, often foreign adjuncts, we are your visiting lecturers, we are your non-tenure-track faculty, we are your Distinguished Writers, we are your American Quarter Horses who have already experienced firsthand a world of injustice and cruelty that is untenable and have set out to mend it because there is no other way to conduct our lives.

We must commit, as a collective, to bringing a fierce energy to our classrooms, where, always, there will be students who develop an intensity of discomfort in their intestines, and others whose guts will finally be identified as being part of the body they inhabit. For we are not in the business of creating a concert of crows cawing in the same register; rather, we are committed to the art of tapping the music of a menagerie of feathered creatures worthy of a Babylonian garden who together create the rhythms to which we can all dance. And yes, in that orchestra there is room for a bench of blackbirds voicing their singular note, but that note no longer grates on our ears. We are here for the iridescence of many, not the dull shades of uniformity.

There is no other way to be a professor, a title whose etymology comes from the Latin *profiteri*, which is to lay claim to, and to declare openly. To be, in a word, public. This is not a profession for the faint of heart, for the cowardly whose concerns are to do with notions of safety and security absent from the scrutiny of the young people before them or the judgement of their fellow human beings now and in the future. Teach, from the Middle English *techen*, which is to show, train, direct, warn, from the Proto-Germanic *taikijana* and Proto-Indo-European *dejge*—which is to declare, to tell—and the German *ziehen*, which is to accuse, to blame. Students are not served by those who are willing to abdicate the responsibilities that, if they have been forgotten by many of us, might be remembered if we only consider the very terms that define our lines of work: *professor, teacher.* Line edits are the least of our tasks.

What Is Courage?

In the wake of the *Charlie Hebdo* shooting, I read a tweet that kind of broke my heart. Someone I know and like said they did not believe in boycotts because they had "fought too hard to be included." The person in question was referring to the controversy that erupted in the American literary world over PEN giving their prestigious Freedom of Expression Award to *Charlie Hebdo*.

I've thought about that statement since. What does it mean to "be included"? By whom? To what purpose, and to what end?

It made me think about the fight itself—for whom and what do we fight? When we fight for inclusion, is it just for ourselves? Would I, Ru Freeman, like to "be included"? Where? At the PEN gala? I have been. I've been one of those table hosts, and I enjoyed it. Then, as on many other occasions, I've thought about where I came from, who I am, how much I enjoy the glamor and jazz of being in such places, but also about the immense loneliness I feel at such moments. The public person, the representative of my kind—South Asian, of color, the international, the woman, the Sri Lankan—puts on both the ball gown and the star performance. But that same person understands that at all times I am but the face of all those other identities, and of all the other people who look like me or talk like me or think like me or share my various parts and orientations. What I do does not impact me alone. And I am far too old and far too wise to believe that the fame of a New York minute is a rule meant only for other people. I'm far too old not to know that when the lights dim, I walk home as myself, a woman of many identities, and many complexities, not Ru Freeman the Table Host at the PEN Gala, circa 2013 or 2025.

Knowing these things, I have often advised people who have asked that in the end what we are left with—what anybody is left with—is their integrity. The table at which I sat included some of New York's finest philanthropists; I knew their work thanks to my own stint in development and fundraising with major donors. The reward for their gift to PEN was being consumed as we talked, and I, good soldier that I am, changed seats through the various courses to make sure that I had a chance to make a personal connection with each one, to express, through some combination of charm and intelligence, that I valued their support on behalf of PEN. But I am not only the good soldier. And the glitz of the corporate presentation that year grated on my nerves. (There is a reason why I love the American Friends Service Committee—nobody there looks like they're rolling out a multimillion-dollar initiative for Nike when they are raising money to help the poor in the most remote parts of Afghanistan.) But that was not the place to express my small sentiment of dismay. It would have served no purpose. It could not have helped the people who were struggling under the weight of censorship across America or the world. It would have been a pointless and graceless gesture. And man, was I not enjoying my ball gown and my wine at my first black-tie gala?

But what would I have done if I had been asked to represent PEN during a ceremony that awarded a badge of courage to a group that denigrates most of the population of the world? Whose raison d'être for being present at the gala was that they had persisted in ridiculing and taunting a marginalized and mostly misunderstood minority? Would this not have been the time to think about those other identities that I embody? If I had ever belonged to any group, of any size, that had been denied the respect and regard and rights accorded to everyone else, that had been brutalized and collectively dismissed at every turn, particularly in America, would not my conscience trouble me enough to stand with those who more closely embody the hardships I may have undergone? The answer would have been clear to me: forget the ball gown and the wine and the little table tents that tell the assembled all about me and my literary achievements.

So what is belonging and inclusion? And in whose hands do we place the right to include us, and to stand in judgement about our merits?

I read a lot of posts and interviews with the writers who chose to sign the letter of dissent, keeping in mind that a letter of dissent is like the words penned by judges of the courts: it allows the majority ruling to go forward, but it articulates the reasons why the particular judge/s disagree. It has no teeth with regard to the particular ruling, but it informs the legal arguments yet to be made in other cases. In other words, as an organization like PEN ought to understand better than any other, a letter of dissent permits the freedom of speech and conscience. This particular letter of dissent expressed exactly that, and no more. The vilification of the six table hosts—

and therefore the other signatories, of whom I am one—permitted by PEN, and articulated in fact by some of PEN's most recognized names, including Mr. Salman Rushdie, is the real blow to freedom of speech.

To claim that the award had nothing to do with the denigration of Muslims while quoting Ayaan Hirsi Ali[61] is like saying you aren't racist but quoting George Zimmerman, who murdered American teenager Trayvon Martin because he was Black.

What Ali said could have been said by anybody. That PEN chose to use her as a quotable human being at a gala where they have sworn they were making an award that has nothing to do with Islamaphobia is nothing short of not just a bucket but an entire dry oil well full of bovine excrement.

To return to this idea that crawling through the needle to be "included" requires the setting aside of one's conscience or silencing the voice one possesses and can use to speak for the voiceless and the "un-included"—a condition with which the freshly "included" must surely be familiar—I quote the writer Conner Habib: "I am not one of the widely celebrated writers on the list. I, like many of the 204 signatories, am not a household name. I am not wealthy or luxuriously free to sign petitions." In other words, some writers choose to do what is not easy because they value the tenor of our community more than they value the fleeting moment of "inclusion."

Habib goes on to make several excellent points about his decision to sign the letter of dissent or, as he puts it more accurately, disassociation. As does Amitava Kumar, another writer who knows of what he speaks, in his conversation during "The Takeaway" with John Hockenberry.

Amitava takes on both the matter of PEN mobilizing its surrogates to attack the writers who wish to disassociate themselves from this award, and the matter of choosing to celebrate *Charlie Hebdo* while ignoring the murder, say, of Pakistani activist Sabeen Mahmud,[62] among other things. And he asks this question: "Does it take courage to stand up at a glittery gala in NYC and toast *Charlie Hebdo*? I don't think it does. So what does it take more courage to stand up for today?"

---

[61] @PENamerican quoted Hirsi Ali in a tweet:"'Every important freedom that Western individuals possess rests on free expression.' - Ayaan hirsi Ali #PENgala." For more on Hirsi Ali, read Leung, Michele. "Why Aayan Hirsi Ali Gets A Conservative Media Spotlight." *Media Matters*, April 11, 2014.

[62] Parshley, Lois. "The Life and Death of Sabeen Mahmud." *The New Yorker*, April 28th, 2015.

It is a question that should have been answered by an overwhelming majority of us writers. As history repeatedly warns us, nuance and courage unexpressed when it is required but seemingly unrelated become the nuance and courage that is lacking when the stakes are much higher. Almost two years later, to the day, of the events in Paris and our collective cowardice as we parsed the entirety of it, our inexcusably misplaced sympathies for the crass and blasphemous, America went on to inaugurate Donald Trump to the White House.

Which Would You Choose?

Perhaps it is because I've been immersed in the history of these two peoples—the Palestinians and the Americans—for so long, perhaps it is because I have been dismayed by the US government's official move of its embassy in Israel to Jerusalem and its "awarding" of the Golan Heights to Israel in contravention of international law, but I am reminded today of a day when I asked my daughter this question: which would you choose?

She was already one foot and half her heart out the door, poised to leap off the tall building and take flight, safe in the knowledge that wherever she went, no matter how far away and under what circumstances, a depthless store of love waited to welcome her back. It was a discussion about politics but, more importantly, about what it meant to take a stand about an issue.

Some history. A month prior, she had decided (this math and science child who talked about how she was not a writer—*like you? oh my god! never!*—yet was an editor of her high school newspaper) to write an opinion piece about Palestine. Needless to say, she met with a lot of resistance, all aimed at (a) whittling down the space she had to write, and (b) providing rebuttals. Given the many, unrelated, struggles she had to overcome over the preceding years, I eventually asked her as kindly as I could if she wanted to withdraw her article. I explained that she didn't have to fight the battles I take on, that she was sixteen years old and didn't possess the knowledge that she needs to speak about this particular issue, and that life could become tough for her at her mostly Jewish high school. I explained, only half jokingly, that one of our dearest friends had told me that he only began speaking out about this issue after he got tenure and decided that he didn't need any more friends. "If everybody did that, nobody would say anything," said she. Of course.

I'm an adoring mother, but not an easygoing one. Thus it was that once she did her research and wrote that article and received the backlash I knew she would (before it even went to print), and when she hid in the bathroom because she was going to backtrack and didn't want to tell me, I held her feet to the literal fire. This is what it means, I told her, to speak out about something. You want to do it, you better be sure you are going to stand your ground. It was an ugly morning, full of tantrums and tears, including mine, though mine were private, shut up in a stall at a swim meet, where I cried for the weight of never knowing if what I say and do will make them stronger or imperil their lives; a predicament, I understood then, that my own parents had found themselves in many times.

The article appeared and was discussed in classrooms by the more enlightened teachers. The students in those classes greeted it with divergent opinions but were united in their appreciation for the research she had done and the courage she had displayed. Nothing she said was particularly controversial, and much of what she said I—and many Palestinian activists—would have trouble with. Nonetheless, it seems, a "friend" of hers (who had previously made an effort to block the formation of an Amnesty International chapter at the high school on grounds of anti-Semitism) launched an insidious attack on her, not under her own steam but that of her older brother, long gone from the high school.

So we had The Talk. It came full circle to what our responsibilities are when we choose to take on a cause. I didn't believe that her fellow editors were ill-intentioned, that theirs was a malicious attempt to thwart her, but thwarted she would be if she said nothing. I spoke again of our tenured friend, the one who has taken many difficult stands over this issue, a few of which have included the sacrifice of professional acclaim. Would she lose her editorship, she asked. I didn't think so (and man, if she did, I'd have fought that battle to the bitter end). But it allowed me to mention what it is we talk about when we talk about taking on a cause. You cannot take on a cause and remain impervious to what the cause demands of you. You cannot take on a cause yet back down when it becomes uncomfortable for you personally. And perhaps more important to understand than both those things is that every cause is bigger than the people who choose to speak for it, and that the moment you speak, it is no longer about the stand or the personal risks you take but about the people for whom you speak.

Omar Barghouti, founder of the Boycott Divestment and Sanctions (BDS) movement, has spoken about the Palestinian campaign for the Academic & Cultural Boycott of Israel (PACBI) and the need for American academics and artists to support the boycott of Israel. Several artists, including Alice Walker and Sarah Schulman, have done so. Some others, like David Grossman, have called upon writers to join in the call for peace, a peace that may or may not be the peace desired by Palestinians who rightly point out that peace within a system where there are lesser humans and more perfect humans is no peace at all, and the text of the declaration makes assertions that are problematic at many levels, but at least they are refusing to remain silent.

I don't know how this particular life lesson will play out for her. I am glad that she forwent a chance to stay home and study for the ACTs or tend to half a dozen other academic demands and accompanied me to the University of Pennsylvania that week to listen to Omar Barghouti speak. I am glad that though she rolled her eyes at me for being directionally challenged, and complained about the freezing cold, and uttered a disdainful "never!" to the young guy who walked us to our destination and asked her if she was considering his university for college, she still sat and listened to that talk, and had the humility to reveal the depths of her ignorance by whispered questions (to me) about the most rudimentary of details.

Perhaps, I thought then, she will determine that speaking out about difficult subjects, something this reserved child, so unlike her mother, has embraced, and for which I remain forever in awe, for it is harder for her than it is for me, is not the particular gift she has to give the world. Maybe, I thought, that article would be the sum total of her contribution to this cause. But if it was, I hoped it would not be because she feared for her own physical or emotional comfort. For if that is the rationale, no matter how justified given her youth and her commitments to multiple other areas of her life, I hoped that she would ask herself this question: if she could choose to be a child in Jenin who risks death by bouncing a rock off the hull of an approaching 66 ton Merkava whose driver has not been occasioned the opportunity to set much store by her humanity, or to be a child who risks a degree of reprobation and perhaps even ostracism by speaking out against injustice at an elite American high school she will soon leave behind, which would she choose? Which would you? If change can come to America, it must come through the bravery that is embraced despite our discomfort with its repercussions.

Seven years ago she was conflicted, but pushed through. Six years ago she went on to conduct a grant-funded series of interviews with former combatants from the Liberation Tigers of Tamil Eelem and reconciliation efforts in the Northern province of postwar Sri Lanka. Five years ago she decided that she was a literature and politics double major after all. Four years ago she went to Palestine with the Palestine Festival of Literature, sold books at their events, and met Barghouti in person. Three years ago she worked with the American Council of State Legislators, a conservative organization, learning what inspired people to go into public service. For two years after she worked for the Center on Law and Policy, presenting bills protecting the poor against evictions in front of the Colorado senate and chairing the women's legislative breakfast. She worked nights at a pizza joint and registered her peers to vote every chance she got, served on multiple committees and boards. Today she works in the courts in Butte County, California, as outspoken about the importance of vaccines as she is in building common ground with a swath of the local demographic that is against them, and is deciding between offers from law schools. She moves easily within hierarchies, with confidence and compassion. She knows the names and stories of both janitors and judges. *I'm not giving up*, she says when I inquire about her future plans. For the sake of this girl at the center of my heart, I wrap my faith around her sisters and her peers from Parkland, Florida, to Mingora, Pakistan, from Ramallah, Palestine, to Davos, Sweden. *Bon courage.*

Marry an American

Sometimes, on a long drive alone, I find myself singing a song I'd learned as a child in another country: "God Bless America." Then, it was just one song among many. Now, it carries a resonance I'd not have believed possible.

A long time ago my mother made me apply to American colleges by pointing out that Sri Lankan universities had been closed for three years due to political unrest in the country, and, more importantly, that she would let me marry the boyfriend of the time if I just went away for a year. I laughed at her plot and decided to prove her wrong: I'd get that full scholarship, but I'd never change my mind about the boy. She won. I came, I met another boy. I suppose that is why she, a teacher of literature, underlined a certain quote in one of the texts we studied in school for our high school exams, these words from Benvolio to Romeo in Shakespeare's *Romeo and Juliet*:

> *Go thither; and, with untainted eye,*
> *Compare her face with some that I shall show,*
> *And I will make thee think thy swan a crow.*

My Sri Lankan swan turned crow in the face of the beautiful all-American boy I met on a college campus in Maine. But setting out on the grand adventure of romance is not the same thing as setting out on the dangerous escapade of marriage to someone from a different culture. My mother loved my husband—he was, without a doubt, everything she wanted in a partner for her only daughter—and he, in turn, humored her. When she visited, they gardened together, laughed together, alternately tolerated and admired me together. But my mother only saw my life as she wanted to: a life of perfection and great accord in a country of seeming order and prosperity, conducted among intellectual peers and peerless granddaughters.

But the difficulties of the life of my heart I concealed from her, and often from myself. Whatever I felt about the imbalance in my marriage to a wonderful man who happened to live in his own country, among his own people, while I was so far from mine, I learned to cloak in political rants.

But my grievances ran deeper than ideology.

I hail from a country where nobody worries about the triumvirate of concerns that were supposed to paralyze me now as an American: education, health care, and a roof over my head. Sri Lankan children are inculcated with a deep regard for and love of education, and it is provided free through university; one of the most heartening sights you will ever see are the parents readying their children at public faucets in the shanty towns, and those children pouring out in their hand-me-down uniforms on their way to school. We did not have the kind of equipment that can prolong life for ninety-year-olds, or separate conjoined fetuses, but the quality of general medicine—also provided free—is equivalent to that in America. Money is a fluid commodity, going to the person who needs it most. We lend and borrow ceaselessly and are unconstrained by the fears of destitution that terrorize Americans.

It was a way of being that was perpetually at odds with my American life. I was never far from the thought that though I was deeply immersed in the life and culture of this country, it would take enormous willpower to continuously seek the things that sustain my heart. To live far away from where one is born, particularly when the two countries are different in such critical ways, is to go around with a constant dislocation of the mind. The littlest things reminded me of this. Back in Sri Lanka, for instance, we rarely say "please" or "thank you." Both are regarded as creating distance between the person who has needed assistance and the one who has had the opportunity to help, because both reference the request, not the connection between the two people. Yet my husband swore by these words, and I learned to say them in the interest of marital harmony.

We choose our adventures as young people on a whim. How easily I had gone from doubling my courses and shortening my college years so I could get back home to persuading myself to live here. How could I have not seen the strain of loneliness that would run through such a life? How, when the romance of weddings and first apartments settles down, what is left would be the conduct of a life that would unfold at a great and aching distance from the people who cared about it the most, my parents and older brothers? How could I have not known that though I would find ways to celebrate the transition of my daughters from girls to young women, cajoling letters and gifts from the older American women in their lives as well as their aunts and grandmother back home, that it wouldn't compare to the solemnity and joy that surrounded the rituals that take place in my island country among extended relatives who hand down their own jewelry as blessing?

I have made an art of thriving in the United States. I am more informed about its politics, more engaged in its civic life, and more committed to building community wherever I find myself than the now ex-husband whose American ancestry is steeped in the beginnings of its colonial enterprises. I was asked, after my swearing in, why I wanted to be a citizen of this country. With my youngest daughter a few months old in my arms, I said I wanted to demonstrate to them what it means to be a citizen, to be proud of their country. It's a responsibility I take seriously. No matter the size of the campaign, whether it is local or national, it is I who can be found walking the streets, knocking on doors, often with my daughters in tow, I who take them with me into the voting booths, I who help them with their placards and teach them the reasons for their slogans, and I who insist that they read, night after night, the landmark cases that changed the United States. Between the two of us, it is I, not their father, who embraces the chance to travel to the farthest corners of this country, who engages all manner of Americans in conversation, and whose American friends can be found from coast to coast. It is also I who teach my daughters their place, as Americans, in a world bigger than America.

I have many things in my American life: a house that provides shelter for my family and refuge to those who need it, innumerable friends, a solid career, an instinctive familiarity with the customs of this country, public acclaim, and the adoration of many whose instincts I respect. It is a life I would not now exchange, for I have made of my own need to build bridges—between myself and others, between countries—a vocation as a novelist whose eye is trained steadfastly on the ties that bind and break but must always be mended. It is my way of reconciling the gift that was given to me by my parents, to be a force of good in the world, with the fact of their distance from it.

Still, in my quietest moments, when I held my history in my hands, my advice returned to these words: *Marry an American*, I would say to my American daughters. Perhaps one of them will choose to disregard my advice, leave their country forever, and experience another culture in the way that I have done. Indeed, the middle daughter has set off for the United Kingdom to study film, acquiring facility in French and Arabic, and has in mind that after that, she will conduct her life in a country that will require her to raise multilingual kids. Perhaps her sisters, too, will choose to play a different game, with foreign rules, using somebody else's deck of cards. Perhaps they will learn to experience other truths, and to know that those truths are rooted in simple routines (from what we use to brush our teeth to how we board a train) as much as they are rooted in the larger frameworks we each use to explain life and death—how we are born, how we consider the genders, how we express faith—and that no one way is better or worse than another. But for the sake of their hearts, I hope that they will not. I wish for their travel to be round trip, for their imagination to soar among works of fiction and the literature of translation. For their sake, and mine, I hope their feet turn ever homeward, that they will recognize that there is a diversity of thought and culture and experience among their own countrymen that would make for an equally thrilling life, and that if travel is necessary, they will do so in the company of another who carries the same passport.

I was holding those thoughts when, in post-lockdown NYC, I stood up in the ferry boat and serenaded the Statue of Liberty with the then-song-now-anthem that my mother had made me learn. We were passing just beneath Lady Liberty on the New York Harbor, on a boat filled with new friends and strangers. One of my companions, the writer Colum McCann, took a knee beside me in protest. There we both were, utterly foreign and completely American, wrapped in the tumultuous discords and divergent politics of this immigrant country, still casting our professional lot together because we were fundamentally united to work for a common good.

I thought about my daughters, the way each of them has shaped herself in similar, seemingly contradictory fashion. One can sing that anthem at state track meets and also march at the head of thousands in Philadelphia, refusing to back off with her tear-streaked face inches from armed police. Another can hold her own in debates with legislators on public policy across two states, navigate countries where she does not speak the native language, and also use that voice at protests against the brutality of evictions. One can create art that is featured on screens, in magazines, and in galleries, grace catwalks, win the trust of a family whose oldest son was murdered by the British police so she can bring their story to life, and also go undercover to hang banners of protest from the rooftops of international Pharma companies refusing to share their COVID vaccine patents with the very brown and black people on whose backs those vaccines were tested.

I change my wish for them. I hope they will go where they will, choose partners as they please. They were raised by me. They grew up in this country. They have the moral fiber and skills in spades to create a place that they can call home. They can begin again. And again.

Home Spun

I

This is how it is written. There is no linear narrative possible. It is inconvenient, the way that reality muddles life. Think of a leaf of mint; use the wrong instrument, one with teeth on the end, perhaps, and you release not the rising fresh but the bitterness of chlorophyll. I am that leaf, the absinthian a half note away from the neoteric. This is why: I did not come here intending to stay. I do not stay here because I have no wish to leave.

II

I am home, my mother still in this life, and I wade out to sea, scooping sand from a sudden dip a little farther than it is safe for me, a non-swimmer, to be. Each time the waves bury me, drag me farther out to sea, and the sand is more water than solid. That gathering, and the way it pours through my fingers, reminds me of what can never be made tangible: what is left behind, what remains, the shift of memory.

III

When I mention the relevance of place with reference to a book I've been given by my American husband, Anne Fadiman's *The Spirit Catches You and You Fall Down*, which tells the story of the clash between two couples, one Hmong, one American, and the culture-directed misunderstandings between them that result in an American-born Hmong child becoming braindead at seven years of age, a book imbued not only with the worth of its contents but by the personal note from its author, my first signed book, my father uses the word *deracinate*. This is an email communication, the kind that amplifies the power of words, punctuation, and font size as if history alone provides inadequate weight. It is an accusation of sorts, for this life I have chosen.

IV

Deracinate: a term that does its job, communicating the surgical precision of the crime, for it is a word full of malignance, even as its smooth articulation presses down hard on the severed limbs below. When I picture the transaction, I see it through glass. The water on the top lies still and reflective, sure of the opaque solidity of the idea upon which it rests, this notion of clinical separation between act and result. But below that, beating against the underside like lotuses seeking light, are those flailing arms and legs that reached out and held hands and walked and danced beside in the somewhere else that cannot be accommodated in the pictures cast upon that cold water above.

Into that water shine different faces, the topography of change, they who in turn look in and see themselves and me, too, a different color but still the same. In that mirror we see, together, the plants that grow here, the food that is cooked here, the roads that run here, the people who live here. Ricocheting off that impermeable surface are the words that are spoken here, songs that are sung here, speeches that are made here, and all of those sounds create the emotive melodies of our days. Around its banks we join hands to move in a new dance; we smile and celebrate our common bonds, and I hold tight because unlike my friends, if I do not, I will fall in and I will drown.

What they do not see, these companions of my days, is the real truth to the conduct of my life.

V

I stand apart from the crowd that has gathered around an open-air stage on a college campus in Maine. I wear blue jeans sold in my country for their intimation of current trends in *a place called America* rather than for style and a faded cotton shirt belonging to the boyfriend abandoned back home with the fervent promise of eventual return. I have no interest in getting involved beyond what I require of myself—something easy, within reach: academic excellence.

The next day, though, as I sit on the bleachers inside the gym with my dorm mates, someone mispronounces my name over a loudspeaker.

Apparently, in a moment of zeal for the oncoming adventure of an American college experience on a full scholarship, I had signed up to sing at the freshman talent show. I hear for the first time not my name, but the voice that will accompany me from then on, the voice of the outside heard from the inside, whispering these words: *What Will They Think of You?*

What will they think of you if you do, if you do not, if you speak or remain silent, if you get up to dance or sit by the wall, if you come in or stay out, if you get drunk or abhor alcohol, if you accept or refuse, if you smile or frown, if you pass or fail, if you know or are ignorant, run or walk, wear black or colors, speak loudly or mutter, swear or use the words of angels…

I get up, propelled by a force I cannot resist, walk over to the center of the brilliantly lit basketball court, take the microphone, and, after making a self-deprecating comment about possibly not remembering all the lyrics, pour my heart and soul into my Sri Lankan rendition of Joan Baez's version of Bob Dylan's "Forever Young." Sustained applause is orchestrated by the MC for the evening, Arvelle "Ozzie" Jones, Jr., a slender, six-foot African American from Philadelphia, who will one day be a beloved luminary in the independent theater circuit between New York City, Washington, DC, and Philadelphia, but is, for now, one among a dozen or so minority students who blaze a particularly fiery trail through a mostly snow-filled campus in a former mill town in Maine.

VI

I am among friends who, I learn, are described as being Of Color. I gravitate toward the Black students on campus more than I do toward the international students; I acknowledge, but I am sanguine about the fact, that I am resented for this. I learn the history of my new friends, read their stories, perform in their plays, dance at their dances, listen to their music, and grow to champion their causes. I do not know then that I will do this unceasingly as long as I am here.

I learn that I, too, am A Person of Color, though I have, thus far, only ever been no more and no less than a person in another country. It is nearly impossible to be a person from another country and also A Person of Color, for the one defines a set of preconditions and realities and Q&As and calls and responses that cannot be used on the other. In my interiority, I am first a person, then a woman, and last A Person of Color. In the physical world I inhabit, I am first and last A Person of Color with a sandwich filling called *immigrant* oozing out the sides and gumming everybody's fingers at a party with no napkins in sight.

VII

We come, often with no intention to stay. We come not to the land of opportunity but because some opportunity wagered, created, fought for, bought, or sold *back home* enabled us to be here. We come not to take away or judge, but to travel our own life's path through the wider universe of experience of which this, your-country-never-mine, could signify our every experience or the experience of lack. We stay, sometimes, so long that there is no home that we inhabit except that which is *back home*. When we are there, home is this place. When we are here, home is there. Home is a notion where nothing is perfect so long as it contains only one of our sets of circumstances. Our lives are a perpetual preparation to arrive at or depart from. We save money for gifts and plane tickets. We don't have retirement plans. Where would we retire to? Retirees look toward heaven, and where would heaven be for an immigrant but along a road between homes?

Our metaphysical space is like a house of many rooms where only one is furnished and available for entertaining our hosts. Our décor for that one room is chosen so as to cause the least offense, and yet to offer Them a taste of whom we once were. We use our accents and our spices to charm, but we leave our religions and our notions of child-rearing out. In those other rooms that they, you, do not see and, perhaps, are incurious about are the stories that complete the rest of who we are. We visit those rooms alone.

VIII

The World Series involves America and, in 1992 and 1993, a single team from Canada. I think of World Series games that involve a good part of the world and last for days between two teams with eleven players each, all dressed in white "longs" and white shirts. The word *oval* means, first, a field of grass, then the shape of a face, and last a figure related to geometry. But there is no equivalence between long on and left field. Mid wicket is farther away than third base. Silly mid on is not quite the same as shortstop. I cheer for the Red Sox and, later, for the Phillies. I quiet the names Kumar Sangakkara and Muttiah Muralitharan. I wear t-shirts that say Hunter Pence and Ryan Howard.

IX

The cop who pulls me over is decked in aviator sunglasses. He bellows at me to *get back in my car and stay there* while he coddles the blond teenage girl who, en route to obtain her driving permit, no less, has crashed into the side of my car. I fall back on the comforting refrain of the immigrant: *this would never happen to me in my own country.* Well, it may, or may not, depending upon who is in power at the time. This is the only difference: I would be present, entirely, not observing from above, in a holding pattern over my own life, commenting upon and analyzing the whys and wherefores of such moments.

X

The ambiance at the Mexican restaurant is familiar, and therefore comforting to me: pared down, bare walls, uncovered wood tables, durable tin plates, and cheap, good food served without fanfare or flourish by a young girl with other things on her mind. My then husband and my girls—who have inherited his pigmentation—are the only people not wrapped up in the gift of brown skin. A week later, arriving for a first swim with a new team in a new town, my shy oldest daughter hangs behind me as I walk around the pool to talk to the coach.

"It's easy for you," she says afterward when I cajole her to try and do some of the talking herself, "you can talk to anybody." A conversation which leads, in the convoluted way mother-daughter conversations do, to her declaring that she had enjoyed the Mexican food at the restaurant but hadn't felt comfortable there. "I felt like it was only for Mexican people."

"And why is that?"

"Because nobody looked like me."

"Well, that's interesting," I tell her. "That's how I feel every day of my life." And then I follow that up with this: "I just don't think about it. If I thought about it all the time, I'd go mad. So I just forget about it and keep on going."

But these are the fictions of parenthood, the tall tales that are uttered in the spirit of hope; hope that life for our children will be different with regard to all the hard things that social interaction brings with it. I lie, because I *do* think about it.

XI

I cut someone off on the narrow streets of our startlingly well-heeled Philadelphia suburb, and I imagine a xenophobic slur being uttered in the car behind me. I let someone cut in front of me, waiting patiently for their left turn as my green light nears yellow, and I am buoyed by the thought that a sudden happiness may have darted across their minds on the wings of this meditation: *foreigners are nice people.* They do not raise their palm in acknowledgement or toot their thanks, and I imagine that a sense of entitlement may have bewitched them: of course I would let them get ahead of me, that's my proper place, behind them.

I cannot remember a particular word to affix to a story I am relating or I'm tired and a malapropism slips out, and I cringe. A series of excuses light up behind my eyes, and I articulate them in silence: I'm really very smart, I don't always speak this way, in fact I rarely make mistakes. My English is very good. In fact, my English is probably better than most people here for whom English is their first language. How long will it take to restore myself to my former standing as an exemplary immigrant of impeccable virtue, the highest among which would be my command of this language that I often wish to evict from my brain?

XII

The acquisition of language is the crucible of loss and gain. To retain a former self, I must mispronounce, be less fluent, stumble a little, continue to think and dream and curse in my native tongue. To ascend the strata of a country that covets the English language, I must strive not simply for good

English but a superior eloquence. Lucidity in this foreign tongue elevates us immigrants: we are no longer better than the average come-lately, we become an enhanced version of the Americans we have no wish to become.

XIII

What is this except an alternate life unrolling always in comparison to the past in a place that is not *that* place?

XIV

The realtor says, "We must begin with bathrooms. You have five in the family, so you need two bathrooms and a powder room for guests."

I grew up in a household of five in a home whose usual head count was closer to a dozen, and where we managed to eat, drink, and send our children to college without the convenience of three cisterns.

The realtor says, "Every house, if it does not come with one already, needs a modern kitchen."

I have only one friend with a modern kitchen who enjoys cooking. Every other modern kitchen appears to be a clone of some other modern kitchen lifted from the pages of a glossy magazine whose clarion call to a life of simplicity appears to require the destruction of the planet to afford it. Such kitchens come complete with granite countertops and marble floors and Italian tile splash guards and gleaming cast-iron pots dangling like missiles overhead and islands and barstools for people who make fair-trade coffee on $200 machines and dine out. I try, but I cannot translate the term "foodie" into Sinhala. The closest equivalent would be, unfortunately, "greed."

In the immigrant kitchens of my friends, and mine, there seems to be a steady output of home cooking, mostly based around the staples of rice and curry or various legumes created from South American recipes and, also, pizza with unusual toppings, and hand-rolled breads and birthday cakes presented on battered foil-lined trays. I wonder about my future life in a house with a modern kitchen. Will the acquisition of one finally and unequivocally make me feel *at home*?

After waiting in vain for a response from me, the realtor says, "It would really help the resale value."

XV

A home is not sold. The particular bit of land upon which a home might sit, regardless of size or condition, is passed down, through the family, no matter the need or inconvenience or indeed legal battles that often come with such gifts.

I do not know how to turn my back on the land that, unlike houses, which can be built, rebuilt, or torn down, remains there, with fixed coordinates, reminding me of that neighborhood, those neighbors, the path down to those stores at which my family ran credit, the peculiarities of the vendors who visit and call out their wares, bearing oil cakes or fish or bread or papaws or green leaves for *mallun*, or even parchment and string for fortune telling, on their heads. It is only *that* particular bullock-drawn cart that comes to visit the inhabitants of that relentlessly small square of land, *that* cart with *that* red and white barrel of kerosene oil for sale. A postman, the same one who has come year after year, whose bell can be heard twenty houses down and is louder, nearer, here sometimes, passes our land. To contemplate selling is to contemplate not living while life is in our bodies, for how does one inhabit a place that is to belong to someone not of your own family?

If there is lichen on the boundary walls and broken glass stuck into wet cement when it goes up as security against burglaries that are exciting to entertain but have never been experienced, if the windows do not shut all the way and nobody has thought of building screens to keep out encephalitis-carrying mosquitoes, what does it matter? The food is still good, the household dramas unfold, children grow up and go away and return and accept, with grace or the lack of it, but still, accept, the gift of land.

XVI

Will my daughters stay, I wonder? Will they return, and if they do, for what is it that they would come? Weddings? Funerals? Or simply, like their all-American peers, to take care of the business of sifting through our accumulations when we are moved from a house we raised children in to a place of tending to ashes?

XVII

Albert Camus once argued in a short essay written in 1940 that Sisyphus's fate was not always futile, and, indeed, we immigrants whose task it is to roll that effortful ball up the hill of assimilation each day tend to agree. Some days, the journey is joyful; our steps are light, and the work of reflecting this culture back to our friends sits easily upon shoulders, steady in our knowledge that we are, fundamentally, unchanged from whom we once were and, also, one and the same with those born-here Americans whose lives entwine with ours. On other days it is full of despair. On those days the hill is a dangerous precipice, the ball leaden and the summit merely a vantage from which we dream of hurling it and ourselves to whatever end God has in mind for us.

XVIII

In the name of the Buddhist life into which I was born and whose serene places of worship I can no longer find, I seek out a faith tradition that looks toward what is the same in all of us, to silent contemplation of our movements, and responsibilities toward life rather than those external realities that keep us from each other. In Quaker meetings attended by people all related, intimately, to the routines of my life in a small town in Central Maine, I find quiet and family, but no relief from bearing the weight of difference in solitude. In Philadelphia, within the simple and temple-like silence of a large meeting filled with the as-yet-unmet, I find welcome and recognition but no family. That search for family, which reaches far beyond spouses and children, is what drives some of us to recreate claustrophobic marketplaces and collections of restaurants where we go to forget where we are, and is what drives me to turn again and again to my American friends for a helping hand, with the sometimes impossible request that they, too, step toward.

XIX

The parameters of American friendships have become my unlearned lesson. I fail repeatedly to remember, before it is too late, that American relationships exist on a scale constructed of civility, balanced in equal part by give and take, and I choose instead to go from one great conversation to embracing like family, loyalty wrapping around each hapless acquaintance in a vice of expectation that they will never be able to reciprocate. I forget, too often, that disagreement is dangerous, and that contradiction or a demand for truth can be fatal. I lose some whom I have thought of as friends. I see them recoil before some deficiency of tone in my voice, its inflections edged with a hitherto-concealed sting. At such moments I find myself lacking in the ability to recall myself to my surroundings, these realities, theirs and mine, but rather watch myself as I sharpen my words, uncharitably flaying them for being American, simultaneously driving them away and challenging them to prove me wrong, for not knowing me, not wanting to know me, for the repeated disappointment that there will never be an American friend able to set their own upbringing aside so as to treat me not as a friend, whose lapses can break our bonds, but as family, whose lapses must always be forgiven.

XX

I discover that my Black friends are no more Sri Lankan than my Caucasian future-husband from Connecticut. Needing to fix my high-heeled shoes before the beginning of a debate tournament where I am, oddly enough, a member of the only team representing North America at an international tournament hosted by Canada—a tournament to which I arrive only by covering myself with a blanket and pretending to be asleep at the border crossing during a time when such things are possible—I ask Jason, a private school–raised African American, to hold my books.

"What do you think I am? Your servant?" he asks. "Hold your own books!"

We are teammates. I grin, but I am shocked. I am used to friends moving seamlessly in and out of my orbit, picking and propping up what needs to be, supporting, navigating, speaking, and standing up for me, often without my ever having to speak a word. And here is this boy: my friend, almost my color, a person who, surely, feels just as marginalized in this country as I do, and he will not help me. Not even if I ask. Is it that private school? I wonder. Is it the history I am not completely familiar with? I take that confusion with me into the future, unable to reconcile the connection I feel with a Black man or woman with the fact that they do not speak my language. You are like me, I want to say. You must know what I mean.

XXI

We are like prayers: there when we are needed. We can be counted on to be ardent about our civic participation, our way of confirming to you, and to ourselves, that we are, indeed, *not* hovering somewhere above ourselves but right here on earth, invested in the fortunes of *this* common place. We volunteer at our children's schools, we don't litter, we march in parades and we sing the national anthem from start to finish. We vote. And, before we vote, we educate ourselves about issues and politicians. We are consistently, meticulously well informed. We are, but we try not to out-do you who are born here because that could be perceived as presumptuous. It is a fine balance between belonging and usurpation, and we not only do not wish to be accused of the latter, we do not wish to commit the sacrilege of the former, sacrilege not of taking what you think is yours, but of disloyalty to what we consider to be ours: our memory of belonging to another place.

XXII

Consider this: if an American were to visit Myanmar for a time, meet and marry a Burmese man, and raise children there, would that American no longer consider America to be his or her home? Would they be less American? And if not, then why am I faced so often with the well-intentioned who question the right of us elsewhere-people to long for the countries in which we were born? No passport, no pledge, no vote, no law, no years of volunteerism or military service can turn me into an American. The best I can do, and that I work hard to do, is to pretend that I am, for the exclusive love demanded of me by America, a demand that takes no note of who I really am and where I come from, a demand lacking in empathy, makes loving this country if not impossible then a quest that must be set aside at night and renewed each daybreak.

XXIII

One cannot come from a country whose recorded history harkens back more than two thousand five hundred years and be expected to cherish with no reservation the nationality of one whose dominant history is but two hundred and fifty years old, and which largely leaves out the contributions of immigrants who were not of the chosen hue, religious affiliation, or temperament.

XXIV

I am asked to do a presentation about Sri Lanka at a local library. The task: ten minutes to tell a group of children about my country.

"How long is the history of America?" I begin.

A few hands go up. "Thousand years!" "Two hundred years!" "Hundreds of years!"

"Could you tell me the history of America in ten minutes?"

"No!" they say, laughing at the very idea.

"My country's history is ten times as long, so I couldn't possibly tell you all about it in ten minutes, could I?"

And, also, this:

"What countries are next to North America?"

"Mexico!" "Canada!"

"Do any of you born here consider yourselves to be Mexican or Canadian?"

"No way!"

"Well, Sri Lanka is next to India, and we Sri Lankans get very offended when we are called Indians."

They cede both points with the sweetest of smiles.

Children are easily taught, their hearts open to the things that they can visualize and touch and feel: the idea of boundaries, the difference between numbers, 250 versus 2,500, the curving script of their names written out for them in Sinhala, the taste of milk toffee made with not just cardamom and roasted cashews but with both sweetened condensed milk *and* sugar, a game played by hiding a middle finger among the other fingers.

XXV

What do I say to the adult who asks me, en route to filling up his glass and mine with a supposedly remarkable Cabernet Sauvignon, "So, tell me, wasn't there a civil war in Sri Lanka? What was that about? How did that get started exactly?"

Here is what I want to say:

"I'd love to explain the current situation in Sri Lanka, but first could you explain the repercussions today of slavery in America and the civil war in between? And oh, could you keep it to five minutes? Surely, it can't be *that* complicated. Half a glass please, thanks!"

Here's what I do say:

"Yes, it's been going on for a while. *The New York Times* [or some other varietal of newspapers in America] did a piece recently. Did you see it?"

"No, I didn't. Was it good? Don't get a lot of time to read, you know."

"Yes, life gets busy. Don't I know it. I really wanted to see X actor in Y movie but every time I tried…" Etc., etc.

And I have avoided confrontation the way Americans do, becoming most American in the very moment in which I am most conspicuously not. I aim in those moments for the recognition of effort rather than the reality of ignorance. At least he wants to let me know he knows where I come from, and he knows something about what was going on there, I tell myself. And why, I ask myself, should these people know anything about my country? How does my presence here become a requirement for them to become more educated about the world? Those are the excuses I use to glide on, staying smooth, on message, allowing the exoticization and somehow assuaging the unalterable fact that I, we, grew up knowing a lot about this country, its location, its history, its gifts, and its perpetrations.

XXVI

"I'll see you when we invade your country someday," John S. III, one of the boys who lives across from my room in our co-ed dorm, quips on the eve of the first invasion of Iraq. John, a Texan, has spent an hour participating in a candlelit vigil around the college duck pond in protest of Bush the Senior.

John's roommate Josh Kennedy, lyricist, cartoonist, son of a poet, and I, we who regularly share the tea that I have brought from Sri Lanka that he pours into his un-cracked American flag cup for me and the cracked one for himself, says nothing. Earlier that day, he had been with me as I tried to place a call to my parents back home. On the line I heard the voice of the operator—exasperated perhaps with the fact that her counterpart in Sri Lanka could not understand her—say, loudly and clearly: *This Is the United States of America.* I recall the chill that went up my spine at that voice, those words. The unchecked, horrific, inexorable weight of her declaration to the braided, cotton sari–clad young woman in my tiny island country at the other end.

XXVII

During a political campaign that I have joined in an effort to help a candidate with a name that reminds America of that world of which we are a part, I work down a long list and place a call to a fellow South Asian in Texas, a Mr. Veeraseshamamba. I pronounce that name completely, rolling it out like a gilt-edged invitation, even though I know that he probably goes by a lesser moniker: Veer, for instance, or V. The woman who answers does not speak English, but she takes down my number, repeating the numerals after me several times, breaking now and then into what I assume to be an Indian dialect, though I do not understand it. I imagine a mother visiting, perhaps, here for a graduation or a marriage. I dwell for a moment in the old importance of phone calls, the rarity of a telephone, the further miracle of one ringing, the deep excitement of a long-distance call, the group that might gather around the speaker, the voice raised so it could be better heard across the miles, the sharpness of the dialogue trimmed for effect and financial prudence. I think about international telephone calls and words written over the internet. And the way neither can diminish the immense solidarity that I feel with this other permanent visitor who only happens to be the parent of a voter in an American election.

XXVIII

I get a letter from a reader. He writes this way:

I am a 75 year old federal employee and I was in the U.S. Marines in my youth. I consider myself a tough character unfazed by life's challenges. Get the picture? When I read your story about "The Folks at Moe's Diner," your story brought tears to my eyes. What a wonderful story. May you have great success in your writing career

—M.S.

Somewhere above my head, in my visible life, the water ripples; somewhere up there, the usual reflections disintegrate. For a moment, home is a place, and it is here.

Acknowledgments

My gratitude is boundless.

Colum McCann, comrade, colleague, older and younger brother, dear friend, may our journeys be ever proximate in spirit and heart.

Phil Brady, your first words of acceptance were all the proof I needed of safety and care in entrusting this book to Etruscan Press. I couldn't have asked for a better reader.

John Hennessy, whose faith in the value of my work has never faltered. Among the many gifts you have given me, this one is priceless.

Charles Rice-Gonzalez, beloved friend. So long as you stand, I have both safety and home.

Arjuna and Malinda Seneviratne, my older brothers, indefatigable in their goodness and their fight for an inclusive justice. My sisters-in-law, Manjula Dharmasiri and Samadanie Kiriwandeniya, equally undiminished warrior-women. A generation of young people walk taller because of the four of you.

My father, Gamini Seneviratne, who demonstrated the value of speaking in many languages even if the words were sourced from the same alphabet, and the responsibility that comes with occupying a podium.

My late mother, Indrani Seneviratne, who modeled what it is to be both fierce and loving, unapologetic and generous, brave and kind, as a woman, as a teacher, and as a mother. I am because she was.

My daughters, Duránya, Hasadrī, and Kisārā Freeman. You continue to be my inspiration. The passion of the Herath and Seneviratne side of your lineage burns bright within you. Let the world continue to be purified by that fire.

Versions of the following essays have appeared in the following publications:

"Many Rights, Few Responsibilities," *Virginia Quarterly Review* (September, 2020)

"Our Security Is, by Definition, Indivisible," adapted from the preface to *Indivisible: Global Leaders on Shared Security* (Interlink, 2018)

"#MeToo Is Not Enough," *Chronicle of Higher Education* (April, 2018)

"Extraordinary Rendition," adapted from the preface to *Extraordinary Rendition: (American) Writers on Palestine* (O/R Books, 2015, Interlink, 2016)

"Memory, Loss" Disquiet International Prize for Literature, *Ninth Letter* (2017)

"A Brief for the Defense of a White Man," *The Normal School* (2017)

"Everything but the Ranch," *Panorama: The Journal of Intelligent Travel* (2016)

"Hero," *Electric Literature* (2016)

"This Brown, This Green," *The House That Made Me* (Spark Press, 2016; Grant Jarrett, Ed.)

"Pineapple & Roasted Nuts," *The Guardian* (2015)

"When in Doubt, Climb the Roof," *Shaping the World: Women Writers on Themselves* (Hay House, 2015; Manju Kapur, Ed.)

"Glory," *Me, My Hair and I: Twenty-Seven Women Untangle an Obsession* (Algonquin Press, 2015; Elizabeth Benedict, Ed.)

"Silk," *NPR: You Must Read This* (June, 2014)

"One Book to Rule Them All," *AWP Writer's Notebook* (2014)

"What Is Feminism?" *Virginia Quarterly Review* (2012)

"Worth It," *Spent* (Seal Publishing, 2014; Kerry Cohen, Ed.)

"Home Spun," *Ocean State Review* (2014); nominated for a Pushcart Prize

"Uncle Moe's Diner," *The Reader's Digest* (2014)

"Playing the Game," *The Nation, Sri Lanka* (2013)

"Dear Natalie Gyte: I Hope You Dance," *The Huffington Post* (February 17th, 2103)

"Why I Travel," *AWP Writer's Notebook* (2013)

"Osama Bin Laden and America's Celebration of Death," in *Kayan News, Iran* (2011)

"In All Things, Absent," in *R.kv.r.y Journal* (2010)

"Staying Hungry on Enid Blyton," *Pebble Lake Review* (2010)

"The First Mistake: Barack Obama's Silence on Gaza," *Common Dreams* (January 12th, 2009)

"I Am Not Now, Nor Have I Ever Been, an Adolescent," *Crab Orchard Review* vol. 12, no. 2, special issue on The In-Between Age: Writers on Adolescence (2008)

"I Cannot Weep for Mariane Pearl," *Spectrum* (2007)

"Ahmadinejad v. Bush: The Village Druid v. The Zygote," *Common Dreams* (May 10th, 2006)

About The Author

Ru Freeman is an award-winning multi-hyphenate Sri Lankan and American novelist, poet, editor, and critic whose work appears internationally and in translation. She is the author of the short-story collection *Sleeping Alone* and the novels *A Disobedient Girl* and *On Sal Mal Lane,* a New York Times Editors' Choice Book, and the editor of two anthologies, *Extraordinary Rendition: (American) Writers on Palestine* and *Indivisible: Global Leaders on Shared Security.* She holds an MFA in poetry and an MA in labor studies, researching female migrant labor in the countries of Kuwait, the UAE, and the Kingdom of Saudi Arabia. She has worked at the Institute for Policy Studies in Washington, DC, the South Asia office of the American Federation of Labor and Congress of Industrial Organizations (AFL-CIO), and for the American Friends Service Committee (AFSC) on social justice initiatives around sanctuary and human rights. She teaches creative writing in the US and abroad.

Books from Etruscan Press

Etruscan Press Is Proud of Support Received From

Wilkes University

Youngstown State University

Ohio Arts Council

The Stephen & Jeryl Oristaglio Foundation

Community of Literary Magazines and Presses [clmp]

National Endowment for the Arts

Drs. Barbara Brothers & Gratia Murphy Endowment

The Thendara Foundation

Founded in 2001 with a generous grant from the Oristaglio Foundation, Etruscan Press is a nonprofit cooperative of poets and writers working to produce and promote books that nurture the dialogue among genres, achieve a distinctive voice, and reshape the literary and cultural histories of which we are a part.

etruscan press
www.etruscanpress.org

Etruscan Press books may be ordered from

Consortium Book Sales and Distribution
800.283.3572
www.cbsd.com

Etruscan Press is a 501(c)(3) nonprofit organization.
Contributions to Etruscan Press are tax deductible
as allowed under applicable law.
For more information, a prospectus,
or to order one of our titles,
contact us at books@etruscanpress.org.